The Big Diabetic Cookbook for Beginners

500 Simple

Low-Carb and Low-Sugar Diabetic Recipes with 28-Day Meal Plan for Type 2 Diabetes to Keep a Healthy Lifestyle

Mitchell Cato

Copyright © 2025 By Mitchell Cato
All rights reserved.

No part of this book may be reproduced, transmitted, or distributed in any form or by any means without permission in writing from the publisher except in the case of brief quotations embodied in critical articles or reviews.

Legal & Disclaimer

The content and information in this book is consistent and truthful, and it has been provided for informational, educational and business purposes only.

The illustrations in the book are from the website shutterstock.com, depositphoto.com and freepik.com and have been authorized.

The content and information contained in this book has been compiled from reliable sources, which are accurate based on the knowledge, belief, expertise and information of the Author. The author cannot be held liable for any omissions and/or errors.

Table of Content

INTRODUCTION ·· 1

CHAPTER 1: UNDERSTANDING DIABETES: A CHRONIC JOURNEY WITH BLOOD SUGAR ··· 2

CHAPTER 2: THE ROLE OF DIET IN DIABETES ································· 4

CHAPTER 3 BREAKFAST RECIPES ·· 12

CHAPTER 4 GRAIN AND RICE RECIPES ·· 19

CHAPTER 5 BEANS AND LEGUMES RECIPES ···································· 27

CHAPTER 6 SALAD RECIPES ··· 34

CHAPTER 7 FISH AND SEAFOOD RECIPES ······································· 40

CHAPTER 8 POULTRY RECIPES ·· 46

CHAPTER 9 VEGETABLE RECIPES ·· 54

CHAPTER 10 BEEF, LAMB AND PORK RECIPES ······························· 61

CHAPTER 11 SOUP AND STEW RECIPES ·· 68

CHAPTER 12 APPETIZER AND SIDES RECIPES ································ 74

CHAPTER 13 SMOOTHIE RECIPES ·· 81

CHAPTER 14 SNACK AND DESSERT RECIPES ·································· 87

CHAPTER 15 SAUCE AND DRESSING RECIPES ································ 93

APPENDIX 1: BASIC KITCHEN CONVERSIONS & EQUIVALENTS ········ 98

APPENDIX 2: THE DIRTY DOZEN AND CLEAN FIFTEEN ···················· 99

APPENDIX 3: RECIPES INDEX ·· 100

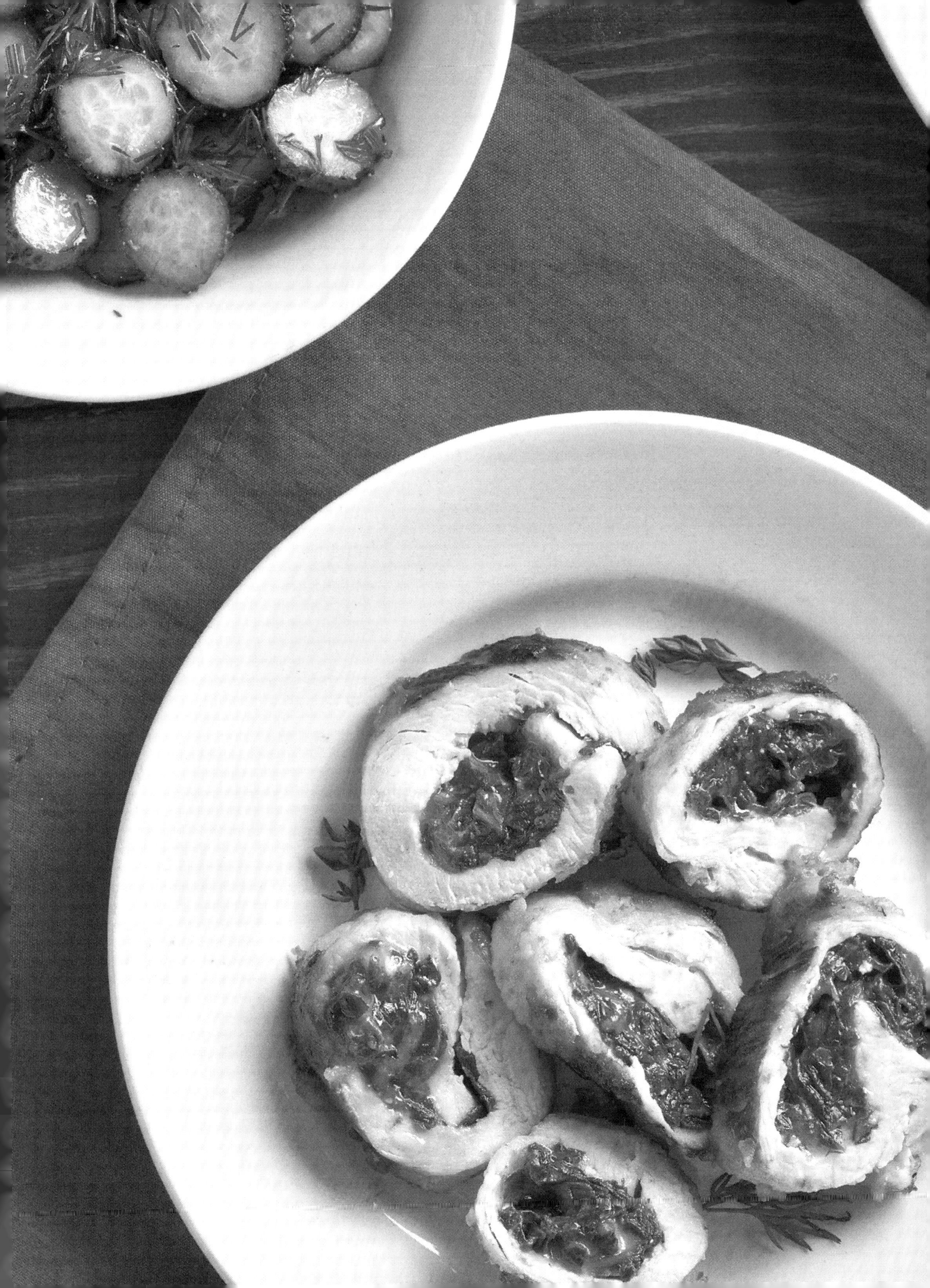

INTRODUCTION

Hello there, my name is Mitchell Cato, and I'm here to share a part of my life's journey that has transformed not only my culinary perspective but my entire lifestyle. Five years ago, life took an unexpected turn when I, a 47-year-old chef working in a bustling restaurant, was diagnosed with type 2 diabetes. The initial emotions of sadness and fear gripped me, and for the next six months, I wrestled with what felt like a daunting challenge. But with the support of my loving son and the guidance of a compassionate doctor, I discovered that diabetes could be managed through a combination of mindful eating, a positive outlook, and maintaining a healthy lifestyle.

The doctor's advice marked the beginning of my deep dive into the world of diabetes management. Armed with prescriptions and a determination to take control of my health, I embarked on a journey that would not only change my life but also my culinary career. As a chef, I was no stranger to the art of food, flavors, and creativity in the kitchen. With time, I learned to channel my expertise into crafting delicious dishes that were not only satisfying but also aligned with my new dietary needs.

The path was not always easy, but I gradually mastered the dos and don'ts of a diabetic diet. The experience I gained over the years has been invaluable, shaping the way I view food, health, and the harmonious relationship they share. Today, I am not only free from medications but also filled with vitality and the knowledge that a well-balanced diet and a mindful lifestyle are the keys to a healthy life.

And now, dear friends, I am thrilled to announce my upcoming cookbook. This book is a culmination of my personal experiences, insights, and, of course, a treasure trove of recipes that have helped me along the way. It's a guide to transforming your relationship with food and embracing a lifestyle that not only manages diabetes but celebrates the joy of nourishing your body.

In this cookbook, I will cover the basics of diabetes, providing a clear understanding of what foods to embrace and which ones to approach with caution. I'll share practical tips and effective measures for crafting a diabetic-friendly diet that doesn't compromise on taste or creativity. With over 500 meticulously crafted recipes, the book is divided into 13 chapters based on ingredients and food forms. This organization ensures that you can swiftly find recipes that resonate with your cravings and dietary preferences.

Whether you're seeking breakfast inspiration that kickstarts your day with vitality, hearty and wholesome soups that comfort your soul, or delightful desserts that allow you to indulge guilt-free, each chapter will be your culinary companion on this transformative journey. From succulent seafood dishes to vibrant vegetable creations, every recipe has been thoughtfully designed to help you savor the joy of eating while nourishing your body from within.

CHAPTER 1: UNDERSTANDING DIABETES: A CHRONIC JOURNEY WITH BLOOD SUGAR

Diabetes, a journey I've walked for the past five years, is a chronic condition that intimately intertwines with our body's intricate dance of blood sugar levels. It's like composing a symphony where the notes of glucose need to be finely orchestrated to maintain harmony within. In this condition, the body struggles with either producing insufficient insulin or utilizing it ineffectively, causing blood sugar levels to rise.

Type 2 diabetes, the path I tread, often emerges in adulthood, fueled by a combination of genetics, lifestyle, and environmental factors. It's not just about skipping sweets - carbohydrates play a pivotal role, as they metamorphose into glucose upon digestion. With diabetes, this transformation becomes a tightrope walk - too much glucose floods the bloodstream, while too little starves our cells.

Blood sugar management becomes an art, requiring strategic food choices, regular exercise, and sometimes medications. Elevated blood sugar levels, a concern, can lead to a host of complications - from cardiovascular woes to nerve damage. However, with vigilance and a holistic approach, diabetes can be tamed.

So, my friends, let's journey into the intricate world of diabetes, where understanding the nuances of blood sugar and adopting a balanced lifestyle create the masterpiece of well-being.

Exploring Diabetes: From Type 1 and Type 2 to Gestational

As we delve deeper into the realm of diabetes, it's essential to unravel its varied forms: Type 1, Type 2, and Gestational. Type 1 diabetes, often diagnosed in childhood, is a result of the immune system mistakenly attacking insulin-producing cells, leading to a deficiency of this vital hormone. This type necessitates insulin injections for life to regulate blood sugar levels.

Type 2 diabetes, the path I've navigated, emerges predominantly in adulthood due to a mix of genetics and lifestyle factors. Here, the body either doesn't produce enough insulin or can't use it effectively. Lifestyle modifications, including diet and exercise, can often manage Type 2 diabetes. We're going to talk about in this cookbook is Type 2 diabetes.

Gestational diabetes, a fleeting companion, occurs during pregnancy when hormonal changes compromise insulin usage. Though it usually resolves post-delivery, it requires careful monitoring to safeguard both mother and child's health.

Understanding these nuances, my friends, empowers us to make informed choices on our diabetes journey. Whether managing the lifelong path of Type 1, finding equilibrium with Type 2, or navigating the temporary presence of gestational diabetes, knowledge is our greatest ally in ensuring our health and well-being.

Unraveling Diabetes: Causes and Risks We Face

In my years of battling diabetes, I've come to understand the intricate tapestry of causes and risk factors that can weave this condition into our lives. While genetics certainly plays its part, lifestyle choices are equally influential. Sedentary habits and poor dietary decisions can act as triggers for Type 2 diabetes, the path I've walked. Excess weight, especially around the waistline, heightens the risk by increasing insulin resistance.

Type 1 diabetes, on the other hand, often emerges due to an autoimmune response where the body's immune system misguidedly attacks its insulin-producing cells. Environmental factors may also play a role, though research is ongoing.

For gestational diabetes, hormonal changes during pregnancy can induce insulin resistance, potentially affecting both mother and baby.

Understanding these intricacies reminds us that while some factors may lie beyond our control, the power to influence our diabetes journey through mindful lifestyle choices remains firmly in our hands. It's a harmonious symphony of genetics, lifestyle, and awareness that guides us toward a healthier, more empowered existence.

Navigating Diabetes: Symptoms, Diagnosis and the Watchful Eye

When diabetes entered my life, it brought along a host of signals - a gentle reminder that our bodies communicate, urging us to pay attention. Symptoms of diabetes can vary, from unquenchable thirst and frequent urination to persistent fatigue and unexplained weight loss. These signs, when heeded, can serve as beacons guiding us to seek medical evaluation.

Diagnosis involves more than just a label; it's a roadmap to understanding our body's needs. Blood tests, particularly fasting glucose and A1C tests, help healthcare providers decipher our blood sugar levels over time. These numbers unveil the intricate dance of our metabolism and provide insights into the effectiveness of our management strategies.

But the journey doesn't stop at diagnosis - it's a commitment to vigilant monitoring. Regular blood sugar checks, lifestyle adjustments, and close collaboration with healthcare professionals become our tools for empowerment. Monitoring isn't merely about numbers; it's about staying attuned to our body's rhythms and taking proactive steps to keep them in harmony.

Through my own experience, I've realized that regular monitoring isn't a burden; it's an act of self-care. It's a way of acknowledging the importance of our well-being and ensuring that we're the composers of our own health narrative.

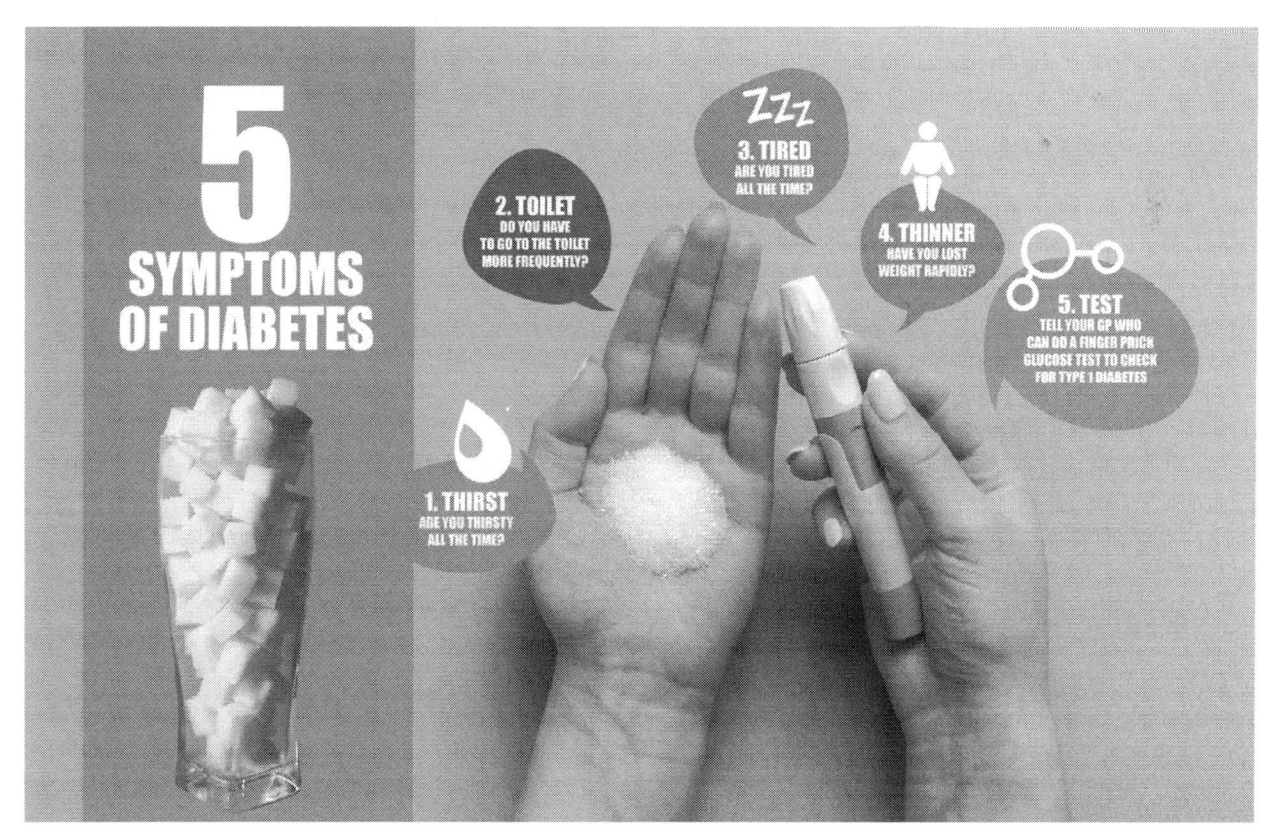

5 SYMPTOMS OF DIABETES

1. **THIRST** — Are you thirsty all the time?
2. **TOILET** — Do you have to go to the toilet more frequently?
3. **TIRED** — Are you tired all the time?
4. **THINNER** — Have you lost weight rapidly?
5. **TEST** — Tell your GP who can do a finger prick glucose test to check for Type 1 diabetes

CHAPTER 2: THE ROLE OF DIET IN DIABETES

The Dance of Flavors and Glucose: How Food Affects Blood Sugar

As a chef who has embraced the intricate art of flavors, I've also come to intimately understand the delicate choreography between the food we savor and the blood sugar levels within us. Every meal is a performance, where each ingredient plays a vital role in this dance.

Carbohydrates, our primary energy source, have the most profound impact. They transform into glucose after digestion, causing blood sugar levels to rise. The speed at which this happens depends on the type of carbohydrate - refined ones like sugary treats create swift spikes, while complex ones like whole grains offer a gradual elevation.

Proteins and fats, though slower to influence blood sugar, still play their part. Proteins have a minimal impact, while fats can slow digestion, leading to steadier blood sugar levels.

Portion sizes matter too. Excessive intake, even of healthy foods, can still lead to unexpected spikes. Balancing meals with a mix of carbohydrates, lean proteins, and healthy fats is crucial, as is spreading out food intake across the day.

Experimentation becomes our ally. Monitoring blood sugar levels after meals helps us understand the unique response of our bodies to different foods. This knowledge, gained through a blend of culinary intuition and scientific inquiry, empowers us to craft meals that not only tantalize our taste buds but also honor our health.

Remember, each plate is an opportunity - a chance

to embrace the symphony of flavors while nurturing our bodies with the harmony they deserve.

Decoding the Glycemic Index: A Maestro's Guide to Meal Planning

As a chef who's danced through the realms of ingredients and tastes, I've discovered the symphony that is the Glycemic Index (GI), a conductor of sorts in the world of meal planning for diabetes. The GI is a scale that reveals how different carbohydrates impact blood sugar levels after consumption.

Foods with a high GI, like sugary cereals, can cause rapid spikes in blood sugar, akin to a crescendo in a musical piece. On the other hand, foods with a low GI, such as whole grains and legumes, create gentler rises, like soothing melodies that linger.

Understanding the GI equips us with a tool for crafting harmonious meals. It guides our choices, helping us select foods that sustain energy and prevent abrupt sugar spikes. Balancing high-GI items with low-GI counterparts is key - it's about finding the right notes to compose a meal that maintains stability.

However, the GI isn't the sole maestro in this orchestra. Portion sizes, meal composition, and individual responses also play pivotal roles. This journey, as intricate as a musical score, requires experimentation, mindfulness, and the willingness to embrace the art of meal planning as a symphony of flavors and health.

So, my fellow culinary enthusiasts, let's wield the Glycemic Index as our baton, orchestrating meals that resonate not only on our palates but within the very rhythms of our bodies.

Wholesome Delights: A Bounty of Diabetes-Friendly Foods

In my culinary journey through diabetes, I've unearthed a treasure trove of foods that not only tantalize the taste buds but also nurture our health. Here's a comprehensive list, divided into different kinds, of the beneficial gems for individuals with diabetes:

1. Vibrant Vegetables:
- Leafy greens (spinach, kale, collard greens)
- Non-starchy vegetables (broccoli, cauliflower, bell peppers)
- Tomatoes (rich in lycopene)

2. Fantastic Fruits:
- Berries (blueberries, strawberries, raspberries)
- Apples (with skin for added fiber)
- Citrus fruits (oranges, grapefruits)

3. Wholesome Whole Grains:
- Quinoa (protein-packed)
- Brown rice (fiber-rich)
- Oats (soluble fiber champion)

4. Lean Proteins:
- Skinless poultry (chicken, turkey)
- Fatty fish (salmon, mackerel, sardines)
- Plant-based proteins (tofu, legumes, lentils)

5. Healthy Fats:
- Avocados (heart-healthy monounsaturated fats)
- Nuts and seeds (almonds, walnuts, chia seeds)
- Olive oil (for cooking and dressing)

6. Dairy Delights:
- Low-fat Greek yogurt (protein source)

Skim or low-fat milk (calcium boost)
Cottage cheese (high-protein, low-carb option)

7. Flavorful Herbs and Spices:
- Cinnamon (may help improve insulin sensitivity)
- Turmeric (anti-inflammatory properties)

- Garlic (for added depth of flavor)

8. Hydrating Beverages:

- Water (the ultimate thirst quencher)
- Herbal teas (unsweetened and soothing)
- Infused water (with slices of citrus or cucumber)

Embracing these nourishing choices doesn't mean compromising on taste; in fact, it's an invitation to explore a world of flavors that elevate both our palates and well-being. Remember, the culinary canvas is vast, and within it lies a palette of colors that can enrich our lives as we savor each bite with gratitude and health in mind.

Steering Clear: Navigating Away from Unhealthy Culinary Waters

As a seasoned chef on a diabetes journey, I've become adept at spotting the culinary pitfalls that can derail our health. Here's my guide, divided into different kinds, to identify foods high in unhealthy fats, added sugars, and sodium - the ones that should be limited or avoided:

1. Sneaky Unhealthy Fats:

- Fried foods (crispy delights often soaked in unhealthy fats)
- Processed meats (sausages, hot dogs, deli meats)
- Margarine and hydrogenated oils (trans fats in disguise)

2. Hidden Added Sugars:

- Sugary beverages (sodas, fruit-flavored drinks)
- Commercially baked goods (pastries, cookies, cakes)
- Breakfast cereals (check labels for hidden sugars)

3. Salty Culprits - High Sodium Foods:

- Canned soups (often loaded with sodium)
- Processed snacks (chips, pretzels, crackers)
- Deli meats and packaged sausages (sodium-rich for preservation)

4. Sugary Sauces and Dressings:

- Barbecue sauce (sweet and high in sugars)
- Ketchup (often sugar-laden)
- Store-bought salad dressings (opt for homemade with healthier oils)

5. Creamy Indulgences:

- Full-fat dairy products (butter, whole milk, full-fat cheeses)
- Cream-based sauces (laden with saturated fats)
- Ice cream (sugar and saturated fat duo)

6. Processed Convenience Foods:

- Frozen meals (typically high in sodium and unhealthy fats)
- Instant noodles (excessive sodium)
- Packaged snacks (often loaded with unhealthy ingredients)

Awareness is our ally when it comes to steering clear of these culinary pitfalls. By reading labels, preparing meals at home, and choosing fresh, whole ingredients, we can safeguard our health and delight in the true flavors of life. Remember, the journey to wellness is paved with choices, and with each mindful decision, we inch closer to a healthier, happier existence.

Stocking Up for Success: My Diabetic-Friendly Pantry Essentials

As a chef who's embraced the nuances of a diabetic diet, my pantry is a well-orchestrated symphony of ingredients that balance flavor, nutrition, and blood sugar management. Here's my curated pantry list for a diabetes-friendly culinary journey:

1. Whole Grains:
- √ Brown rice
- √ Quinoa
- √ Whole wheat pasta
- √ Oats (rolled or steel-cut)
- √ Whole grain flour for baking

2. Lean Proteins:
- √ Canned tuna or salmon
- √ Dried beans (black, kidney, chickpeas)
- √ Lentils
- √ Lean poultry (chicken, turkey)
- √ Tofu

3. Healthy Fats:
- √ Extra-virgin olive oil
- √ Avocado oil
- √ Nuts (almonds, walnuts)
- √ Seeds (chia, flaxseed)
- √ Nut butters (unsweetened)

4. Canned Goods:
- √ Low-sodium broth (chicken, vegetable)
- √ Canned vegetables (tomatoes, green beans)
- √ Canned fruit (in water or juice, no added sugar)

5. Spices and Seasonings:
- √ Cinnamon
- √ Turmeric
- √ Garlic powder
- √ Dried herbs (oregano, thyme)
- √ Black pepper

6. Condiments and Sauces:
- √ Low-sodium soy sauce
- √ Mustard
- √ Vinegar (balsamic, apple cider)
- √ Salsa (no added sugar)
- √ Hot sauce (if you like a kick)

7. Whole Food Sweeteners:
- √ Stevia (liquid or powder)
- √ Monk fruit extract

8. Beverages:
- √ Herbal teas (unsweetened)
- √ Coffee
- √ Water (stay hydrated!)

9. Snacks:
- √ Nuts and seeds (portioned for snacking)
- √ Whole grain crackers
- √ Popcorn kernels (for air-popping)

10. Grains for Baking:
- √ Whole wheat flour
- √ Almond flour (for gluten-free baking)
- √ Baking powder
- √ Baking soda

This pantry lineup reflects my dedication to balancing flavors, nutrition, and blood sugar stability. Armed with these essentials, you'll have the foundation to create vibrant, delicious meals that align with your diabetes management goals. Remember, the pantry isn't just a storage space - it's a culinary playground where you compose your health and happiness, one ingredient at a time.

Crafting Harmony: A Step-by-Step Guide to a Balanced Meal Plan

In my culinary voyage through diabetes management, I've honed the art of composing meals that not only please the palate but also respect the needs of our bodies. Here's my step-by-step guide to designing a balanced meal plan:

Step 1: Foundation of Carbohydrates

Start with whole grains, starchy vegetables, or legumes as your carbohydrate source. These provide sustained energy and fiber that aids digestion.

Step 2: Lean Proteins Take Center Stage

Pair your carbs with lean proteins like poultry, fish, tofu, or beans. Protein maintains satiety and helps manage blood sugar levels.

Step 3: Load *Up on Vibrant Vegetables*

Fill half your plate with non-starchy vegetables like greens, bell peppers, and broccoli. These are low in carbs and rich in nutrients.

Step 4: Embr*ace Healthy Fats*

Incorporate sources of healthy fats, like avocados, nuts, or olive oil, for flavor and to keep you satisfied.

Step 5: The *Right* Portions

Pay attention to portion sizes. Use measuring tools or your hand's size as a guide for proteins, grains, and fats.

Step 6: Mindful Sn*acking*

Plan balanced snacks with protein and fiber, like a handful of nuts with some carrot sticks.

Step 7: Stay Hy*drated*

Water is essential. Stay hydrated throughout the day for optimal bodily functions.

Step 8: Sweet Sensati*ons*

If you're indulging in sweets, do so in moderation and consider natural sweeteners like stevia.

Step 9: Re*gular Monitoring*

Continuously monitor blood sugar levels after meals to understand how your body responds.

Step 10: Flexib*ility and Variety*

Don't be afraid to explore new ingredients and recipes. Variety ensures you get a wide range of nutrients.

Remember, meal planning isn't just about following a set of rules; it's about finding the symphony of flavors and nutrients that resonate with your individual needs. Each plate is an opportunity to nourish not only your body but also your spirit, so embark on this culinary journey with curiosity and creativity as your guides.

Savoring Success: Navigating Dining Out with Health in Mind

Embarking on the path of diabetes management, I've learned that dining out doesn't need to be a challenge. With a few savvy strategies, you can make healthier choices and savor the experience of eating away from home:

- **Scout the Menu Ahead**

Before you even arrive, peruse the menu online. This helps you plan your choices and avoid impulsive decisions.

- **Mindful Starters**

Opt for broth-based soups, salads with vinaigrette on the side, or vegetable-based appetizers to kick off your meal.

- **Choose Lean Proteins**

Lean meats like grilled chicken, fish, or lean cuts of beef are smart choices. Ask for grilled, baked, or steamed preparations.

- **Tame the Portions**

Many restaurants serve large portions. Consider sharing a dish or requesting a to-go box at the beginning to control portion sizes.

- **Side Swap**

Swap out carb-heavy sides for steamed veggies, side salads, or a small serving of whole grains.

- **Dressing on the Side**

Ask for dressings and sauces on the side. This way, you can control the amount you use.

- **Water Wisdom**

Start with water or unsweetened tea. It helps you stay hydrated and prevents overconsumption of sugary beverages.

- **Customization is Key**

Don't hesitate to ask for modifications to meet your dietary needs. Most restaurants are accommodating.

- **Choose Whole Grains**

If there's a choice, opt for whole-grain options like brown rice or whole wheat bread.

- **Plan Dessert Wisely**

If you're indulging in dessert, consider sharing or choosing fruit-based options with limited added sugars.

- **Practice Mindful Eating**

Eat slowly, savor each bite, and listen to your body's cues of fullness.

- **Sip Strategically**

Limit alcohol intake, as it can affect blood sugar levels. If you choose to drink, do so in moderation and pair it with food.

Dining out can be a delightful experience that aligns with your health goals. Armed with these strategies, you'll be equipped to navigate restaurant menus with confidence, making choices that celebrate both flavor and wellness. Remember, every meal away from home is an opportunity to nurture your body while enjoying the pleasure of good company and great food.

28-Day Meal Plan

Embarking on 4 week-long culinary adventure that embraces both flavor and health is my specialty. Here's a 28-day meal plan, curated from my personal experience, to guide you on your diabetes management journey:

Week-1	Breakfast	Lunch	Dinner	Snack/Dessert
Day-1	Open-Faced Breakfast Egg Sandwich	Veggie and Haddock Foil Packets	Classic Coleslaw	Brown Rice Pudding
Day-2	Spicy Egg Muffins	Tomato and Beans with Baby Spinach	Maple-Glazed Spareribs	Buffalo Bites
Day-3	Healthy Country Breakfast Sausage	Ground Turkey Spinach Stir-Fry	Greek Quinoa Bowl	Vanilla Avocado Peach Smoothie
Day-4	Best Healthy French Toast	Cauliflower Tater Tots	Stir-Fried Chicken and Broccoli	Easy Banana Mug Cake
Day-5	Tofu and Mushroom Omelet	Nut Buckwheat Pilaf	Lemon Chicken and Zucchini Soup	Pita Pizza with Feta and Cucumber
Day-6	Easy Breakfast Quesadillas with Egg	Cauliflower and Beef Soup	Tomato and Peach Salad	Banana Blueberry Smoothie
Day-7	Spring Asparagus and Radicchio Brunch Plate	Salmon with Lemon Mustard	Simple Curried Squash	Crispy Apple and Pecan Bake

Week-2	Breakfast	Lunch	Dinner	Snack/Dessert
Day-8	Delicious Apple Pancakes	One-Pot Creamy Tuscan Chicken	Healthy Southwestern Salad	Fruit and Beet Smoothie
Day-9	Kiwifruit, Peach and Yogurt Bowl	Thyme-Sesame Crusted Halibut	Chermoula Beet Roast	Roasted Chickpeas with Herbs
Day-10	Mediterranean Scramble with Feta Cheese	Feta and Red Onion Couscous Pilaf	Creamy Broccoli and Cauliflower Soup	Strawberry Sorbet
Day-11	Healthy Whole Grain Pancakes	Paprika Pork with Brussels Sprouts	Garlicky Tofu and Brussels Sprouts	Green Smoothie with Berry and Banana
Day-12	Cauliflower Hash Brown	Endive and Shrimp with Walnuts	Italian Eggplant Parmesan	Toffee Apple Mini Pies
Day-13	Breakfast Zucchini	Farro Risotto with Mushroom	Thai Fish Curry	Date and Almond Balls with Seeds
Day-14	Almond Butter and Dates Power Bars	Fresh Raspberry Spinach Salad	Slaw and Chicken Stir-Fry	Healthy Green Smoothie

Week-3	Breakfast	Lunch	Dinner	Snack/Dessert
Day-15	Mini Basil Broccoli Frittatas	Steak with Green Beans	Healthy Tuna Salad	Almond Flour Crackers
Day-16	Healthy English Muffin with Berries	Roasted Eggplant and White Bean	Italian Chicken Cacciatore	Healthy Green Smoothie Bowl
Day-17	Easy Breakfast Egg Burrito	Nourishing Vegetable Stew	Couscous with Veggies	Chia and Raspberry Pudding
Day-18	Quinoa Bowl with Blackberry	Fish Fillets with Asparagus	Balsamic Brussels Sprouts	Chickpea Tortillas
Day-19	Spinach and Tomato Baked Egg Cups	Harissa Chicken Thighs with Yogurt	Greens and Beans Stuffed Mushrooms	Avocado Smoothie
Day-20	Zucchini Fritters	Pea and Carrot Rice	Appetizing Tuna Patties	Peanut Butter Pie
Day-21	Delicious Apple Pancakes	Honey Roasted Carrots and Parsnips	Pepper and Tomato Salad	Peach Bruschetta with Tarragon

Week-4	Breakfast	Lunch	Dinner	Snack/Dessert
Day-22	Healthy Strawberry Parfait Oatmeal	Simple Oatmeal Chicken Tenders	Triple Bean Chili	Spinach and Berries Smoothie
Day-23	Pumpkin and Yogurt Bread	Barley Kale and Squash Risotto	Shrimp Magic	Crispy Apple Chips
Day-24	Chicken Breakfast Burritos	Italian Chickpea and Carrot Soup	Quick Summer Chicken Salad	Roasted Cherry Tomato with Parmesan
Day-25	Cauliflower Hash Brown	Pepper and Black Bean Tacos	Beef Picadillo	Orange and Peach Ambrosia
Day-26	Quinoa Bowls with Avocado and Egg	Mahi-Mahi Fillets with Peppers	Green Beans with Shallot	Almond Cheesecake Bites
Day-27	Veggie Stuffed Omelet	Herb Turkey Cutlets	Lentils with Spinach	Quick Healthy Peaches and Greens Smoothie
Day-28	Healthy Veggie Egg Scramble	Egg Salad Lettuce Wraps	Roasted Colorful Bell Peppers	Mini Peppers Stuffed with Black Bean

Each day is a canvas for you to create vibrant, nutritious meals that elevate both your health and your culinary experience. Remember, variety is the spice of life - feel free to modify and experiment with these ideas to suit your tastes and preferences. Bon appétit on your journey to diabetes wellness!

CHAPTER 3 BREAKFAST RECIPES

Best Healthy French Toast 13
Almond Butter and Dates Power Bars 13
Cauliflower Hash Brown 13
Easy Breakfast Egg Burrito 13
Chicken Breakfast Burritos 13
Healthy Strawberry Parfait Oatmeal 13
Easy Breakfast Quesadillas with Egg 14
Quick Protein Bowl 14
Kiwifruit, Peach and Yogurt Bowl 14
Delicious Apple Pancakes 14
Healthy Veggie Egg Scramble 14
Mini Basil Broccoli Frittatas 15
Healthy Country Breakfast Sausage 15
Healthy Whole Grain Pancakes 15
Air Fryer Breakfast Bake 15
Open-Faced Breakfast Egg Sandwich 15
Mediterranean Scramble with Feta Cheese 15
Breakfast Zucchini 16
Healthy Apple Cinnamon Overnight Oats 16
Spinach and Tomato Baked Egg Cups 16
Pumpkin and Yogurt Bread 16
Veggie Stuffed Omelet 16
Fried Almond Butter with Banana 17
Quick Avocado Egg Sandwiches 17
Healthy English Muffin with Berries 17
Spring Asparagus and Radicchio Brunch Plate 17
Homemade Breakfast Chicken Sausage 17
Spicy Egg Muffins 17
Quinoa Bowl with Blackberry 18
Quinoa Bowls with Avocado and Egg 18
Tofu and Mushroom Omelet 18
Zucchini Fritters 18

Best Healthy French Toast

Prep Time: 5 minutes, Cook Time: 10 minutes, Serves: 4

- 4 egg whites
- 1 whole egg
- 8 slices whole grain bread (at least ½–1 inch thick)
- 1 cup unsweetened almond milk
- ½ tsp. ground cinnamon
- 1 tsp. vanilla extract
- ¼ tsp. ground nutmeg
- ½ tsp. powdered stevia

1. In a shallow bowl, whisk together the egg whites, whole egg, almond milk, cinnamon, vanilla, nutmeg, and stevia. Soak each slice of bread in the mixture for about 1 minute per side, let the bread absorb the liquid and flavors. 2. Heat a griddle pan until very hot, and coat with olive oil spray. Place each soaked slice of bread on the griddle pan, and cook about 3 minutes on each side, or until browned and crunchy. 3. Serve immediately.

Calories: 305, Protein: 15g, Fat: 7g, Carbs: 49g, Fiber: 6g, Sugar: 0.3g, Sodium: 438 mg

Almond Butter and Dates Power Bars

Prep Time: 30 minutes (includes chilling time), Cook Time: 20 minutes, Serves: 8

- 1¾ cups pitted dates
- ⅓ cup unsweetened raisins
- ¼ cup all-natural almond butter
- ¼ cup whole raw apricots
- ½ cup instant oats

1. Add the dates in a small bowl and cover with warm water. Let sit for 10 minutes, then drain. 2. Mix the dates, almond butter, raisins, apricots, and oats in a blender, and process to a paste. 3. Using a kitchen mallet lightly pound the mixture into an 8-by-8-inch nonstick baking pan in an even layer. 4. Transfer to the freezer and chill for 15 minutes to set. Slice into bars and serve immediately, or store in the refrigerator for up to 2 weeks or in the freezer for up to 3 months.

Calories: 215, Fat: 6g, Protein: 3g, Carbs: 40g, Fiber: 5g, Sugar: 14g, Sodium: 13mg

Cauliflower Hash Brown

Prep Time: 20 minutes, Cook Time: 10 minutes, Serves: 4

- 2 cups cauliflower, finely grated, soaked and drained
- 2 tbsps. xanthan gum
- Salt, to taste
- Pepper powder, to taste
- 2 tsps. chili flakes
- 1 tsp. garlic
- 1 tsp. onion powder
- 2 tsps. vegetable oil

1. Preheat the Air fryer to 300°F (149°C) and grease an Air fryer basket with oil. 2. Heat vegetable oil in a nonstick pan and add cauliflower. 3. Sauté for about 4 minutes and dish out the cauliflower in a plate. 4. Mix the cauliflower with xanthum gum, salt, chili flakes, garlic and onion powder. 5. Mix well and refrigerate the hash for about 20 minutes. 6. Place the hash in the Air fryer basket and air fry for about 10 minutes. 7. Flip the hash after cooking half way through and dish out to serve warm.

Calories: 291, Fat: 2.8g, Carbs: 6.5g, Sugar: 4.5g, Protein: 6.6g, Sodium: 62mg

Easy Breakfast Egg Burrito

Prep Time: 5 minutes, Cook Time: 8 minutes, Serves: 1

- 1 tbsp. extra virgin olive oil
- 2 egg whites
- 1 whole egg
- 1 100% whole wheat tortilla
- 2 tbsps. chopped white onion
- 1 clove garlic, minced
- 1 cup spinach
- ⅛ cup shredded low-fat cheddar cheese
- Cracked black pepper
- ¼ cup rinsed and drained canned black beans
- 1 tbsp. chopped fresh cilantro
- ¼ cup chopped Roma tomato
- 1 tbsp. prepared low-sodium salsa, optional

1. Heat the oil in a medium pan over medium heat. Add the onion and garlic, and cook for about 30 seconds. 2. Meanwhile, whisk together the egg whites and whole egg. Add the eggs, spinach, cheese, and pepper. Cook until the eggs are no longer runny, about 2 to 3 minutes. Remove the pan from the heat. 3. Warm the tortilla in a flat pan over medium heat. Place the beans in a small pot, and bring to a simmer. 4. Set the warm tortilla on a plate, and spoon the beans into the middle of the tortilla, in a line. Add the vegetable and egg mixture, and top with cilantro, tomato, and salsa (if using). 5. Fold into a burrito, and enjoy immediately.

Calories: 460, Protein: 28g, Fat: 24g, Carbs: 39g, Fiber: 9g, Sugar: 1g, Sodium: 709mg

Chicken Breakfast Burritos

Prep Time: 5 minutes, Cook Time: 10 minutes, Serves: 5

- Nonstick cooking spray
- 10 tbsps. shredded reduced-fat Cheddar cheese
- 8 ounces (227g) lean ground chicken
- 6 large eggs
- 2 cups baby spinach
- 5 (6-inch) whole wheat tortillas
- ½ tsp. freshly ground black pepper
- ½ tsp. onion powder
- ½ tsp. paprika
- 1 garlic clove, minced

1. Whisk the eggs in a large bowl. Add the spinach and set aside. 2. Coat a large skillet with cooking spray and heat over medium heat. Add the ground chicken, pepper, onion powder, paprika, and garlic and cook, stirring often, until it's no longer pink. 3. Reduce the heat. Add the whisked eggs and continue to cook, stirring often but not constantly, until no liquid egg is visible. Remove from the heat. 4. Evenly distribute the egg and chicken mixture among the tortillas, leaving a 1-inch border around the edges. Sprinkle each with 2 tbsps. of Cheddar cheese. Fold up the bottoms, then the edges, and roll tightly without the contents spilling. Use toothpicks to secure if necessary.

Calories: 307, Total Fat: 14g, Carbs: 22g, Fiber: 3g, Protein: 25g, Sodium: 355mg

Healthy Strawberry Parfait Oatmeal

Prep Time: 10 minutes, Cook Time: 5 minutes, Serves: 1

- ⅔ cup rolled oats
- ½ cup water
- ¼ cup nonfat milk
- ½ cup low-fat unsweetened yogurt
- ½ cup sliced strawberries
- 1 sugar-free cookie

CHAPTER 3 BREAKFAST RECIPES

1. Mix the oats, water and milk in a small saucepan and heat over medium heat. When it starts to boil, heat to low and cook for 3 minutes. Stir occasionally, with the pan uncovered, for just 3 minutes. 2. Remove from heat and spoon the oats into 2 parfait glasses. Top each serving with yogurt and strawberries, and then crumble the cookie over the top.

Calories: 430, Protein: 23g, Fat: 15.7g, Carbs: 73.6g, Fiber: 3g, Sugar: 8g, Sodium: 254 mg

Easy Breakfast Quesadillas with Egg

Prep Time: 10 minutes, Cook Time: 15 minutes, Serves: 4

1½ tbsps. extra-virgin olive oil	cheese, divided
Nonstick cooking spray	½ cup crumbled low-fat feta cheese
4 large eggs	½ medium onion, diced
4 (6-inch) whole wheat tortillas, divided	1 medium red bell pepper, diced
	⅛ tsp. salt
½ cup shredded part-skim low-moisture mozzarella	⅛ tsp. freshly ground black pepper
	4 cups baby spinach

1. In a large skillet, heat the oil over medium heat. Add the onion and bell pepper and sauté for about 5 minutes, or until soft. 2. In a medium bowl, whisk together the eggs, salt, and black pepper. Stir in the spinach and feta cheese. Add the egg mixture to the skillet and scramble for about 2 minutes, or until the eggs are cooked. Remove from the heat. 3. Coat a clean skillet with cooking spray and add 2 tortillas. Place one-quarter of the spinach-egg mixture on one side of each tortilla. Sprinkle each with ⅛ cup of mozzarella cheese. Fold the other halves of the tortillas down to close the quesadillas and brown for about 1 minute. Flip and cook for another minute on the other side. Repeat with the remaining 2 tortillas and mozzarella cheese. 4. Cut each quesadilla in half or wedges. Divide among 4 storage containers or reusable bags.

Calories: 453, Total Fat: 28g, Carbs: 28g, Fiber: 4.5g, Protein: 23g, Sodium: 650mg

Quick Protein Bowl

Prep Time: 10 minutes, Cook Time: 5 minutes, Serves: 1

¼ cup uncooked old-fashioned oats	½ medium banana, thinly sliced
¾ cup low-fat cottage cheese	
1 tbsp. almond butter	

1. Add the banana, oats, almond butter, and cheese in a bowl and combine all the ingredients together. Serve immediately!

Calories: 346, Fat: 12g, Protein: 28g, Carbs: 47g, Fiber: 7g, Sugar: 8g, Sodium: 690mg

Kiwifruit, Peach and Yogurt Bowl

Prep Time: 5 minutes, Cook Time: 20 minutes, Serves: 2

½ cup diced fresh kiwifruit	yogurt
½ cup diced fresh peach	Fresh mint leaves
½ cup diced fresh banana	1 tsp. cider
1 cup low-fat unsweetened coconut	

1. Mix the kiwifruit, peach, banana and yogurt in a bowl and whisk gently. Divide into 2 individual bowls. 2. Add each serving with a small drizzle of cider. Garnish with a couple fresh mint leaves.

Calories: 256, Protein: 7.65g, Fat: 4.75g, Carbs: 47.91g, Fiber: 7g, Sugar: 12g, Sodium: 92 mg

Delicious Apple Pancakes

Prep Time: 5 minutes, Cook Time: 5 minutes, Serves: 16 pancakes

¼ cup extra-virgin olive oil, divided	2 tsps. baking powder
1 cup 1% milk	1 tsp. baking soda
2 large eggs	1 tsp. ground cinnamon
1 medium Gala apple, diced	2 tbsps. maple syrup
1 cup whole wheat flour	¼ cup chopped walnuts

1. Set aside 1 tsp. of oil to use for oiling a griddle or skillet. In a large bowl, stir together the flour, baking powder, baking soda, cinnamon, milk, eggs, apple, and the remaining oil. 2. Heat a griddle or skillet over medium-high heat and coat with the reserved oil. Working in batches, pour in about ¼ cup of the batter for each pancake. Cook until browned on both sides. 3. Place 4 pancakes into each of 4 medium storage containers and the maple syrup in 4 small containers. 4. To serve, sprinkle each serving with 1 tbsp. of walnuts and drizzle with ½ tbsp. of maple syrup.

Calories: 378, Total Fat: 22g, Carbs: 39g, Fiber: 5g, Protein: 10g, Sodium: 65mg

Healthy Veggie Egg Scramble

Prep Time: 7 minutes, Cook Time: 10 minutes, Serves: 4

2 tbsps. extra virgin olive oil	¼ cup chopped red bell pepper
3 whole eggs	½ cup chopped broccoli
3 egg whites	2 tbsps. water
1 cup mixed greens (such as collard greens, mustard greens, and kale)	1 large clove garlic, minced
	⅛ tsp. sea salt
¼ cup chopped red onion	Pinch of cracked black pepper

1. Wash the greens and pat dry, cut off thick part of stems, and cut the leaves into 1-inch pieces. Chop the onion, bell pepper, and broccoli into small pieces of about the same size. 2. Heat a large nonstick skillet over medium to high heat and add the oil once the pan is hot. Add the greens once the oil is hot and sauté for about 3 minutes or until the greens start to wilt. 3. Pour in the water and cover the pan with a lid, steam for 2 to 3 minutes. Remove the lid, add the broccoli, bell pepper, onion, and garlic. 4. Meanwhile, in a medium bowl, whisk together the eggs, egg whites, salt, and pepper. Once the onion is translucent, add the whisked egg mixture. Stir to evenly break up and distribute the eggs. 5. Cook until the eggs are no longer runny but still look a little bit wet, turn off the heat, and serve immediately.

Calories: 145, Protein: 9g, Fat: 11g, Carbs: 4g, Fiber: 1g, Sugar: 0.7g, Sodium: 178mg

Mini Basil Broccoli Frittatas

Prep Time: 10 minutes, Cook Time: 20 minutes, Serves: 4

Olive oil, for greasing the muffin cups	1 scallion, white and green parts, chopped
¼ cup unsweetened almond milk	Pinch sea salt
8 eggs	Pinch freshly ground black pepper
½ tsp. chopped fresh basil	
½ cup shredded fresh spinach	
½ cup chopped broccoli	

1. Preheat the oven to 350°F(180°C). 2. Use olive oil to lightly grease a 6-cup muffin tin, set it aside. 3. Add the almond milk, eggs and basil into a medium bowl, whisk them together until frothy. 4. Add the spinach, broccoli and scallion, stir well. In the muffin cups, spoon with the egg mixture. 5. Bake until the frittatas are golden, puffed and cooked through, about 20 minutes. 6. With sea salt and pepper to season and serve warm.

Calories: 132, Total Fat: 9g, Saturated Fat: 3g, Carbs: 2g, Fiber: 1g, Protein: 12g, Sodium: 318mg

Healthy Country Breakfast Sausage

Prep Time: 25 minutes, Cook Time: 15 minutes, Serves: 6

½ tsp. black pepper	½ tsp. ground sage
½ lb. (227g) ground turkey breast	½ tsp. paprika
½ tsp. allspice	¼ tsp. dry mustard
½ tsp. minced garlic	¼ tsp. onion powder
½ lb. (227g) lean ground pork loin	

1. In a large bowl, add all the ingredients and mix well to make a sausage pie. 2. Prepare a large frying pan and heat it over medium-low heat. Spray canola oil lightly on the pot with canola oil spray. Heat the pan for one minute while placing the sausage pie in the frying pan. Turn on medium heat and fry for about 5 minutes on each side until the sausage pie is completely browned. Take out from the pot and serve while hot. 3. Optional: You can add chili powder. Use Italian seasoning herbs instead of the spices listed above to make mild Italian sausage.

Calories: 137, Fat: 5.03g, Protein: 21.17g, Carbs: 0.6g, Fiber: 0.1g, Sugar: 0g, Sodium: 69 mg

Healthy Whole Grain Pancakes

Prep Time: 15 minutes, Cook Time: 15 minutes, Serves: 4

½ cup chopped toasted almonds or walnuts	1 small banana, mashed
2 cups unsweetened almond milk	2 tsps. baking powder
	½ tsp. ground cinnamon
1 tsp. vanilla extract	¼ cup unsweetened applesauce
¼ cup old-fashioned oats	¼ tsp. sea salt
1¼ cups whole wheat flour	3 tbsps. brown sugar substitute

1. Add the vanilla extract, almond milk, and applesauce in a medium bowl, mix together. Then place the banana, wheat flour, oats, baking powder, almonds or walnuts, and cinnamon in a larger bowl, combining together, season with salt and sugar substitute. Put the wet ingredients to the dry ingredients, and stir constantly until smooth. 2. Take out the pan, heat it over medium heat, and spray the pan with olive oil evenly. Use a spoon to divide the batter into four portions, spread evenly on the pan, and fry for 2 to 3 minutes. Turn them when the batter starts to bubble on top and continue frying for about a minute. Repeat the above steps. Finally, remove the pan from the heat and stack the cooked pancakes on a covered plate. Serve while hot.

Calories: 301, Fat: 10g, Protein: 9g, Carbs: 55g, Fiber: 9g, Sugar: 14g, Sodium: 483mg

Air Fryer Breakfast Bake

Prep Time: 15 minutes, Cook Time: 25 minutes, Serves: 2

4 eggs	½ cup bell pepper, diced
1 slice whole grain bread, torn into pieces	½ tsp. kosher salt
1½ cups baby spinach	1 tsp. hot sauce
⅓ cup low-fat cheddar cheese, shredded	

1. Preheat the Air fryer to 250ºF (121°C) and grease a 6-inch soufflé dish with nonstick cooking spray. 2. Whisk together eggs, salt and hot sauce in a bowl. 3. Dip the bread pieces, spinach, ¼ cup cheddar cheese and bell pepper in the whisked eggs. 4. Pour this mixture into prepared soufflé dish and sprinkle with remaining cheese. 5. Transfer into the Air fryer basket and bake for about 25 minutes. 6. Remove from the Air fryer basket and let it rest for 10 minutes before serving.

Calories: 249, Fat: 15.7g, Carbs: 10.3g, Sugar: 3.4g, Protein: 18.2g, Sodium: 979mg

Open-Faced Breakfast Egg Sandwich

Prep Time: 5 minutes, Cook Time: 5 minutes, Serves: 1

1½ tsps. extra virgin olive oil	2 egg whites, beaten
1 slice 100% whole wheat bread	½ cup spinach
2 thick tomato slices	Cracked black pepper, to taste
1 thin slice low-fat cheddar cheese	1 tsp. brown mustard

1. Preheat the oven or toaster oven to 400°F(205°C). Heat a small nonstick pan on medium heat. Add oil to the hot pan and when the oil is hot, add the egg whites. 2. Scramble the eggs while cooking, then add the spinach and season to taste with pepper. Spread mustard onto the bread, add the tomato and scrambled eggs, and top with cheese. 3. Heat in the oven until the cheese melts, about 2 minutes.

Calories: 286, Protein: 20g, Fat: 12g, Carbs: 27g, Fiber: 4g, Sugar: 0.1g, Sodium: 515mg

Mediterranean Scramble with Feta Cheese

Prep Time: 15 minutes, Cook Time: 10 minutes, Serves: 4

1 medium clove garlic, minced	⅛ cup chopped red onion
2 tbsps. extra virgin olive oil	1 whole egg
¼ cup sliced red bell pepper	2 egg whites
¼ cup rinsed and drained, chopped canned artichoke hearts	⅛ tsp. cracked black pepper
	⅛ tsp. dried oregano
	⅛ cup low-fat feta cheese

CHAPTER 3 BREAKFAST RECIPES

1. Prepare a small non-stick pan, heat it over medium heat, and pour oil into the pan. When the oil is hot, put onion and garlic and stir fry for about 1 minute. Then add the bell pepper strips and the artichoke heart, and fry for another 3 minutes, until the onion is translucent and the bell pepper is soft. 2. Put the egg whites and eggs in a small bowl, beat the egg whites and eggs, season with oregano and black pepper. Pour the eggs into the pot and stir evenly with a spatula. Cook for 3 to 4 minutes until the egg no longer runs. Remove the pan from the heat, place the feta on the egg, and close the lid until the feta starts to melt. Enjoy warm.

Calories: 424, Fat: 37g, Protein: 21g, Carbs: 5g, Fiber: 1g, Sugar: 1g, Sodium: 572mg

Breakfast Zucchini

Prep Time: 5 minutes, Cook Time: 25 minutes, Serves: 4

- 4 zucchinis, diced into 1-inch pieces, drained
- 2 small bell peppers, chopped medium
- 2 small onions, chopped medium
- Cooking oil spray
- Pinch salt and black pepper

1. Preheat the Air fryer to 350°F (177°C) and grease the Air fryer basket with cooking spray. 2. Season the zucchini with salt and black pepper and place in the Air fryer basket. 3. Roast for about 20 minutes, stirring occasionally. 4. Add the onion and bell pepper and roast for 5 more minutes. 5. Remove from the Air fryer and mix well to serve warm.

Calories: 146, Fat: 0.5g, Carbs: 3.8g, Sugar: 5.5g, Protein: 4g, Sodium: 203mg

Healthy Apple Cinnamon Overnight Oats

Prep Time: 15 minutes, plus overnight to soak, Cook Time: 0, Serves: 3

- 2 medium Gala apples, diced
- 1½ cups rolled oats
- 3 tbsps. coarsely chopped walnuts
- 3 tbsps. coconut sugar
- 1½ cups 1% milk
- 1½ tbsps. ground cinnamon
- Pinch ground nutmeg

1. Put the diced apples in a storage container. 2. Mix the oats, walnuts, coconut sugar, cinnamon, and nutmeg in a large bowl. Divide evenly among 3 mason jars and seal the jars. 3. The evening before you plan to have this for breakfast, add ½ cup of milk to each jar of oat mixture and let sit in the refrigerator overnight. 4. In the morning, top each with ½ cup of diced apples.

Calories: 368, Total Fat: 9g, Carbs: 66g, Fiber: 9g, Protein: 11g, Sodium: 69mg

Spinach and Tomato Baked Egg Cups

Prep Time: 15 minutes, Cook Time: 15 minutes, Serves: 5

- Nonstick cooking spray
- 10 large eggs
- 2½ ounces (71g) shredded reduced-fat Cheddar cheese
- 2½ cups chopped spinach
- 1 medium tomato, diced
- 1 garlic clove, minced
- ½ tbsp. chopped fresh parsley
- ½ tbsp. chopped fresh chives
- ¼ tsp. freshly ground black pepper

1. Preheat the oven to 400°F(204°C). Coat 10 cups of a muffin tin with cooking spray or line with silicone muffin liners or paper liners. 2. Crack the eggs into a large bowl. Add the garlic, parsley, chives, and pepper and whisk well. Then stir in the Cheddar cheese, spinach, and tomato. 3. Divide the egg mixture evenly among the muffin cups, filling about two-thirds full. 4. Bake for about 15 minutes, or until set. Let cool. 5. Place 2 egg cups into each of 5 storage containers.

Calories: 232, Total Fat: 18g, Carbs: 2g, Fiber: 0.5g, Protein: 17g, Sodium: 258mg

Pumpkin and Yogurt Bread

Prep Time: 10 minutes, Cook Time: 15 minutes, Serves: 4

- 2 large eggs
- 8 tbsps. pumpkin puree
- 6 tbsps. banana flour
- 4 tbsps. nonfat plain Greek yogurt
- 6 tbsps. oats
- 2 tbsps. honey
- 2 tbsps. vanilla essence
- Pinch of ground nutmeg

1. Preheat the Air fryer to 360°F (182°C) and grease a loaf pan. 2. Mix together all the ingredients except oats in a bowl and beat with the hand mixer until smooth. 3. Add oats and mix until well combined. 4. Transfer the mixture into the prepared loaf pan and place in the Air fryer. 5. Bake for about 15 minutes and remove from the Air fryer. 6. Place onto a wire rack to cool and cut the bread into desired size slices to serve.

Calories: 212, Fat: 3.4g, Carbs: 36g, Sugar: 20.5g, Protein: 6.6g, Sodium: 49mg

Veggie Stuffed Omelet

Prep Time: 5 minutes, Cook Time: 10 minutes, Serves: 1

- 1 tbsp. extra virgin olive oil
- 2 egg whites
- 1 whole egg
- ¼ cup coarsely chopped broccoli
- 2 tbsps. chopped red onion
- 1 clove garlic, minced
- ¼ cup chopped zucchini
- ⅛ cup shredded low-fat cheddar cheese
- ⅛ tsp. sea salt
- ⅛ tsp. cracked black pepper

1. Heat a medium-sized nonstick pan over medium heat and add the oil once the pan is hot. When the oil is hot, add the broccoli and cook for a minute before adding the onion, garlic, and zucchini. Sauté for 3 to 4 minutes. 2. In a small bowl, whisk together the egg whites and whole egg and season with salt and pepper. 3. Turn heat to low and add the whisked eggs to the pan with the vegetables, making sure to tilt the pan so the eggs evenly cover the vegetables. After 30 seconds, turn the heat off, flip the omelet, and spread the cheese on half of the omelet. 4. Fold the other half over the cheese, and cover the pan with a lid. Let it steam for 1 to 2 minutes, or until the cheese melts. 5. Serve immediately.

Calories: 279, Protein: 20g, Fat: 20g, Carbs: 6g, Fiber: 2g, Sugar: 0.8g, Sodium: 580mg

Fried Almond Butter with Banana

Prep Time: 10 minutes, Cook Time: 5 minutes, Serves: 1

⅛ tsp. ground cinnamon
2 tbsps. almond butter
2 slices 100% whole wheat bread
1 small banana, sliced

1. In a pan, put each slice of almond butter bread in the pan and bake for 2-3 minutes. 2. Then take out the toasted bread and place the banana slices neatly on top. Sprinkle with cinnamon at the end. Enjoy while it's hot!

Calories: 484, Fat: 21g, Protein: 19g, Carbs: 56g, Fiber: 12g, Sugar: 21g, Sodium: 421mg

Quick Avocado Egg Sandwiches

Prep Time: 5 minutes, Cook Time: 15 minutes, Serves: 4

2 small avocados, halved and pitted
2 tbsps. nonfat plain Greek yogurt
8 large eggs, hard-boiled, peeled and chopped
8 whole wheat bread slices (or your choice)
Juice of 1 large lemon
¼ tsp. salt
½ tsp. freshly ground black pepper
3 tbsps. finely chopped fresh dill
3 tbsps. finely chopped fresh parsley

1. Scoop the avocados into a large bowl and mash. Mix in the yogurt, lemon juice, salt, and pepper. Then combine the eggs, dill, and parsley. 2. Store the bread and salad separately in 4 reusable storage bags and 4 containers and assemble the night before or when serving. 3. To serve, divide the mixture evenly among 4 of the bread slices and top with the other slices to make sandwiches.

Calories: 488, Total Fat: 22g, Carbs: 48g, Fiber: 8g, Protein: 23g, Sodium: 597mg

Healthy English Muffin with Berries

Prep Time: 10 minutes, Cook Time: 5 minutes, Serves: 1

1 tbsp. low-fat cream cheese
4 strawberries, thinly sliced
½ cup blueberries, mashed
1 100% whole wheat English muffin, halved

1. Prepare a pan, put in the prepared English muffins, heat over medium heat for 2 to 3 minutes. 2. Then take it out of the pan and place it on a plate. Spread the cream cheese evenly on the fried muffins, and then put fruits on top. Enjoy while it's hot!

Calories: 231, Fat: 4g, Protein: 8g, Carbs: 43g, Fiber: 8g, Sugar: 11g, Sodium: 270mg

Spring Asparagus and Radicchio Brunch Plate

Prep Time: 10 minutes, Cook Time: 30 minutes, Serves: 2

8 stalks young fresh asparagus, trimmed and chopped
1 red onion, sliced
½ cup (120mL) water
½ cup radicchio, chopped
2 boiled eggs, peeled
1 cup unsweetened almond milk
1 tsp. Dijon mustard
1 tsp. vanilla
1 tbsp. fresh mint leaves
¼ tsp. nutmeg
fresh ground black pepper

1. Pour ½ cup of water to a boil in a pan large enough to hold the asparagus. Add the asparagus and radicchio, cover with a lid and reduce the heat to medium-low. 2. Check the vegetables for tenderness after 5 minutes, the asparagus should be bright green but still slightly crisp. Cook an additional 1 or 2 minutes if necessary. 3. In the meantime, chop the eggs coarsely in a microwave-safe, medium-sized mixing bowl - this is easily done using 2 knives. Add the milk, mustard and vanilla and whisk lightly. Add in the mint and nutmeg. Gently add the onion. 4. Warm the egg and milk mixture, covered with a paper towel, in the microwave for about 45 seconds. 5. Transfer the asparagus and radicchio onto 2 plates with a slotted spoon and then spoon the warm egg and milk mixture over each serving. Spread with fresh ground black pepper to season.

Calories: 208, Protein: 13.48g, Fat: 11.16g, Carbs: 15.2g, Fiber: 8g, Sugar: 0.5g, Sodium: 167mg

Homemade Breakfast Chicken Sausage

Prep Time: 15 minutes, Cook Time: 15 minutes, Serves: 8

Extra-virgin olive oil, for brushing
2 scallions, sliced
1½ pounds (680 g) ground chicken
1 tbsp. chopped fresh sage
½ tsp. ground nutmeg
1 tbsp. Dijon mustard
1 tsp. salt
¼ tsp. freshly ground black pepper

1. Preheat the oven to 400°F(205°C). Use the olive oil to brush a rimmed baking sheet. 2. Add the scallions, chicken, sage, nutmeg, mustard, salt and pepper into a medium bowl. Combine gently until the chicken is thoroughly distributed with all the ingredients. 3. Scoop the mixture into 24 small mounds with a 1-ounce ice cream scoop or spoon, transfer them onto the prepared baking sheet. 4. Gently flatten each mound into a patty shape with the back of a spatula or your fingers. 5. Bake for 10 to 15 minutes, until firm to the touch. 6. After baking, remove from the oven and serve warm.

Calories: 130, Total Fat: 7 g, Total Carbs: <1g, Sugar: <1g, Fiber: <1g, Protein: 15g, Sodium: 390mg

Spicy Egg Muffins

Prep Time: 25 minutes, Cook Time: 40 minutes, Serves: 6

4 tbsps. chopped green onion, white ends discarded
½ cup chopped green bell pepper
4 cups chopped spinach
½ cup chopped red bell pepper
3 whole eggs
14 egg whites
Pinch of paprika
¼ tsp. dried oregano
⅛ tsp. cracked black pepper
2 tbsps. finely chopped fresh parsley
⅛ tsp. chile pepper flakes

1. Preheat the oven to 375°F in advance. Put spinach, green peppers, red peppers, and onions in a large bowl and mix well. In a separate large bowl, whisk together egg whites, whole eggs, chili flakes, oregano, parsley, pepper, and chili powder. 2. Spray each muffin tin evenly with olive oil spray, making sure to spray on the sides as well. Scoop the vegetable mixture into each muffin cup, about half of the muffin cup. 3. Then slowly pour about ⅓ cup of egg mixture into each muffin cup so as not to replace the vegetables. 4. Place the muffin tin on the grill in the middle of the oven and bake for 25 to 30 minutes until the eggs no longer run. Remove from the oven immediately to avoid over-bake or dry the eggs. Enjoy.

Calories: 93, Fat: 3g, Protein: 14g, Carbs: 4g, Fiber: 1g, Sugar: 1g, Sodium: 181mg

Quinoa Bowl with Blackberry

Prep Time: 20 minutes, Cook Time: 20 minutes, Serves: 4

2 tsps. canola oil	½ cup nonfat milk
Nutmeg	1 cup water
¾ cup quinoa	1 tsp. vanilla
½ orange, peeled	2 cups fresh blackberries

1. Rinse the quinoa and drain. Heat the oil in a medium-sized non-stick pan, add the quinoa, roast the quinoa on medium high heat for about 1 minute, stirring constantly. Cut the peeled oranges into small pieces and remove all seeds. 2. Add a little nutmeg and processed oranges to the quinoa, stir and then add water. Simmer on low heat for about 11 minutes, until the quinoa is almost soft but still a bit crispy in the middle. Add milk, blackberries and vanilla, stir gently, and simmer for 2 or 3 minutes until the quinoa grains are translucent. 3. Remove from the pot to a bowl and enjoy while it is hot!

Calories: 271, Fat: 4.5g, Protein: 7.3g, Carbs: 51.8g, Fiber: 3g, Sugar: 5g, Sodium: 24mg

Quinoa Bowls with Avocado and Egg

Prep Time: 10 minutes, Cook Time: 25 minutes, Serves: 5

5 hard-boiled eggs, peeled and sliced	½ tsp. freshly ground black pepper
3 avocados, pitted, sliced, and coated with lemon juice	½ tsp. ground cumin
	½ tsp. garlic powder
3¾ cups cooked quinoa	1 tbsp. chopped fresh cilantro
½ tsp. onion powder	2 small tomatoes, diced
	½ large red onion, chopped

1. In a large bowl, season the cooked quinoa with the onion powder, pepper, cumin, and garlic powder. Add the cilantro, tomatoes, and onion and mix well. 2. Divide the quinoa mix among 5 storage containers as a base for the breakfast bowl, then divide the avocados evenly into the bowls. Top each with a whole sliced egg.

Calories: 388, Total Fat: 20g, Carbs: 40g, Fiber: 10g, Protein: 15g, Sodium: 90mg

Tofu and Mushroom Omelet

Prep Time: 15 minutes, Cook Time: 28 minutes, Serves: 2

¼ of onion, chopped	2 tsps. canola oil
8 ounces silken tofu, pressed and sliced	1 garlic clove, minced
3½ ounces fresh mushrooms, sliced	Salt and black pepper, to taste
3 eggs, beaten	
2 tbsps. low-fat milk	

1. Preheat the Air fryer to 360°F (182°C) and grease an Air Fryer pan. 2. Heat oil in the Air Fryer pan and add garlic and onion. 3. Air fry for about 3 minutes and stir in the tofu and mushrooms. 4. Season with salt and black pepper and top with the beaten eggs. 5. Bake for about 25 minutes, poking the eggs twice in between. 6. Dish out and serve warm.

Calories: 224, Fat: 14.5g, Carbs: 6.6g, Sugar: 3.4g, Protein: 17.9g, Sodium: 214mg

Zucchini Fritters

Prep Time: 15 minutes, Cook Time: 7 minutes, Serves: 4

10½ ounces zucchini, grated and squeezed	2 eggs
7 ounces low-fat Halloumi cheese	1 tsp. fresh dill, minced
¼ cup whole wheat flour	Salt and black pepper, to taste

1. Preheat the Air fryer to 360°F (182°C) and grease an Air Fryer basket. 2. Mix together all the ingredients in a large bowl. 3. Make small fritters from this mixture and place them on the prepared Air Fryer basket. 4. Bake for about 7 minutes. 5. Dish out and serve warm.

Calories: 250, Fat: 17.2g, Carbs: 10g, Sugar: 2.7g, Protein: 15.2g, Sodium: 330mg

CHAPTER 4 GRAIN AND RICE RECIPES

Cranberry and Almond Quinoa Pilaf ········· 20
Apple and Pecan Quinoa Salad ··············· 20
Feta and Red Onion Couscous Pilaf ········· 20
Greek Quinoa Bowl ···························· 20
Brown Rice with Collard and Scrambled Egg ··· 20
Quinoa with Spinach ·························· 21
Easy Coconut Quinoa ························· 21
Mint and Pea Risotto ·························· 21
Sautéed Beluga Lentil and Zucchinis ········ 21
Couscous with Balsamic Dressing ··········· 21
Nut Buckwheat Pilaf ·························· 21
Lentil and Bulgur Pilaf ························ 22
Millet Pilaf with Lime ························· 22
Eggplant and Bulgur Pilaf ···················· 22
Farro Risotto with Mushroom ················ 22
Pearl Barley with Peppers ···················· 22
Pepper and Egg Oatmeal Bowl ··············· 22
Spicy Chicken Bulgur ························· 23

Farro and Avocado Bowl ······················ 23
Couscous with Veggies ······················· 23
Simple Wild Brown Rice ······················ 23
Vegetable Fried Millet ························ 23
Pea and Carrot Rice ··························· 24
Mushroom Rice with Hazelnut ··············· 24
Wild Rice and Basmati Pilaf ·················· 24
Wild Rice, Almonds, and Cranberries Salad ····· 24
Barley Kale and Squash Risotto ·············· 24
Farro and Cherry Salad ······················· 24
Mushroom Farro Bowl ························ 25
Za'atar-Spiced Bulgur Wheat Salad ·········· 25
Lentils with Spinach ·························· 25
Mushroom Alfredo Rice ······················ 25
Wild Rice and Basmati Pilaf ·················· 25
Mediterranean Couscous Salad ·············· 26
Simple Brown Rice Pilaf ······················ 26

Cranberry and Almond Quinoa Pilaf

Prep Time: 2 minutes, Cook Time: 10 minutes, Serves: 3

1 cup quinoa, rinsed
2 cups water
1 cup dried cranberries
½ cup slivered almonds
¼ cup salted sunflower seeds

1. Combine the water and quinoa in the Instant Pot. 2. Lock the lid. Select the Manual mode and set the cooking time for 10 minutes at High Pressure. 3. Once cooking is complete, do a quick pressure release. Carefully open the lid. 4. Add the cranberries, almonds, and sunflower seeds and gently mix until well incorporated. Serve warm.

Calories: 311, Fat: 10.5g, Protein: 7.2g, Carbs: 50g, Fiber: 5.5g, Sugar: 20g, Sodium: 48mg

Apple and Pecan Quinoa Salad

Prep Time: 7 minutes, Cook Time: 8 minutes, Serves: 4 to 6

1 cup quinoa, rinsed
1 cup water
¼ tsp. salt, plus more as needed
2 apples, unpeeled and cut into large dices
2 tbsps. freshly squeezed lemon juice
1 tbsp. rice vinegar
2 celery stalks, halved lengthwise and chopped
½ bunch scallions, green and light green parts, sliced
¾ to 1 cup dried cranberries, white raisins, and regular raisins
2 tbsps. avocado oil
½ to 1 tsp. chili powder, plus more as needed
Pinch freshly ground black pepper
½ to 1 cup chopped pecans
½ cup chopped fresh cilantro

1. Combine the quinoa, water, and salt in the Instant Pot. 2. Secure the lid. Select the Manual mode and set the cooking time for 8 minutes at High Pressure. 3. Once cooking is complete, do a natural pressure release for 10 minutes, then release any remaining pressure. Carefully open the lid. 4. Transfer the quinoa to a large salad bowl. Refrigerate for 5 minutes to cool. 5. Mix the apples, lemon juice, and vinegar in a small resealable container. Cover and shake lightly to coat the apples, then refrigerate. 6. Remove the cooled quinoa and stir in the celery, scallions, cranberry-raisin mix, oil, and chili powder. Taste and season with more salt and pepper, as needed. Add the apples and lemon-vinegar juice into the salad and stir well. 7. Serve topped with the pecans and cilantro.

Calories: 346, Fat: 21g, Protein: 5g, Carbs: 39g, Fiber: 5g, Sugar: 17g, Sodium: 78mg

Feta and Red Onion Couscous Pilaf

Prep Time: 5 minutes, Cook Time: 5 minutes, Serves: 4

2 tbsps. vegetable oil
1 tsp. cumin seeds
1 tsp. ground turmeric
1 cup frozen peas and carrots
1 cup Israeli couscous
½ cup diced yellow onion
1 tsp. kosher salt
1 tsp. garam masala
1 cup water
½ cup chopped red onion
½ cup crumbled low-fat feta cheese
Black pepper, to taste

1. Press the Sauté button on the Instant Pot and heat the oil. 2. Once the oil is hot, stir in the cumin seeds and turmeric, allowing them to sizzle for 10 seconds. Turn off the Instant Pot. 3. Add the peas and carrots, couscous, yellow onion, salt, garam masala, and water. Stir to combine. 4. Lock the lid. Select the Manual mode and set the cooking time for 3 minutes at High Pressure. 5. When the timer beeps, perform a natural pressure release for 5 minutes, then release any remaining pressure. Carefully remove the lid. 6. Stir in the red onion and feta cheese. Season to taste with black pepper and serve.

Calories: 320, Fat: 12g, Protein: 9g, Carbs: 42g, Fiber: 4g, Sugar: 4g, Sodium: 586mg

Greek Quinoa Bowl

Prep Time: 10 minutes, Cook Time: 13 minutes, Serves: 4

1 tbsp. olive oil
3 cloves garlic, minced
1 cup chopped red onion
½ cup quinoa
2 cups chopped tomatoes
2 cups spinach, torn
2 cups chopped zucchini
2 cups vegetable broth
½ cup chopped black olives
½ cup pine nuts

1. Set your Instant Pot to Sauté and heat the olive oil. 2. Add the garlic and onion and sauté for approximately 5 minutes, stirring frequently. 3. Add the remaining ingredients, except for the pine nuts, to the Instant Pot and stir to combine. 4. Secure the lid. Select the Manual mode and set the cooking time for 8 minutes at High Pressure. 5. Once cooking is complete, do a natural pressure release for 10 minutes, then release any remaining pressure. Carefully open the lid. 6. Fluff the quinoa and stir in the pine nuts, then serve.

Calories: 359, Fat: 19g, Protein: 10g, Carbs: 41g, Fiber: 7g, Sugar: 8g, Sodium: 702mg

Brown Rice with Collard and Scrambled Egg

Prep Time: 15 minutes, Cook Time: 20 minutes, Serves: 4

1 tbsp. extra-virgin olive oil
1 bunch collard greens, stemmed and cut into chiffonade
1 carrot, cut into 2-inch matchsticks
1 red onion, thinly sliced
½ cup low-sodium vegetable broth
2 tbsps. coconut aminos
1 garlic clove, minced
1 cup cooked brown rice
1 large egg
1 tsp. red pepper flakes
1 tsp. paprika
Salt, to taste

1. Heat the olive oil in a Dutch oven or a nonstick skillet over medium heat until shimmering. 2. Add the collard greens and sauté for 4 minutes or until wilted. 3. Add the carrot, onion, broth, coconut aminos, and garlic to the Dutch oven, then cover and cook for 6 minutes or until the carrot is tender. 4. Add the brown rice and cook for 4 minutes. Keep stirring during the cooking. 5. Break the egg over them, then cook and scramble the egg for 4 minutes or until the egg is set. 6. Turn off the heat and sprinkle with red pepper flakes, paprika, and salt before serving.

Calories: 154, Fat: 6g, Protein: 6g, Carbs: 22g, Fiber: 6g, Sugar: 2g, Sodium: 78mg

Quinoa with Spinach

Prep Time: 5 minutes, Cook Time: 2 minutes, Serves: 4

1½ cups quinoa, rinsed
1½ cups water
4 cups spinach
1 bell pepper, chopped
3 stalks of celery, chopped
¼ tsp. salt

1. Combine all ingredients in the Instant Pot. 2. Secure the lid. Select the Manual mode and set the cooking time for 2 minutes at High Pressure. 3. Once cooking is complete, do a natural pressure release for 10 minutes, then release any remaining pressure. Carefully open the lid. 4. Fluff the quinoa and serve.

Calories: 280, Fat: 3g, Protein: 10g, Carbs: 53g, Fiber: 6g, Sugar: 3g, Sodium: 196mg

Easy Coconut Quinoa

Prep Time: 15 minutes, Cook Time: 25 minutes, Serves: 4

2 tsps. extra-virgin olive oil
1 sweet onion, chopped
1 tbsp. grated fresh ginger
2 tsps. minced garlic
1 cup low-sodium chicken broth
1 cup unsweetened coconut milk
1 cup quinoa, well rinsed and drained
Sea salt, to taste
¼ cup shredded, unsweetened coconut

1. Place a large saucepan over medium-high heat and add the oil. 2. Sauté the onion, ginger, and garlic until softened, about 3 minutes. 3. Add the chicken broth, coconut milk, and quinoa. 4. Bring the mixture to a boil, then reduce the heat to low and cover. Simmer the quinoa, stirring occasionally, until the quinoa is tender and most of the liquid has been absorbed, about 20 minutes. 5. Season the quinoa with salt, and serve topped with the coconut.

Calories: 355, Fat: 21.1g, Protein: 9.1g, Carbs: 35.1g, Fiber: 6.1g, Sugar: 4.0g, Sodium: 33mg

Mint and Pea Risotto

Prep Time: 5 minutes, Cook Time: 20 minutes, Serves: 2

2 tbsps. coconut oil
1 onion, peeled and diced
½ tsp. garlic powder
½ cup barley
1 cup vegetable broth, divided
Salt and pepper, to taste
½ cup fresh peas
¼ tsp. lime zest
¼ cup chopped fresh mint leaves

1. Press the Sauté button on the Instant Pot and heat the oil. 2. Add the onion and stir-fry for 5 minutes. 3. Add garlic powder and barley and cook for 1 minute more. 4. Pour in ½ cup of vegetable broth and stir for 3 minutes until it is absorbed by barley. 5. Add the remaining ½ cup of broth, salt, and pepper. 6. Secure the lid. Select the Manual mode and set the cooking time for 10 minutes at High Pressure. 7. Once cooking is complete, do a natural pressure release for 10 minutes, then release any remaining pressure. Carefully open the lid. 8. Stir in peas, lime zest, and mint and let sit for 3 minutes until heated through. Serve immediately.

Calories: 401, Fat: 13g, Protein: 7g, Carbs: 62g, Fiber: 12g, Sugar: 6g, Sodium: 685mg

Sautéed Beluga Lentil and Zucchinis

Prep Time: 15 minutes, Cook Time: 10 minutes, Serves: 4

2 tbsps. olive oil
2 large zucchinis, chopped
4 garlic cloves, minced
½ tbsp. dried oregano
½ tbsp. curry powder
Salt and ground black pepper, to taste
2 cups canned beluga lentils, drained
¼ cup chopped parsley, divided
½ cup chopped basil
1 small red onion, diced
2 tbsps. balsamic vinegar
1 tsp. Dijon mustard

1. Set the Instant Pot to Sauté mode. Heat the oil and sauté the zucchinis until tender. 2. Mix in the garlic and cook until fragrant, 30 seconds. Top with oregano, curry, salt, and pepper. Allow to combine for 1 minute, stirring frequently. 3. Pour in lentils, cook for 3 minutes, and stir in half of parsley, basil, and onion. Sauté until onion softens, about 5 minutes. 4. Meanwhile, in a bowl, combine vinegar with mustard and pour mixture over lentils. Plate and garnish with remaining parsley.

Calories: 289, Fat: 9g, Protein: 14g, Carbs: 40g, Fiber: 13g, Sugar: 7g, Sodium: 291mg

Couscous with Balsamic Dressing

Prep Time: 10 minutes, Cook Time: 5 minutes, Serves: 6

For the Dressing:
¼ cup extra-virgin olive oil
2 tbsps. balsamic vinegar
1 tsp. honey
Sea salt and freshly ground black pepper, to taste
For the Couscous:
1¼ cups whole-wheat couscous
Pinch sea salt
1 tsp. almond butter
2 cups boiling water
1 scallion, white and green parts, chopped
½ cup chopped pecans
2 tbsps. chopped fresh parsley

To Make the Dressing: 1. Whisk together the oil, vinegar, and honey. 2. Season with salt and pepper and set it aside. To Make the Couscous: 3. Put the couscous, salt, and almond butter in a large heat-proof bowl and pour the boiling water on top. Stir and cover the bowl. Let it sit for 5 minutes. Uncover and fluff the couscous with a fork. 4. Stir in the dressing, scallion, pecans, and parsley. 5. Serve warm.

Calories: 250, Fat: 12.9g, Protein: 5.1g, Carbs: 30.1g, Fiber: 2.2g, Sugar: 1.1g, Sodium: 77mg

Nut Buckwheat Pilaf

Prep Time: 10 minutes, Cook Time: 11 minutes, Serves: 4

1 tbsp. olive oil
4 garlic cloves, minced
1 red bell pepper, diced
2¼ cups chicken broth
1 cup roasted buckwheat groats
½ cup yellow lentils
¾ tsp. dried thyme
Salt and black pepper, to taste
1 cup chopped dried figs
½ cup toasted walnuts
½ cup chopped dried apricots
½ cup chopped cilantro

1. Press the Sauté button on the Instant Pot and heat the oil. Add the garlic and bell pepper to the pot and sauté for 5 minutes. Stir in the chicken broth, buckwheat groats, lentils, thyme, salt

and pepper.2.Close and secure the lid. Select the Manual mode and set the cooking time for 6 minutes on High Pressure. Once the timer goes off, use a natural pressure release for 10 minutes, then release any remaining pressure. Carefully open the lid.3.Stir in the figs, walnuts, apricots and cilantro. Spoon the pilaf into bowls and enjoy.

Calories: 502, Fat: 17g, Protein: 16g, Carbs: 72g, Fiber: 13g, Sugar: 19g, Sodium: 672mg

Lentil and Bulgur Pilaf

Prep Time: 5 minutes, Cook Time: 10 minutes, Serves: 6

2 tbsps. vegetable oil	1¾ cups water, divided
1 large onion, thinly sliced	1 cup whole-grain red wheat bulgur
1½ tsps. kosher salt	½ cup dried red lentils
½ tsp. ground cinnamon	¼ cup chopped fresh parsley
½ tsp. ground allspice	Toasted pine nuts (optional)

1.Press the Sauté button on the Instant Pot and heat the oil.2.Once the oil is hot, add the onion and salt. Cook, stirring occasionally, until the onion is browned, about 5 minutes.3.Stir in the cinnamon and allspice and cook for 30 seconds.4.Add ¼ cup of water to deglaze the pot, scraping up the browned bits. Add the bulgur, lentils, and remaining 1½ cups of water.5.Lock the lid. Select the Manual mode and set the cooking time for 5 minutes at High Pressure.6.When the timer beeps, perform a natural pressure release for 10 minutes, then release any remaining pressure. Carefully remove the lid.7.Stir gently to fluff up the bulgur. Stir in the parsley and pine nuts (if desired), then serve.

Calories: 255, Fat: 7g, Protein: 10g, Carbs: 41g, Fiber: 10g, Sugar: 2g, Sodium: 590mg

Millet Pilaf with Lime

Prep Time: 5 minutes, Cook Time: 10 minutes, Serves: 4

1 cup chopped green onions	1 cup water
1 cup millet	1 cup chopped fresh cilantro or parsley
1 tsp. kosher salt	
1 tbsp. olive oil	Zest and juice of 1 lime

1.In the Instant Pot, combine the green onions, millet, salt, olive oil, and water.2.Lock the lid. Select the Manual mode and set the cooking time for 10 minutes at High Pressure.3.When the timer beeps, perform a natural pressure release for 10 minutes, then release any remaining pressure. Carefully remove the lid. 4.Stir in the cilantro and lime zest and juice and serve.

Calories: 258, Fat: 5g, Protein: 7g, Carbs: 47g, Fiber: 6g, Sugar: 1g, Sodium: 594mg

Eggplant and Bulgur Pilaf

Prep Time: 10 minutes, Cook Time: 60 minutes, Serves: 4

1 tbsp. extra-virgin olive oil	4 cups low-sodium chicken broth
½ sweet onion, chopped	1 cup diced tomato
2 tsps. minced garlic	Sea salt and freshly ground black pepper, to taste
1 cup chopped eggplant	
1½ cups bulgur	2 tbsps. chopped fresh basil

1.Place a large saucepan over medium-high heat. Add the oil and sauté the onion and garlic until softened and translucent, about 3 minutes.2.Stir in the eggplant and sauté 4 minutes to soften.3.Stir in the bulgur, broth, and tomatoes. Bring the mixture to a boil.4.Reduce the heat to low, cover, and simmer until the water has been absorbed, about 50 minutes.5.Season the pilaf with salt and pepper.6.Garnish with the basil, and serve.

Calories: 300, Fat: 4g, Protein: 14g, Carbs: 54g, Fiber: 12g, Sugar: 7g, Sodium: 358mg

Farro Risotto with Mushroom

Prep Time: 10 minutes, Cook Time: 30 minutes, Serves: 3

½ cup farro	2 tbsps. onion powder
2 tbsps. barley	Salt and pepper, to taste
3 cups chopped mushrooms	4 garlic cloves, minced
1 tbsp. red curry paste	1½ cups water
1 jalapeño pepper, seeded and chopped	2 tomatoes, diced
	Chopped cilantro, for serving
1 tbsp. shallot powder	Chopped scallions, for serving

1.Combine all the ingredients, except for the tomatoes, cilantro, and scallion, in the Instant Pot.2.Secure the lid. Select the Manual mode and set the cooking time for 30 minutes at High Pressure.3.Once cooking is complete, do a quick pressure release. Carefully open the lid.4.Stir in the tomatoes and let sit for 2 to 3 minutes until warmed through. Sprinkle with the cilantro and scallions and serve.

Calories: 282, Fat: 2g, Protein: 8g, Carbs: 61g, Fiber: 10g, Sugar: 6g, Sodium: 298mg

Pearl Barley with Peppers

Prep Time: 5 minutes, Cook Time: 25 minutes, Serves: 2

1 tbsp. sesame oil	1 jalapeño pepper, deseeded and chopped
½ yellow onion, chopped	
1 garlic clove, minced	1½ cups vegetable broth
1 bell pepper, deseeded and chopped	¾ cup pearl barley, rinsed
	2 tbsps. chopped chives

1.Set the Instant Pot to the Sauté mode and heat the oil. Add the onion to the pot and sauté for 3 minutes, or until just tender and fragrant. Add the garlic, bell pepper and jalapeño pepper to the pot and sauté for 2 minutes, or until fragrant. Stir in the vegetable broth and pearl barley.2.Lock the lid. Select the Multigrain mode and set the cooking time for 20 minutes on High Pressure. When the timer goes off, perform a quick pressure release. Carefully open the lid.3.Fluff the pearl barley mixture with a fork. Serve garnished with the chopped chives.

Calories: 366, Fat: 8g, Protein: 8g, Carbs: 64g, Fiber: 13g, Sugar: 8g, Sodium: 805mg

Pepper and Egg Oatmeal Bowl

Prep Time: 5 minutes, Cook Time: 6 to 7 minutes, Serves: 2

1½ cups vegetable broth	2 tsps. olive oil
½ cup steel-cut oats	1 onion, chopped
1 tomato, puréed	2 bell peppers, deseeded and sliced
Kosher salt and freshly ground black pepper, to taste	
	2 eggs, beaten

CHAPTER 4 GRAIN AND RICE RECIPES

1. Add the vegetable broth, oats, tomato, salt and black pepper to the Instant Pot and stir to combine. 2. Set the lid in place. Select the Manual setting and set the cooking time for 3 minutes on High Pressure. When the timer goes off, perform a natural pressure release for 20 minutes, then release any remaining pressure. Open the lid. Transfer the oatmeal to bowls. 3. Heat the olive oil in a skillet over medium-high heat. Add the onion and peppers to the skillet and sauté for 3 to 4 minutes, or until tender. Add the beaten eggs and continue to cook until they are set. 4. Spread the egg mixture over the oatmeal and serve warm.

Calories: 329, Fat: 15g, Protein: 13g, Carbs: 36g, Fiber: 6g, Sugar: 6g, Sodium: 697mg

Spicy Chicken Bulgur

Prep Time: 10 minutes, Cook Time: 19 to 20 minutes, Serves: 2

- ½ tbsp. sesame oil
- ½ pound (227 g) chicken breasts, boneless and skinless, cut into bite-sized pieces
- ½ onion, chopped
- 1 tsp. minced fresh garlic
- 1-inch ginger, peeled and sliced
- 1 Bird's-eye chili pepper, de-seeded and minced
- 1 cup chicken stock
- ½ cup unsweetened coconut milk
- ½ cup bulgur
- 1 tsp. garam masala
- ½ tsp. turmeric powder
- ½ tsp. ground cumin
- Sea salt and ground black pepper, to taste
- 1 tbsp. chopped fresh coriander

1. Set the Instant Pot to the Sauté mode and heat the sesame oil. Add the chicken breasts to the pot and sear for 3 to 4 minutes, or until lightly browned. Transfer to a plate and set aside. 2. Add the onion to the pot and sauté for 5 minutes, or until just softened and fragrant. Stir in the garlic and continue to sauté for 1 minute. 3. Return the cooked chicken breasts to the pot and stir in the remaining ingredients, except for the coriander. 4. Set the lid in place. Select the Manual setting and set the cooking time for 10 minutes on High Pressure. When the timer goes off, perform a natural pressure release for 10 minutes, then release any remaining pressure. Open the lid. 5. Transfer the chicken mixture to bowls and serve topped with fresh coriander

Calories: 465, Fat: 14g, Protein: 34g, Carbs: 50g, Fiber: 8g, Sugar: 4g, Sodium: 472mg

Farro and Avocado Bowl

Prep Time: 5 minutes, Cook Time: 25 minutes, Serves: 4

- 3 cups water
- 1 cup uncooked farro
- 1 tbsp. extra-virgin olive oil
- 1 tsp. ground cumin
- ½ tsp. salt
- ½ tsp. freshly ground black pepper
- 4 hard-boiled eggs, sliced
- 1 avocado, sliced
- ⅓ cup nonfat plain Greek yogurt
- 4 lemon wedges

1. In a medium saucepan, bring the water to a boil over high heat. 2. Pour the farro into the boiling water, and stir to submerge the grains. Reduce the heat to medium and cook for 20 minutes. Drain and set aside. 3. Heat a medium skillet over medium-low heat. When hot, pour in the oil, then add the cooked farro, cumin, salt, and pepper. Cook for 3 to 5 minutes, stirring occasionally. 4. Divide the farro into four equal portions, and top each with one-quarter of the eggs, avocado, and yogurt. Add a squeeze of lemon over the top of each portion.

Calories: 333, Fat: 16.1g, Protein: 15.1g, Carbs: 31.9g, Fiber: 7.9g, Sugar: 2g, Sodium: 360mg

Couscous with Veggies

Prep Time: 15 minutes, Cook Time: 5 minutes, Serves: 4 to 6

- 1 tbsp. olive oil
- ½ large onion, chopped
- 2 bay leaves
- 1 large red bell pepper, chopped
- 1 cup grated carrot
- 1¾ cups Israeli couscous
- 1¾ cups water
- ½ tsp. garam masala
- 2 tsps. salt, or more to taste
- 1 tbsp. lemon juice
- Chopped cilantro, for garnish

1. Set your Instant Pot to Sauté and heat the olive oil. 2. Add the onion and bay leaves and sauté for 2 minutes. 3. Stir in the bell pepper and carrot and sauté for another 1 minute. 4. Add the couscous, water, garam masala, and salt. Stir to combine well. 5. Lock the lid. Select the Manual mode and set the cooking time for 2 minutes at High Pressure. 6. When the timer beeps, perform a natural pressure release for 10 minutes, then release any remaining pressure. Carefully remove the lid. 7. Fluff the couscous and stir in the lemon juice. Taste and season with more salt, if needed. Garnish with the chopped cilantro and serve hot.

Calories: 259, Fat: 4g, Protein: 7g, Carbs: 49g, Fiber: 4g, Sugar: 4g, Sodium: 884mg

Simple Wild Brown Rice

Prep Time: 2 minutes, Cook Time: 20 minutes, Serves: 6 to 8

- 2 tbsps. olive oil
- 3¾ cups water
- 3 cups wild brown rice
- Salt, to taste

1. Combine the oil, water, and brown rice in the pot. 2. Season with salt. 3. Lock the lid. Select the Multigrain mode, then set the timer for 20 minutes on Low Pressure. 4. Once the timer goes off, do a natural pressure release for 5 minutes. Carefully open the lid. 5. Fluff the rice with a fork. 6. Serve immediately.

Calories: 268, Fat: 7g, Protein: 5g, Carbs: 48g, Fiber: 3g, Sugar: 0g, Sodium: 1mg

Vegetable Fried Millet

Prep Time: 10 minutes, Cook Time: 25 minutes, Serves: 4

- 1 tsp. vegetable oil
- ½ cup thinly sliced oyster mushrooms
- 1 cup finely chopped leeks
- 2 garlic cloves, minced
- ½ cup green lentils, rinsed
- 1 cup millet, soaked and drained
- ½ cup sliced bok choy
- 1 cup chopped asparagus
- 1 cup chopped snow peas
- 2¼ cups vegetable stock
- Salt and black pepper, to taste
- A drizzle of lemon juice
- ¼ cup mixed chives and parsley, finely chopped

1. Press the Sauté button on the Instant Pot and heat the oil. 2. Cook the mushrooms, leeks, and garlic for 3 minutes. Add lentils and millet, stir, and cook for 4 minutes. 3. Stir in the bok choy, asparagus, snow peas, and vegetable stock. 4. Secure the lid. Select the Manual mode and set the cooking time for 10 minutes at High Pressure. 5. Once cooking is complete, do a quick pressure release. Carefully open the lid. 6. Season to taste with salt and pepper. Serve sprinkled with the lemon juice, chives, and parsley.

Calories: 319, Fat: 3g, Protein: 14g, Carbs: 61g, Fiber: 12g, Sugar: 3g, Sodium: 486mg

Pea and Carrot Rice

Prep Time: 10 minutes, Cook Time: 23 minutes, Serves: 4 to 6

- 1 tbsp. olive oil
- 1 clove garlic, minced
- ¼ cup chopped shallots
- 2 cups chicken broth
- 1½ cups basmati rice, rinsed
- 1 cup frozen peas
- ½ cup chopped carrots
- 2 tsps. curry powder
- Salt and ground black pepper, to taste

1. Set your Instant Pot to Sauté and heat the olive oil. 2. Add the garlic and shallots and sauté for about 3 minutes until fragrant, stirring occasionally. 3. Add the remaining ingredients to the Instant Pot and stir to incorporate. 4. Lock the lid. Select the Rice mode and set the cooking time for 20 minutes at High Pressure. 5. Once cooking is complete, do a natural pressure release for 10 minutes, then release any remaining pressure. Carefully remove the lid. 6. Fluff the rice with the rice spatula or fork. Serve warm.

Calories: 308, Fat: 4g, Protein: 6g, Carbs: 59g, Fiber: 3g, Sugar: 2g, Sodium: 526mg

Mushroom Rice with Hazelnut

Prep Time: 20 minutes, Cook Time: 35 minutes, Serves: 8

- 1 tbsp. extra-virgin olive oil
- 1 cup chopped button mushrooms
- ½ sweet onion, chopped
- 1 celery stalk, chopped
- 2 tsps. minced garlic
- 2 cups brown basmati rice
- 4 cups low-sodium chicken broth
- 1 tsp. chopped fresh thyme
- Sea salt and freshly ground black pepper, to taste
- ½ cup chopped hazelnuts

1. Place a large saucepan over medium-high heat and add the oil. 2. Sauté the mushrooms, onion, celery, and garlic until lightly browned, about 10 minutes. 3. Add the rice and sauté for an additional minute. 4. Add the chicken broth and bring to a boil. 5. Reduce the heat to low and cover the pot. Simmer until the liquid is absorbed and the rice is tender, about 20 minutes. 6. Stir in the thyme and season with salt and pepper. 7. Top with the hazelnuts, and serve.

Calories: 240, Fat: 6.1g, Protein: 7.1g, Carbs: 38.9g, Fiber: 0.9g, Sugar: 1.1g, Sodium: 388mg

Wild Rice and Basmati Pilaf

Prep Time: 5 minutes, Cook Time: 35 minutes, Serves: 6

- 2 tbsps. olive oil
- 2 brown onions, minced
- 2 cloves garlic, minced
- 12 ounces (340 g) mushrooms, sliced
- ½ tsp. salt
- 6 sprigs fresh thyme
- 2 cups broth
- 2 cups wild rice and basmati rice mixture
- ½ cup pine nuts
- ½ cup minced parsley

1. Set your Instant Pot to Sauté. Add the olive oil and onions and cook for 6 minutes. 2. Add minced garlic and cook for 1 minute more. Place the remaining ingredients, except for nuts and parsley, into the Instant Pot and stir well. 3. Lock the lid. Select the Manual mode and set the cooking time for 28 minutes at High Pressure. 4. When the timer beeps, perform a natural pressure release for 15 minutes, then release any remaining pressure. Carefully remove the lid. 5. Sprinkle with the pine nuts and parsley, then serve.

Calories: 333, Fat: 12g, Protein: 9g, Carbs: 49g, Fiber: 3g, Sugar: 2g, Sodium: 340mg

Wild Rice, Almonds, and Cranberries Salad

Prep Time: 10 minutes, Cook Time: 45 minutes, Serves: 6

For the Rice:
- 2½ cups chicken bone broth, vegetable broth, or water
- 2 cups wild rice blend, rinsed
- 1 tsp. kosher salt

For the Dressing:
- Juice of 1 medium orange (about ¼ cup)
- 1½ tsps. grated orange zest
- ¼ cup white wine vinegar
- 1 tsp. pure maple syrup
- ¼ cup extra-virgin olive oil

For the Salad:
- ½ cup sliced almonds, toasted
- ¾ cup unsweetened dried cranberries
- Freshly ground black pepper, to taste

For the Rice: 1. Pour the broth in a pot, then add the rice and sprinkle with salt. Bring to a boil over medium-high heat. 2. Reduce the heat to low. Cover the pot, then simmer for 45 minutes. 3. Turn off the heat and fluff the rice with a fork. Set aside until ready to use. For the Dressing: 4. When cooking the rice, make the dressing: Combine the ingredients for the dressing in a small bowl. Stir to combine well. Set aside until ready to use. For the Salad: 5. Put the cooked rice, almonds, and cranberries in a bowl, then sprinkle with black pepper. Add the dressing, then toss to combine well. 6. Serve immediately.

Calories: 126, Fat: 5g, Protein: 3g, Carbs: 18g, Fiber: 2g, Sugar: 2g, Sodium: 120mg

Barley Kale and Squash Risotto

Prep Time: 10 minutes, Cook Time: 15 minutes, Serves: 6

- 1 tsp. extra-virgin olive oil
- ½ sweet onion, finely chopped
- 1 tsp. minced garlic
- 2 cups cooked barley
- 2 cups chopped kale
- 2 cups cooked butternut squash, cut into ½-inch cubes
- 2 tbsps. chopped pistachios
- 1 tbsp. chopped fresh thyme
- Sea salt, to taste

1. Place a large skillet over medium heat and add the oil. 2. Sauté the onion and garlic until softened and translucent, about 3 minutes. 3. Add the barley and kale, and stir until the grains are heated through and the greens are wilted, about 7 minutes. 4. Stir in the squash, pistachios, and thyme. 5. Cook until the dish is hot, about 4 minutes, and season with salt.

Calories: 160, Fat: 1.9g, Protein: 5.1g, Carbs: 32.1g, Fiber: 7g, Sugar: 2g, Sodium: 63mg

Farro and Cherry Salad

Prep Time: 5 minutes, Cook Time: 40 minutes, Serves: 4 to 6

- 3 cups water
- 1 cup whole grain farro, rinsed
- 1 tbsp. extra-virgin olive oil
- 1 tbsp. apple cider vinegar
- 2 cups cherries, cut into halves
- ¼ cup chopped green onions
- 1 tsp. lemon juice
- Salt, to taste
- 10 mint leaves, chopped

1. Combine the water and farro in the Instant Pot. 2. Lock the lid. Select the Manual mode and set the cooking time for 40 minutes at High Pressure. 3. When the timer beeps, perform a quick pressure release. Carefully remove the lid. 4. Drain the farro and transfer to a bowl. Stir in the olive oil, vinegar, cherries, green onions, lemon juice, salt, and mint. Serve immediately.

Calories: 279, Fat: 5g, Protein: 7g, Carbs: 54g, Fiber: 10g, Sugar: 12g, Sodium: 160mg

Mushroom Farro Bowl

Prep Time: 10 minutes, Cook Time: 18 to 19 minutes, Serves: 2

1 tbsp. olive oil	1½ cups vegetable broth
1 onion, chopped	¾ cup farro
1 cup sliced mushrooms	Sea salt and ground black pepper, to taste
1 sweet pepper, chopped	
1 garlic clove, minced	⅓ cup grated low-fat Swiss cheese
½ cup white wine	1 tbsp. chopped fresh parsley

1. Set the Instant Pot on the Sauté mode and heat the oil. Add the onion to the pot and sauté for 3 to 4 minutes, or until softened. Add the mushrooms and pepper and sauté for 3 minutes. Stir in the garlic and continue to sauté for 1 minute. 2. Pour in the white wine to deglaze the pan. Stir in the vegetable broth, farro, salt and black pepper. 3. Lock the lid, select the Manual mode and set the cooking time for 11 minutes on High Pressure. When the timer goes off, do a natural pressure release for 10 minutes, then release any remaining pressure. Open the lid. 4. Transfer the dish to bowls and serve topped with the cheese and fresh parsley.

Calories: 382, Fat: 10g, Protein: 14g, Carbs: 52g, Fiber: 9g, Sugar: 7g, Sodium: 730mg

Za'atar-Spiced Bulgur Wheat Salad

Prep Time: 10 minutes, Cook Time: 2 minutes, Serves: 6

For the Bulgur Wheat:	2 tbsps. freshly squeezed lemon juice
1 cup bulgur wheat	
2¼ cups water, divided	5 cherry tomatoes, finely chopped
For the Salad:	
¼ cup finely chopped cucumber	1 tsp. kosher salt
¼ cup finely chopped fresh parsley	½ tsp. freshly ground black pepper
2 tbsps. finely chopped fresh mint	
2 tbsps. extra-virgin olive oil	1 tsp. za'atar spice blend

1. Combine the bulgur wheat and 1¼ cups of water in a heat-proof bowl. 2. Pour the remaining 1 cup of water into the Instant Pot and insert a trivet. Place the bowl on the trivet. 3. Secure the lid. Select the Manual mode and set the cooking time for 2 minutes at High Pressure. 4. Once cooking is complete, do a natural pressure release for 5 minutes, then release any remaining pressure. Carefully open the lid. 5. Let the bulgur wheat cool for 20 minutes before fluffing it with a fork. 6. Assemble the salad: Add the cucumber, parsley, mint, olive oil, lemon juice, tomatoes, salt, pepper, and za'atar seasoning to the bulgur wheat. Mix gently and serve immediately.

Calories: 167, Fat: 7g, Protein: 3g, Carbs: 25g, Fiber: 5g, Sugar: 1g, Sodium: 391mg

Lentils with Spinach

Prep Time: 15 minutes, Cook Time: 15 minutes, Serves: 2

1 tbsp. olive oil	½ tsp. salt
½ tsp. cumin seeds	¼ cup split pigeon peas, rinsed
¼ tsp. mustard seeds	¼ cup split red lentil, rinsed
3 cloves garlic, finely chopped	1½ cups water
1 green chili, finely chopped	¼ tsp. garam masala
1 large tomato, chopped	2 tsps. lemon juice
1½ cups spinach, finely chopped	Cilantro, for garnish
¼ tsp. turmeric powder	

1. Press the Sauté button on the Instant Pot. Add the oil and then the cumin seeds and mustard seeds. 2. Let the seeds sizzle for a few seconds and then add the garlic and green chili. Sauté for 1 minute or until fragrant. 3. Add the tomato and cook for 1 minute. Add the chopped spinach, turmeric powder and salt, and cook for 2 minutes. 4. Add the rinsed peas and lentils and stir. Pour in the water and put the lid on. 5. Press the Manual button and set the cooking time for 10 minutes on High Pressure. 6. When timer beeps, let the pressure release naturally for 5 minutes, then release any remaining pressure. 7. Open the pot and add the garam masala, lemon juice and cilantro. Serve immediately.

Calories: 283, Fat: 7g, Protein: 15g, Carbs: 42g, Fiber: 16g, Sugar: 3g, Sodium: 603mg

Mushroom Alfredo Rice

Prep Time: 5 minutes, Cook Time: 25 minutes, Serves: 4

2 tbsps. olive oil	1½ tbsps. fresh lemon juice
¾ cup finely chopped onion	Salt and black pepper, to taste
2 garlic cloves, minced	2 ounces (57 g) creamy mushroom Alfredo sauce
1 cup wild rice	
2¾ cups vegetable broth	¼ cup coarsely chopped walnuts

1. Set your Instant Pot to Sauté. Add the oil, onion, and garlic to the pot and sauté for 3 minutes. Stir in the rice and broth. 2. Secure the lid. Select the Manual mode and set the cooking time for 22 minutes at High Pressure. 3. Once cooking is complete, do a natural pressure release for 10 minutes, then release any remaining pressure. Carefully open the lid. 4. Add lemon juice, salt, pepper, and sauce and stir to combine. Garnish with the chopped walnuts and serve.

Calories: 305, Fat: 16g, Protein: 6g, Carbs: 34g, Fiber: 3g, Sugar: 3g, Sodium: 593mg

Wild Rice and Basmati Pilaf

Prep Time: 5 minutes, Cook Time: 35 minutes, Serves: 6

2 tbsps. olive oil	6 sprigs fresh thyme
2 brown onions, minced	2 cups broth
2 cloves garlic, minced	2 cups wild rice and basmati rice mixture
12 ounces (340 g) mushrooms, sliced	
	½ cup pine nuts
½ tsp. salt	½ cup minced parsley

1. Set your Instant Pot to Sauté. Add the olive oil and onions and cook for 6 minutes. 2. Add minced garlic and cook for 1 minute more. Place the remaining ingredients, except for nuts and parsley, into the Instant Pot and stir well. 3. Lock the lid. Select the Manual mode and set the cooking time for 28 minutes at High Pressure. 4. When the timer beeps, perform a natural pressure release for 15 minutes, then release any remaining pressure. Carefully remove the lid. 5. Sprinkle with the pine nuts and parsley, then serve.

Calories: 333, Fat: 12g, Protein: 9g, Carbs: 49g, Fiber: 3g, Sugar: 2g, Sodium: 340mg

Mediterranean Couscous Salad

Prep Time: 20 minutes, Cook Time: 2 minutes, Serves: 6

For the Couscous:
1 cup couscous
2¾ cups water, divided
For the Salad:
½ cup salad greens (such as a mix of spinach, arugula, and red and green lettuce leaves)
4 tbsps. finely chopped carrot
4 tbsps. finely chopped black olives
4 tbsps. finely chopped cucumber
½ cup thinly sliced red onion, marinated in 2 tbsps. each of lemon juice and water for 20 minutes, then drained
½ cup shredded red cabbage, marinated in 2 tbsps. each of lemon juice and water for 20 minutes, then drained
1 tsp. kosher salt
1 tsp. freshly ground black pepper
2 tbsps. extra-virgin olive oil

1. Combine the couscous and 1¼ of cups water in a heatproof bowl. 2. Pour the remaining 1½ cups of water into the Instant Pot and insert a trivet. Place the bowl on the trivet. 3. Secure the lid. Select the Manual mode and set the cooking time for 2 minutes at High Pressure. 4. Once cooking is complete, do a natural pressure release for 5 minutes, then release any remaining pressure. Carefully open the lid. 5. Let the couscous cool for 15 minutes before fluffing with a fork. 6. Assemble the salad: Add the salad greens, carrot, olives, cucumber, onion, cabbage, salt, pepper, and olive oil to the couscous. Mix gently and serve immediately.

Calories: 186, Fat: 6g, Protein: 4g, Carbs: 30g, Fiber: 3g, Sugar: 2g, Sodium: 413mg

Simple Brown Rice Pilaf

Prep Time: 5 minutes, Cook Time: 10 minutes, Serves: 4

½ tbsp. olive oil
1 cup instant brown rice
1 cup low-sodium vegetable broth
1 clove garlic, minced
1 scallion, thinly sliced
1 tbsp. minced onion flakes
⅛ tsp. freshly ground black pepper

1. Mix the vegetable broth, olive oil, garlic, scallion, and minced onion flakes in a saucepan and bring to a boil. 2. Add rice, return mixture to boil, then reduce heat and simmer for 10 minutes. 3. Remove from heat, uncover and let stand for 5 minutes. 4. Fluff with a fork and season with black pepper.

Calories: 100, Total Fat: 2g, Saturated Fat: 0g, Sodium: 35mg, Total Carbs: 19g, Fiber: 2g, Sugar: 1g, Protein: 2g

CHAPTER 5 BEANS AND LEGUMES RECIPES

Herbed Beans and Brown Rice Bowl ············ 28
Rosemary White Beans with Onion ············ 28
Tomato and Beans with Baby Spinach ·········· 28
Herbed Black Beans ························· 28
Lemon Wax Beans ·························· 28
Garlicky Tofu and Brussels Sprouts ············ 28
Green Lentils with Summer Vegetables ········ 29
Crispy Cowboy Black Bean Fritters ············ 29
Super Bean and Grain Burgers ··············· 29
Easy Three-Bean Medley ···················· 29
Crispy Parmesan Bean and Veggie Cups ········ 29
Roasted Eggplant and White Bean ············ 30
Enchilada Black Bean Casserole ·············· 30
Black-Eyed Peas Curry ····················· 30
Dandelion and Beet Greens with Black Beans ·· 30

Thai Green Bean and Soybean ················ 30
Greens and Beans Stuffed Mushrooms ········· 31
Beluga Lentils with Lacinato Kale ············· 31
Navy Bean Pico de Gallo ···················· 31
Black-Eyed Peas with Collard ················ 31
Red Kidney Beans with Green Beans ·········· 31
Vegetarian Kidney Bean Étouffée ············· 32
Pepper and Black Bean Tacos ················ 32
Chickpeas Curry ··························· 32
Triple Bean Chili ··························· 32
Rutabaga and Lentils Rice Bowl ·············· 32
Swiss Chard with Black-Eyed Peas ············ 33
Kale and Black-Eyed Pea Curry ··············· 33
Black Chickpea Curry ······················· 33

Herbed Beans and Brown Rice Bowl

Prep Time: 15 minutes, Cook Time: 15 minutes, Serves: 8

2 tsps. extra-virgin olive oil
½ sweet onion, chopped
1 tsp. minced jalapeño pepper
1 tsp. minced garlic
1 (15-ounce / 425-g) can sodium-free red kidney beans, rinsed and drained
1 large tomato, chopped
1 tsp. chopped fresh thyme
Sea salt and freshly ground black pepper, to taste
2 cups cooked brown rice

1. Place a large skillet over medium-high heat and add the olive oil. 2. Sauté the onion, jalapeño, and garlic until softened, about 3 minutes. 3. Stir in the beans, tomato, and thyme. 4. Cook until heated through, about 10 minutes. Season with salt and pepper. 5. Serve over the warm brown rice.

Calories: 200, Fat: 2.1g, Protein: 9.1g, Carbs: 37.1g, Fiber: 6.1g, Sugar: 2g, Sodium: 40mg

Rosemary White Beans with Onion

Prep Time: 8 minutes, Cook Time: 8 hours, Serves: 16

1 pound (454 g) great northern beans
2 cups low sodium vegetable broth
4 cups water
1 onion, finely chopped
3 cloves garlic, minced
1 large sprig fresh rosemary
½ tsp. salt
⅛ tsp. white pepper

1. Sort over the beans, remove and discard any extraneous material. Rinse the beans well over cold water and drain. 2. In a 6-quart slow cooker, combine the beans, onion, garlic, rosemary, salt, water, and vegetable broth. 3. Cover the slow cooker and cook on low for 6 to 8 hours or until the beans are soft. 4. Remove and discard the rosemary stem. Stir in the mixture gently and serve warm.

Calories: 88, Fat: 0g, Protein: 5g, Carbs: 17g, Fiber: 5g, Sugar: 0g, Sodium: 362mg

Tomato and Beans with Baby Spinach

Prep Time: 5 minutes, Cook Time: 15 minutes, Serves: 2

1 tbsp. extra-virgin olive oil
1 (13-ounce / 369-g) can white cannellini beans
2 cups baby spinach
¾ cup crushed tomatoes
½ cup chicken stock
1 large garlic clove, minced
½ tsp. dried basil
½ tsp. Himalayan salt
Freshly ground black pepper (optional)

1. In a small saucepan, heat the olive oil over medium heat. 2. Add the garlic, tomatoes, basil, and salt, and sauté for 3 minutes. 3. Place the beans, stock, and spinach. 4. Cook for 10 minutes more. The liquid will reduce by half. 5. Season with some freshly ground black pepper, if desired. Serve warm.

Calories: 300, Fat: 8g, Protein: 17g, Carbs: 44g, Fiber: 12g, Sugar: 8g, Sodium: 333mg

Herbed Black Beans

Prep Time: 11 minutes, Cook Time: 9 hours, Serves: 8

3 cups dried black beans, rinsed and drained
6 cups low-sodium vegetable broth
2 onions, chopped
8 garlic cloves, minced
1 tsp. dried basil leaves
½ tsp. dried thyme leaves
½ tsp. dried oregano leaves
½ tsp. salt

1. Mix all the ingredients in a 6-quart slow cooker. Cover the slow cooker and cook on low for 7 to 9 hours, or until the beans have absorbed the liquid and are tender. 2. Remove the bay leaf and discard.

Calories: 250, Fat: 0g, Protein: 15g, Carbs: 47g, Fiber: 17g, Sugar: 3g, Sodium: 253mg

Lemon Wax Beans

Prep Time: 5 minutes, Cook Time: 15 minutes, Serves: 4

2 pounds (907 g) wax beans
2 tbsps. extra-virgin olive oil
Sea salt and freshly ground black pepper, to taste
Juice of ½ lemon

1. Preheat the oven to 400ºF (205ºC). 2. Line a baking sheet with aluminum foil. 3. In a large bowl, toss the beans and olive oil. Season lightly with salt and pepper. 4. Transfer the beans to the baking sheet and spread them out. 5. Roast the beans until caramelized and tender, about 10 to 12 minutes. 6. Transfer the beans to a serving platter and sprinkle with the lemon juice.

Calories: 99, Fat: 7.1g, Protein: 2.1g, Carbs: 8.1g, Fiber: 4.2g, Sugar: 3.9g, Sodium: 814mg

Garlicky Tofu and Brussels Sprouts

Prep Time: 18 minutes, Cook Time: 30 minutes, Serves: 4

Nonstick cooking spray
1 (14-ounce / 397-g) package extra-firm organic tofu, drained and cut into 1-inch pieces
2 tbsps. balsamic vinegar
1 tbsp. extra-virgin olive oil plus 1 tsp.
1 tbsp. garlic, minced
¼ tsp. salt
¼ tsp. black pepper, freshly ground
1 pound (454 g) Brussels sprouts, quartered
½ cup dried cherries
¼ cup roasted salted pumpkin seeds
1 tbsp. balsamic glaze

1. Preheat the oven to 400ºF (205ºC). Line a large baking sheet with foil and coat it with cooking spray. 2. Place the tofu pieces between 2 clean towels. Rest for 15 minutes to wick away additional liquid. 3. In a large bowl, whisk the vinegar, 1 tbsp. of oil, the garlic, salt, and pepper. Add the tofu and Brussels sprouts and toss gently. Transfer the ingredients to the baking sheet and evenly spread into a layer. Roast for 20 minutes. 4. Remove from the oven and toss its contents. Sprinkle the cherries and pumpkin seeds on top of the Brussels sprouts and tofu. Return to the oven and roast for an additional 10 minutes. Remove from the oven and drizzle with balsamic glaze. Toss to coat. 5. Evenly portion into 4 large glass meal-prep containers with lids. Cover and refrigerate.

Calories: 296, Fat: 11g, Protein: 16g, Carbs: 34g, Fiber: 8g, Sugar: 18g, Sodium: 197mg

Green Lentils with Summer Vegetables

Prep Time: 15 minutes, Cook Time: 0 minutes, Serves: 4

3 tbsps. extra-virgin olive oil	um-free green lentils, rinsed and drained
2 tbsps. balsamic vinegar	½ English cucumber, diced
2 tsps. chopped fresh basil	2 tomatoes, diced
1 tsp. minced garlic	½ cup halved Kalamata olives
Sea salt and freshly ground black pepper, to taste	¼ cup chopped fresh chives
2 (15-ounce / 425-g) cans sodi-	2 tbsps. pine nuts

1. Whisk together the olive oil, vinegar, basil, and garlic in a medium bowl. Season with salt and pepper. 2. Stir in the lentils, cucumber, tomatoes, olives, and chives. 3. Top with the pine nuts, and serve.

Calories: 400, Fat: 15.1g, Protein: 19.8g, Carbs: 48.8g, Fiber: 18.8g, Sugar: 7.1g, Sodium: 439mg

Crispy Cowboy Black Bean Fritters

Prep Time: 10 minutes, Cook Time: 25 minutes, Serves: 20 Fritters

1¾ cups whole wheat flour	1 cup salsa
½ tsp. cumin	2 (16-ounce / 454-g) cans no-salt-added black beans, rinsed and drained
2 tsps. baking powder	
2 tsps. salt	
½ tsp. black pepper	1 tbsp. canola oil, plus extra if needed
4 egg whites, lightly beaten	

1. Combine the flour, cumin, baking powder, salt, and pepper in a large bowl, then mix in the egg whites and salsa. Add the black beans and stir to mix well. 2. Heat the canola oil in a nonstick skillet over medium-high heat. 3. Spoon 1 tsp. of the mixture into the skillet to make a fritter. Make more fritters to coat the bottom of the skillet. Keep a little space between each two fritters. You may need to work in batches to avoid overcrowding. 4. Cook for 3 minutes or until the fritters are golden brown on both sides. Flip the fritters and flatten with a spatula halfway through the cooking time. Repeat with the remaining mixture. Add more oil as needed. 5. Serve immediately.

Calories: 115, Fat: 1g, Protein: 6g, Carbs: 20g, Fiber: 5g, Sugar: 2g, Sodium: 350mg

Super Bean and Grain Burgers

Prep Time: 25 minutes, Cook Time: 1 hour 15 minutes, Makes: 12 patties

1 tbsp. olive oil	For the Patties:
½ cup chopped onion	½ cup ground flaxseed
8 cloves garlic, minced	1 tbsp. dried marjoram
1 cup dried black beans	2 tsps. smoked paprika
½ cup quinoa, rinsed	2 tsps. salt
½ cup brown rice	1 tsp. ground black pepper
4 cups water	1 tsp. dried thyme

1. Select the Sauté setting of the Instant Pot and heat the oil until shimmering. 2. Add the onion and sauté for 5 minutes or until transparent. 3. Add the garlic and sauté a minute more or until fragrant. 4. Add the black beans, quinoa, rice and water to the onion mixture and stir to combine. 5. Put the lid on. Set to Manual mode. Set cooking time for 34 minutes on High Pressure. 6. When timer beeps, release the pressure naturally for 15 minutes, then release any remaining pressure. Open the lid. 7. Preheat the oven to 350°F (180°C) and line 2 baking sheets with parchment paper. 8. Mash the beans in the pot, then mix in the ground flaxseed, marjoram, paprika, salt, pepper and thyme. 9. Divide and shape the mixture into 12 patties and put on the baking sheet. 10. Cook in the preheated oven for 35 minutes or until firmed up. Flip the patties halfway through the cooking time. 11. Serve immediately.

Calories: 186, Fat: 4g, Protein: 6g, Carbs: 31g, Fiber: 6g, Sugar: 1g, Sodium: 396mg

Easy Three-Bean Medley

Prep Time: 16 minutes, Cook Time: 8 hours, Serves: 10

1¼ cups dried black beans, rinsed and drained	6 cups low-sodium vegetable broth
1¼ cups dried kidney beans, rinsed and drained	1½ cups water
	1 onion, chopped
1¼ cups dried black-eyed peas, rinsed and drained	1 leek, chopped
	2 garlic cloves, minced
2 carrots, peeled and chopped	½ tsp. dried thyme leaves

1. Mix all of the ingredients in a 6-quart slow cooker. Cover with lid and cook on low for 6 to 8 hours, or until the beans are soft and the liquid is absorbed. Serve warm.

Calories: 284, Fat: 0g, Protein: 19g, Carbs: 56g, Fiber: 19g, Sugar: 6g, Sodium: 131mg

Crispy Parmesan Bean and Veggie Cups

Prep Time: 10 minutes, Cook Time: 5 minutes, Serves: 4

1 cup grated low-fat Parmesan cheese, divided	¼ cup thinly sliced fresh basil
	1 garlic clove, minced
1 (15-ounce / 425-g) can low-sodium white beans, drained and rinsed	½ jalapeño pepper, diced
	1 tbsp. extra-virgin olive oil
	1 tbsp. balsamic vinegar
1 cucumber, peeled and finely diced	¼ tsp. salt
	Freshly ground black pepper, to taste
½ cup finely diced red onion	

1. Heat a medium nonstick skillet over medium heat. Sprinkle 2 tbsps. of cheese in a thin circle in the center of the pan, flattening it with a spatula. 2. When the cheese melts, use a spatula to flip the cheese and lightly brown the other side. 3. Remove the cheese "pancake" from the pan and place into the cup of a muffin tin, bending it gently with your hands to fit in the muffin cup. 4. Repeat with the remaining cheese until you have 8 cups. 5. In a mixing bowl, combine the beans, cucumber, onion, basil, garlic, jalapeño, olive oil, and vinegar, and season with the salt and pepper. 6. Fill each cup with the bean mixture just before serving.

Calories: 260, Fat: 12.1g, Protein: 14.9, Carbs: 23.9g, Fiber: 8g, Sugar: 3.9g, Sodium: 552mg

Roasted Eggplant and White Bean

Prep Time: 6 minutes, Cook Time: 1 hour 10 minutes, Serves: 2

1 (16-ounce / 454-g) can cannellini beans, drained and rinsed	2 garlic cloves, minced
2 small eggplants, cut into ¼-inch slices	3 tbsps. tahini, divided
1 cup hulled barley	2 tbsps. plus 2 tsps. extra-virgin olive oil, divided
1 cup arugula	3 tsps. tamari, divided
3 cups water	Sea salt
Juice of 1½ lemons	Freshly ground black pepper

1. Preheat the oven to 425ºF (220ºC). 2. In a large pot, bring the hulled barley, water, and 2 tsps. tamari to a boil over high heat. Once the barley just starts to boil, turn the heat to low and cover the pot. 3. Cook the barley for about 40 minutes without removing the lid. Take the pot from the heat when most of the water has been absorbed and the barley is tender and chewy. Drain well. 4. Pour the remaining tsp. of tamari, 1 tbsp. of tahini, and the lemon juice to the barley. Fluff with a fork, mixing all ingredients, and keep aside. 5. When the barley is cooking, arrange the eggplant slices in a single layer on a parchment paper–lined baking sheet and drizzle with 2 tbsps. olive oil. Season with the salt and pepper before putting into the oven. Bake the slices for about 20 minutes. 6. Add the arugula, the remaining 2 tsps. olive oil, garlic, and remaining 2 tbsps. Tahini in a medium skillet over medium heat. Cook for about 5 minutes. 7. Place the cannellini beans to the arugula mixture, and cook for about 5 minutes, until the beans are warm. 8. Put the rice, eggplant, and the arugula-bean mixture into three sections of each bowl, or mix all three components of this bowl together. Enjoy!

Calories: 523, Fat: 28g, Protein: 14g, Carbs: 65g, Fiber: 22g, Sugar: 18g, Sodium: 572mg

Enchilada Black Bean Casserole

Prep Time: 15 minutes, Cook Time: 15 minutes, Serves: 6

1 tbsp. extra-virgin olive oil	1 (10-ounce / 283-g) can low-sodium enchilada sauce
½ onion, chopped	1 tsp. ground cumin
½ red bell pepper, seeded and chopped	¼ tsp. salt
½ green bell pepper, seeded and chopped	¼ tsp. freshly ground black pepper
2 small zucchini, chopped	½ cup shredded low-fat Cheddar cheese, divided
3 garlic cloves, minced	2 (6-inch) whole wheat corn tortillas, cut into strips
1 (15-ounce / 425-g) can low-sodium black beans, drained and rinsed	Chopped fresh cilantro, for garnish nonfat plain yogurt, for serving

1. Heat the broiler to high. 2. In a large oven-safe skillet, heat the oil over medium-high heat. 3. Add the onion, red bell pepper, green bell pepper, zucchini, and garlic to the skillet, and cook for 3 to 5 minutes until the onion softens. 4. Add the black beans, enchilada sauce, cumin, salt, pepper, ¼ cup of cheese, and tortilla strips, and mix together. Top with the remaining ¼ cup of cheese. 5. Put the skillet under the broiler and broil for 5 to 8 minutes until the cheese is melted and bubbly. Garnish with cilantro and serve with yogurt on the side.

Calories: 172, Fat: 7.1g, Protein: 8.1g, Carbs: 20.9g, Fiber: 6.9g, Sugar: 3g, Sodium: 566mg

Black-Eyed Peas Curry

Prep Time: 15 minutes, Cook Time: 40 minutes, Serves: 12

1 pound (454 g) dried black-eyed peas, rinsed and drained	4 large carrots, coarsely chopped
	1½ tbsps. curry powder
4 cups vegetable broth	1 tbsp. minced garlic
1 cup coconut water	1 tsp. peeled and minced fresh ginger
1 cup chopped onion	1 tbsp. extra-virgin olive oil
	Kosher salt (optional)
	Lime wedges, for serving

1. In the electric pressure cooker, combine the black-eyed peas, broth, coconut water, onion, carrots, curry powder, garlic, and ginger. Drizzle the olive oil over the top. 2. Close and lock the lid of the pressure cooker. Set the valve to sealing. 3. Cook on high pressure for 25 minutes. 4. When the cooking is complete, hit Cancel and allow the pressure to release naturally for 10 minutes, then quick release any remaining pressure. 5. Once the pin drops, unlock and remove the lid. 6. Season with salt (if using) and squeeze some fresh lime juice on each serving.

Calories: 113, Fat: 3.1g, Protein: 10.1g, Carbs: 30.9g, Fiber: 6.1g, Sugar: 6g, Sodium: 672mg

Dandelion and Beet Greens with Black Beans

Prep Time: 10 minutes, Cook Time: 15 minutes, Serves: 4

1 tbsp. olive oil	½ cup low-sodium vegetable broth
½ Vidalia onion, thinly sliced	1 (15-ounce / 425-g) can no-salt-added black beans
1 bunch dandelion greens, cut into ribbons	Salt and freshly ground black pepper, to taste
1 bunch beet greens, cut into ribbons	

1. Heat the olive oil in a nonstick skillet over low heat until shimmering. 2. Add the onion and sauté for 3 minutes or until translucent. 3. Add the dandelion and beet greens, and broth to the skillet. Cover and cook for 8 minutes or until wilted. 4. Add the black beans and cook for 4 minutes or until soft. Sprinkle with salt and pepper. Stir to mix well. 5. Serve immediately.

Calories: 161, Fat: 4g, Protein: 9g, Carbs: 26g, Fiber: 10g, Sugar: 1g, Sodium: 224mg

Thai Green Bean and Soybean

Prep Time: 16 minutes, Cook Time: 3½ hours, Serves: 8 to 10

1½ pounds (680 g) green beans	½ cup canned unsweetened coconut milk
3 cups fresh soybeans	⅓ cup chopped fresh cilantro
3 bulbs fennel, cored and chopped	1 lemongrass stalk
	2 tbsps. lime juice
1 jalapeño pepper, minced	½ tsp. salt

1. Mix the green beans, soybeans, fennel, jalapeño pepper, lemongrass, coconut milk, lime juice, and salt in a 6-quart slow cooker. Cover the slow cooker and cook on low for 3 to 3½ hours, or until the vegetables are soft. 2. Remove the lemongrass and discard. Scatter the vegetables with the cilantro and serve warm.

Calories: 115, Fat: 5g, Protein: 6g, Carbs: 11g, Fiber: 6g, Sugar: 4g, Sodium: 154mg

Greens and Beans Stuffed Mushrooms

Prep Time: 12 minutes, Cook Time: 16 minutes, Serves: 4

Nonstick cooking spray
4 tbsps. olive oil, divided
4 portabella mushroom caps
½ tsp. salt
½ tsp. black pepper, freshly ground
2 tbsps. garlic, minced
8 cups baby kale
1 cup vegetable broth
2 (15½-ounce / 439-g) cans white cannellini beans, drained and rinsed
¼ cup lemon juice, freshly squeezed
½ cup mozzarella, shredded

1. Preheat the oven to 375ºF (190ºC). Line a baking sheet with foil, coat it with cooking spray.
2. Drizzle 1 tbsp. of oil over the mushroom caps. Flip and drizzle 1 tbsp. of oil on the gill side. Season with salt and pepper. Place in the baking prepared sheet, gill-side up.
3. Roast for 10 minutes.
4. While the mushrooms cook, heat the remaining 2 tbsps. of oil in a cast-iron skillet over medium heat. Add the garlic and cook for 1 minute. Add 1 handful of kale. Once it begins to wilt, add a bit of the vegetable broth. Continue alternating handfuls of kale with a bit of vegetable broth. letting the kale cook down between additions until all of it is added.
5. Stir in the beans and lemon juice. Cook for 2 minutes, stirring frequently, until most of the liquid is evaporated.
6. Remove the roasted mushrooms from the oven. Portion the kale and beans evenly into the mushroom caps.
7. Sprinkle each mushroom cap with 2 tbsps. Of mozzarella. Return the mushrooms to the oven and bake for 3 minutes, or until the cheese has melted and is lightly golden brown.
8. Portion 1 stuffed mushroom into each of 4 glass meal-prep containers. Cover and refrigerate.

Calories: 387, Fat: 19g, Protein: 16g, Carbs: 41g, Fiber: 11g, Sugar: 4.7g, Sodium: 357mg

Beluga Lentils with Lacinato Kale

Prep Time: 15 minutes, Cook Time: 40 minutes, Serves: 6

¼ cup olive oil, plus more for serving
2 shallots, diced
5 cloves garlic, minced
½ tsp. red pepper flakes
½ tsp. ground nutmeg
1 tsp. fine sea salt
2 bunches (about 1 pound / 454 g) lacinato kale, stems discarded and leaves chopped into 1-inch pieces
2 large carrots, peeled and diced
2½ cups water
1 cup beluga lentils, rinsed

1. Select the Sauté setting on the Instant Pot, add the oil, and heat for 1 minute.
2. Add the shallots and garlic and sauté for about 4 minutes until the shallots soften.
3. Add the red pepper flakes, nutmeg, and salt and sauté for 1 minute more.
4. Stir in the kale and carrots and sauté for about 3 minutes, until the kale fully wilts. Stir in the water and lentils.
5. Secure the lid. Select Bean/Chili setting and set the cooking time for 30 minutes at High Pressure.
6. When timer beeps, let the pressure release naturally for 10 minutes, then release any remaining pressure.
7. Open the pot and give the mixture a stir.
8. Ladle the lentils into serving dishes and drizzle with oil. Serve warm.

Calories: 259, Fat: 10g, Protein: 13g, Carbs: 33g, Fiber: 10g, Sugar: 3g, Sodium: 401mg

Navy Bean Pico de Gallo

Prep Time: 20 minutes, Cook Time: 0 minutes, Serves: 4

2½ cups cooked navy beans
1 tomato, diced
½ red bell pepper, seeded and chopped
¼ jalapeño pepper, chopped
1 scallion, white and green parts, chopped
1 tsp. minced garlic
1 tsp. ground cumin
½ tsp. ground coriander
½ cup low-sodium feta cheese

1. Put the beans, tomato, bell pepper, jalapeño, scallion, garlic, cumin, and coriander in a medium bowl and stir until well mixed.
2. Top with the feta cheese and serve.

Calories: 225, Fat: 4.1g, Protein: 14.1g, Carbs: 34.1g, Fiber: 13.1g, Sugar: 3.9g, Sodium: 165mg

Black-Eyed Peas with Collard

Prep Time: 5 minutes, Cook Time: 3 to 4 minutes, Serves: 4 to 6

1 yellow onion, diced
1 tbsp. olive oil
1 cup dried black-eyed peas
¼ cup chopped sun-dried tomatoes
¼ cup tomato paste
1 tsp. smoked paprika
2 cups water
4 large collard green leaves
Salt and freshly ground black pepper, to taste

1. In the Instant Pot, select Sauté mode. Add the onion and olive oil and cook for 3 to 4 minutes, stirring occasionally, until the onion is softened.
2. Add the black-eyed peas, tomatoes, tomato paste, paprika, water, and stir to combine.
3. Close the lid, then select Manual mode and set cooking time for 30 minutes on High Pressure.
4. Once the cook time is complete, let the pressure release naturally for about 15 minutes, then release any remaining pressure.
5. Trim off the thick parts of the collard green stems, then slice the leaves lengthwise in half or quarters. Roll them up together, then finely slice into ribbons.
6. Sprinkle the sliced collard greens with salt and massage it into them with hands to soften.
7. Open the lid. Add the collard greens and ½ tsp. of salt to the pot, stirring to combine and letting the greens wilt in the heat.
8. Serve immediately.

Calories: 184, Fat: 3g, Protein: 8g, Carbs: 32g, Fiber: 8g, Sugar: 4g, Sodium: 373mg

Red Kidney Beans with Green Beans

Prep Time: 10 minutes, Cook Time: 8 to 12 minutes, Serves: 8

2 tbsps. olive oil
1 medium yellow onion, chopped
1 cup crushed tomatoes
2 garlic cloves, minced
2 cups low-sodium canned red kidney beans, rinsed
1 cup roughly chopped green beans
¼ cup low-sodium vegetable broth
1 tsp. smoked paprika
Salt, to taste

1. Heat the olive oil in a nonstick skillet over medium heat until shimmering.
2. Add the onion, tomatoes, and garlic. Sauté for 3 to 5 minutes or until fragrant and the onion is translucent.
3. Add the kidney beans, green beans, and broth to the skillet. Sprinkle with paprika and salt, then sauté to combine well.
4. Cover the skillet and cook for 5 to 7 minutes or until the vegetables are tender. Serve immediately.

Calories: 187, Fat: 1g, Protein: 13g, Carbs: 34g, Fiber: 10g, Sugar: 4g, Sodium: 102mg

Vegetarian Kidney Bean Étouffée

Prep Time: 20 minutes, Cook Time: 28 minutes, Serves: 4

1 tbsp. olive oil
1 cup minced onion
2 cups minced bell pepper
2 tsps. minced garlic
1 cup dried kidney beans, soaked in water for 8 hours, drained
1½ tsps. dried thyme
3 bay leaves
2 tsps. smoked paprika
1 cup water
2 tsps. dried marjoram
½ tsp. ground cayenne pepper
1 (14.5-ounce / 411-g) can crushed tomatoes
1 tsp. dried oregano
Salt and ground black pepper, to taste

1. Select the Sauté setting of the Instant Pot and heat the oil until shimmering. 2. Add the onion and sauté for 5 minutes or until transparent. 3. Add the bell pepper and garlic. Sauté for 5 more minutes or until the bell peppers are tender. 4. Add the beans, thyme, bay leaves, smoked paprika, water, marjoram and cayenne to the pot. Stir to combine. 5. Put the lid on. Select the Manual setting and set the timer for 15 minutes at High Pressure. 6. When timer beeps, use a natural pressure release for 5 minutes, then release any remaining pressure. Open the lid. Remove the bay leaves. 7. Mix in the crushed tomatoes and oregano. Sprinkle with salt and pepper. Set the cooking time for 3 minutes on High Pressure. 8. When timer beeps, release the pressure naturally for 5 minutes, then release any remaining pressure. Open the lid. 9. Serve immediately.

Calories: 288, Fat: 3g, Protein: 12g, Carbs: 56g, Fiber: 15g, Sugar: 11g, Sodium: 645mg

Pepper and Black Bean Tacos

Prep Time: 10 minutes, Cook Time: 23 minutes, Serves: 2

1 tbsp. sesame oil
½ onion, chopped
1 tsp. garlic, minced
1 sweet pepper, deseeded and sliced
1 jalapeño pepper, deseeded and minced
1 tsp. ground cumin
½ tsp. ground coriander
8 ounces (227 g) black beans, rinsed
2 (8-inch) whole wheat tortillas, warmed
½ cup cherry tomatoes, halved
⅓ cup nonfat coconut cream

1. Press the Sauté button and heat the oil. Cook the onion, garlic, and peppers for 3 minutes or until tender and fragrant. 2. Add the ground cumin, coriander, and beans to the Instant Pot. 3. Secure the lid. Choose the Manual mode and cook for 20 minutes at High Pressure. 4. Once cooking is complete, use a natural pressure release for 10 minutes, then release any remaining pressure. Carefully remove the lid. 5. Serve the bean mixture in the tortillas, then garnish with the cherry tomatoes and coconut cream.

Calories: 347, Fat: 14g, Protein: 11g, Carbs: 49g, Fiber: 11g, Sugar: 7g, Sodium: 262mg

Chickpeas Curry

Prep Time: 15 minutes, Cook Time: 35 minutes, Serves: 4

1 cup dried chickpeas
1 tbsp. baking soda
4 cups water, divided
1 tsp. olive oil
1 clove garlic, minced
¼ cup diced onion
½ tsp. hot curry powder
¼ tsp. ground cinnamon
1 bay leaf
½ tsp. sea salt

1. Add the chickpeas, baking soda, and 2 cups of the water to a large bowl and soak for 1 hour. Rinse the chickpeas and drain. 2. In the Instant Pot, heat the oil on Sauté mode. Add the garlic and onion and sauté for 3 minutes. 3. Add the curry, cinnamon, and bay leaf and stir well. Stir in the chickpeas and 2 cups of the water. 4. Cover the lid. Select Manual mode and set cooking time for 32 minutes on High Pressure. 5. When timer beeps, use a natural pressure release for 15 minutes, then release any remaining pressure. 6. Remove the lid and stir in the sea salt. Remove the bay leaf before serving.

Calories: 190, Fat: 3g, Protein: 8g, Carbs: 33g, Fiber: 7g, Sugar: 6g, Sodium: 305mg

Triple Bean Chili

Prep Time: 20 minutes, Cook Time: 60 minutes, Serves: 8

1 tsp. extra-virgin olive oil
1 sweet onion, chopped
1 red bell pepper, seeded and diced
1 green bell pepper, seeded and diced
2 tsps. minced garlic
1 (28-ounce / 794-g) can low-sodium diced tomatoes
1 (15-ounce / 425-g) can sodium-free black beans, rinsed and drained
1 (15-ounce / 425-g) can sodium-free red kidney beans, rinsed and drained
1 (15-ounce / 425-g) can sodium-free navy beans, rinsed and drained
2 tbsps. chili powder
2 tsps. ground cumin
1 tsp. ground coriander
¼ tsp. red pepper flakes

1. Place a large saucepan over medium-high heat and add the oil. 2. Sauté the onion, red and green bell peppers, and garlic until the vegetables have softened, about 5 minutes. 3. Add the tomatoes, black beans, red kidney beans, navy beans, chili powder, cumin, coriander, and red pepper flakes to the pan. 4. Bring the chili to a boil, then reduce the heat to low. 5. Simmer the chili, stirring occasionally, for at least 1 hour. 6. Serve hot.

Calories: 480, Fat: 28.1g, Protein: 15.1g, Carbs: 45.1g, Fiber: 16.9g, Sugar: 4g, Sodium: 16mg

Rutabaga and Lentils Rice Bowl

Prep Time: 15 minutes, Cook Time: 30 minutes, Serves: 4

1 tbsp. olive oil
½ cup chopped onion
2 cloves garlic, minced
3½ cups water
1 cup brown lentils
1 cup peeled and diced rutabaga
1½ cups brown rice
2-inch sprig fresh rosemary
1 tbsp. dried marjoram
Salt and ground black pepper, to taste

1. Select the Sauté setting of the Instant Pot and heat the oil until shimmering. 2. Add the onion and sauté for 5 minutes or until transparent. 3. Add the garlic and sauté a minute more or until fragrant. 4. Add the lentils, rutabaga, brown rice, rosemary, water, and marjoram to the pot and stir to combine. 5. Put the lid on. Set the Manual mode and set cooking time for 23 minutes at High Pressure. 6. When timer beeps, let the pressure release naturally for 10 minutes, then release any remaining pressure. Open the lid. 7. Sprinkle with salt and pepper before serving.

Calories: 438, Fat: 5g, Protein: 16g, Carbs: 83g, Fiber: 15g, Sugar: 3g, Sodium: 9mg

Swiss Chard with Black-Eyed Peas

Prep Time: 15 minutes, Cook Time: 10 minutes, Serves: 6

1 tsp. olive oil
1 medium large onion, thinly sliced
1 small jalapeño, minced
1 cup diced red bell pepper
3 cloves garlic, minced
1½ cups dried black-eyed peas, soaked overnight, drained
1 tsp. chili powder
2 tsps. smoked paprika
4 dates, finely chopped
1½ cups water
1 (15-ounce / 425-g) can fire-roasted tomatoes with green chiles
2 cups chopped Swiss chard
Salt, to taste

1. Select the Sauté setting of the Instant Pot and heat the oil until shimmering. 2. Add the onion and sauté for 5 minutes or until transparent. 3. Add the peppers and garlic. Sauté for a minute more or until fragrant. 4. Add the black-eyed peas, chili powder, and smoked paprika, and stir. Add the dates and water. 5. Put the lid on. Set to Manual mode and set cooking time for 3 minutes at High Pressure. 6. When timer beeps, let the pressure release naturally for 5 minutes, then release any remaining pressure. Open the lid. 7. Add the tomatoes and Swiss chard. Set cooking time for 1 minute on High Pressure. 8. When cooking is complete, quick release the pressure and open the lid. 9. Sprinkle with salt and serve.

Calories: 233, Fat: 1g, Protein: 12g, Carbs: 47g, Fiber: 10g, Sugar: 14g, Sodium: 349mg

Kale and Black-Eyed Pea Curry

Prep Time: 15 minutes, Cook Time: 30 minutes, Serves: 4

1 tbsp. olive oil
½ tsp. cumin seeds
1 medium red onion, chopped
4 cloves garlic, finely chopped
1-inch piece ginger, finely chopped
1 green chili, finely chopped
2 large tomatoes, chopped
½ tsp. turmeric powder
1 tsp. coriander powder
¼ tsp. garam masala
1 tsp. salt
1 cup dried black-eyed peas, soaked in water for 3 hours, drained
2 cups water
3 cups kale, chopped
2 tsps. lime juice

1. Press the Sauté button on the Instant Pot. Add the oil and the cumin seeds and let them sizzle for a few seconds. 2. Add the onion and sauté for 2 minutes or until soft. 3. Add the garlic, ginger and green chili and sauté for 1 minute or until golden brown. 4. Add the tomatoes and cook for 3 minutes, or until soft. 5. Add the turmeric powder, coriander powder, garam masala and salt. Cook for 1 minute. 6. Fold in the black-eyed peas and water. Lock the lid. 7. Press the Manual button and set the timer for 20 minutes on High Pressure. 8. When timer beeps, let the pressure release naturally for 10 minutes, then release any remaining pressure. 9. Open the pot and press the Sauté button. Add the kale and simmer for 3 minutes. 10. Stir in the lime juice and serve.

Calories: 246, Fat: 4g, Protein: 12g, Carbs: 43g, Fiber: 10g, Sugar: 7g, Sodium: 603mg

Black Chickpea Curry

Prep Time: 15 minutes, Cook Time: 15 minutes, Serves: 6

1 tbsp. olive oil
2 cups minced onion
2 tsps. garam masala
½ tsp. ground coriander
2 tsps. cumin seeds
3 tsps. minced garlic
½ tsp. ground turmeric
½ tsp. ground chile
1 cup black chickpeas, soaked in water for at least 8 hours, drained
1½ cups diced tomatoes
1½ cups water
2 tbsps. grated ginger
2 tsps. crushed curry leaves
Salt, to taste

1. Select the Sauté setting on the Instant Pot, and heat the oil until shimmering. 2. Add the onion and sauté for 5 minutes or until transparent. 3. Add the garam masala, coriander, cumin seeds, garlic, turmeric and chile and sauté for 2 minutes. 4. Add the chickpeas, tomatoes, water, ginger and curry leaves, and stir to combine. 5. Put the lid on. Select the Manual setting and set the timer for 8 minutes on High Pressure. 6. When timer beeps, allow the pressure to release naturally for 5 minutes, then release any remaining pressure. Open the lid. 7. Sprinkle with salt and serve.

Calories: 173, Fat: 4g, Protein: 7g, Carbs: 29g, Fiber: 6g, Sugar: 8g, Sodium: 301mg

CHAPTER 6　　SALAD RECIPES

Healthy Italian Pasta Salad with Pine Nuts ······ 35
Healthy French Lentil Salad ···················· 35
Quinoa Salad with Zucchini, Mint, and Pistachios ···· 35
Fabulous Chicken Salad with Dried Apricots and Almonds ·· 35
Quick Summer Chicken Salad ···················· 35
Roasted Cauliflower with Pomegranate and Pine Nuts ·· 35
Egg Salad Lettuce Wraps ···························· 36
Vinegar Asparagus Salad ··························· 36
Healthy Asian Quinoa Salad ······················· 36
Brown Rice Salad ····································· 36
Savory Mexican Summer Salad ··················· 36
Healthy Tuna Salad ·································· 36
Pepper and Tomato Salad ·························· 36
Classic Blue Cheese Wedge Salad ················ 37
Easy Crab Salad with Endive ······················ 37
Healthy Southwestern Salad ······················ 37
Classic Coleslaw ······································ 37
Fresh Raspberry Spinach Salad ··················· 37
Rice Cauliflower Tabbouleh Salad ················ 37
Tomato and Peach Salad ··························· 38
Moroccan Roast Chili Salad ······················· 38
Healthy Mediterranean Pasta Salad ············· 38
Endive and Shrimp with Walnuts ················ 38
Grilled Romaine Salad with Tomatoes and Walnuts · 38
Garden Salad with Sardine ························ 38
Savory Greek Salad with Lemon Vinaigrette ···· 39
Carrot Salad with Nuts and Coconut Flakes ····· 39
Pomegranate Salad with Avocado ··············· 39
Apple Spinach Salad ································ 39
Lemony Kale Salad ·································· 39
Peppered Shredded Beef Salad ··················· 39
Zucchini and Cherry Tomato Salad ·············· 39

Healthy Italian Pasta Salad with Pine Nuts

Prep Time: 15 minutes, Cook Time: 20 minutes, Serves: 4

4 cups whole wheat penne pasta	2 cups halved cherry tomatoes
¼ cup toasted pine nuts	⅛ tsp. cracked black pepper
4 tbsps. extra virgin olive oil	1 cup chopped low-fat mozzarella cheese
Pinch of sea salt	
1 bunch coarsely chopped fresh basil	

1. Prepare a large pot, pour water into it, boil it, and pour in a little olive oil to prevent the pasta from sticking together. Add the pasta to the boiling water, stir once, and cook for 8 to 10 minutes until hardened. Remove the pasta and set aside for later use. 2. In a large saucepan, add the pine nuts and heat them at medium high temperature, stirring constantly to prevent the pine nuts from burning. Bake for about 2 minutes until the nuts smell buttery and light brown. Turn off the heat and remove from the pot into a bowl. 3. Put the cooked pasta and the remaining ingredients in a large bowl and stir together. Warm pasta will melt the cheese slightly. After stirring well, divide into 4 portions. Serve warm.

Calories: 388, Fat: 15g, Protein: 18g, Carbs: 45g, Fiber: 5g, Sugar: 4g, Sodium: 254 mg

Healthy French Lentil Salad

Prep Time: 20 minutes, Cook Time: 25 minutes, Serves: 4

For the Lentils:	½ tsp. kosher salt
1 cup French lentils	¼ tsp. freshly ground black pepper
1 garlic clove, smashed	2 celery stalks, diced small
1 dried bay leaf	1 bell pepper, diced small
For the Salad:	½ red onion, diced small
2 tbsps. extra-virgin olive oil	¼ cup fresh parsley, chopped
2 tbsps. red wine vinegar	¼ cup fresh mint, chopped
½ tsp. ground cumin	

To Make the Lentils: 1. Put the lentils, garlic, and bay leaf in a large saucepan. Cover with water by about 3 inches and bring to a boil. Reduce the heat, cover, and simmer until tender, 20 to 30 minutes. 2. Drain the lentils to remove any remaining water after cooking. Remove the garlic and bay leaf. To Make the Salad: 3. In a large bowl, whisk together the olive oil, vinegar, cumin, salt, and black pepper. Add the celery, bell pepper, onion, parsley, and mint and toss to combine. 4. Add the lentils and mix well.

Calories: 200, Total Fat: 8g, Saturated Fat: 1g, Cholesterol: 0mg, Sodium: 165mg, Total Carbs: 26g, Fiber: 10g, Sugar: 5g, Protein: 10g

Quinoa Salad with Zucchini, Mint, and Pistachios

Prep Time: 20-30 minutes, Cook Time: 20 minutes, Serves: 4

For the Quinoa:	¼ tsp. freshly ground black pepper
1½ cups water	2 garlic cloves, sliced
1 cup quinoa	Zest of 1 lemon
¼ tsp. kosher salt	2 tbsps. lemon juice
For the Salad:	¼ cup fresh mint, chopped
2 tbsps. extra-virgin olive oil	¼ cup fresh basil, chopped
1 zucchini, thinly sliced into rounds	¼ cup pistachios, shelled and toasted
6 small radishes, sliced	
1 shallot, julienned	
¾ tsp. kosher salt	

To Make the Quinoa: 1. Bring the water, quinoa, and salt to a boil in a medium saucepan. Reduce to a simmer, cover, and cook for 10 to 12 minutes. Fluff with a fork. To Make the Salad: 2. Heat the olive oil in a large skillet or sauté pan over medium-high heat. Add the zucchini, radishes, shallot, salt, and black pepper, and sauté for 7 to 8 minutes. Add the garlic and cook for 30 seconds to 1 minute more. 3. Combine the lemon zest and lemon juice in a large bowl. Add the quinoa and mix well. Add the cooked zucchini mixture and mix well. Then add the mint, basil, and pistachios and gently mix.

Calories: 220, Total Fat: 12g, Saturated Fat: 2g, Cholesterol: 0mg, Sodium: 295mg, Total Carbs: 25g, Fiber: 5g, Sugar: 5g, Protein: 6g

Fabulous Chicken Salad with Dried Apricots and Almonds

Prep Time: 20 minutes, Cook Time: 0, Serves: 3

2½ cups diced cooked chicken	finely diced, or ¼ cup chopped jarred roasted red peppers
⅓ cup chopped dried apricots	½ cup light mayonnaise, or to taste
⅓ cup sliced almonds, toasted	Squeeze of lemon juice, or to taste
2 tbsps. chopped fresh herbs, such as dill	Salt and freshly ground black pepper
2 tbsps. pumpkin or sunflower seeds	
½ red bell pepper, seeded and	

1. Combine all the ingredients in a bowl and mix well. 2. Adjust the seasoning. 3. Refrigerate if not serving immediately.

Calories: 371, Protein: 42g, Carbs: 11g, Fat: 16g, Fiber: 4g, Sodium: 108mg

Quick Summer Chicken Salad

Prep Time: 15 minutes, Cook Time: chill 1 hour, Serves: 6

3 cups cooked, skinless chicken breast	¼ cup chopped almonds
½ cup chopped celery	¼ cup low-fat mayonnaise
½ cup chopped apple	2 tsps. chopped fresh sage
	2 tsps. chopped fresh cilantro

1. Combine all the ingredients in a bowl and stir until combined. 2. Chill for an hour before serving.

Calories: 60, Protein: 3.99g, Fat: 3.1g, Carbs: 4.19g, Fiber: 4g, Sugar: 2g, Sodium: 584mg

Roasted Cauliflower with Pomegranate and Pine Nuts

Prep Time: 20 minutes, Cook Time: 20 minutes, Serves: 4

2 tbsps. extra-virgin olive oil, plus more for drizzling (optional)	½ tsp. kosher salt
1 head cauliflower, trimmed and cut into 1-inch florets	¼ tsp. freshly ground black pepper
5 ounces (142g) arugula	⅓ cup pomegranate seeds
1 tsp. ground cumin	¼ cup pine nuts, toasted

1. Preheat the oven to 425°F(218°C). Line a baking sheet with parchment paper or foil. 2. In a large bowl, combine the cauliflower, olive oil, cumin, salt, and black pepper. Spread in a single layer on the prepared baking sheet and roast for 20 minutes, tossing halfway through. 3. Divide the arugula among 4 plates.

Top with the cauliflower, pomegranate seeds, and pine nuts.4. Serve with Lemon Vinaigrette dressing or a simple drizzle of olive oil.

Calories: 190, Total Fat: 14g, Saturated Fat: 2g, Sodium: 210mg, Total Carbs: 16g, Fiber: 6g, Sugar: 7g, Protein: 6g

Egg Salad Lettuce Wraps

Prep Time: 10 minutes, Cook Time: 0, Serves: 4

¼ cup anti-inflammatory mayonnaise
8 hard-boiled eggs, peeled and chopped
½ red bell pepper, finely chopped
1 tsp. dijon mustard
⅛ tsp. freshly ground black pepper
½ tsp. sea salt
4 large lettuce leaves

1.Add all of the ingredients except the lettuce leaves into a large bowl, mix them together gently to combine.2.Spoon into the lettuce leaves with the mixture.

Calories: 190, Total Fat: 14, Total Carbs: 6g, Sugar: 2g, Fiber: <1g, Protein: 11g, Sodium: 477mg

Vinegar Asparagus Salad

Prep Time: 10 minutes, Cook Time: 5 minutes, Serves: 4

4 tbsps. olive oil
1 tbsp. balsamic vinegar
1 pound asparagus
Sea salt and freshly ground pepper
1 tbsp. lemon zest

1.Either roast the asparagus or, shave it into thin strips with a vegetable peeler.2.Season to taste.3.Toss with the vinegar and olive oil, sprinkle with lemon zest, and serve.

Calories: 148, Fat: 13.66g, Carbs: 5.69g, Protein: 2.6g, Cholesterol: 0mg, Sodium: 4mg, Fiber: 2.7g

Healthy Asian Quinoa Salad

Prep Time: 30 minutes, Cook Time: 25 minutes, Serves: 6

4 cups low-sodium vegetable broth
2 cups uncooked quinoa
1 tbsp. sesame oil
1 tbsp. extra virgin olive oil
1 cup cooked, shelled edamame
⅛ tsp. cracked black pepper
½ cup chopped red bell pepper
⅛ tsp. chile pepper flakes
1 tsp. sesame seeds
¼ cup chopped green onion
½ tsp. grated orange zest
1½ tsps finely chopped fresh mint
2 tbsps. finely chopped fresh Thai basil
Juice of ½ orange
½ cup chopped carrot

1.Rinse the quinoa with clean water (if not pre-rinsed). Put the cleaned quinoa and vegetable soup in a small pot with a lid and bring to a boil over high heat. Then reduce the heat and cook for 10 to 15 minutes until most of the liquid is absorbed by the quinoa. Boiled quinoa is chewy, and when most of the grain has been unfolded and you can see the unfolded germ, it is done. Let the quinoa sit in a covered pot for about 5 minutes. Stir gently with a fork.2.Transfer the cooked quinoa to a large bowl and add the edamame, onion, mint, carrot, pepper, orange zest, Thai basil, orange juice, sesame, sesame oil, olive oil, and black pepper to mix well. It can be eaten when cooled to room temperature or refrigerated.

Calories: 331, Fat: 10g, Protein: 11g, Carbs: 50g, Fiber: 6g, Sugar: 7g, Sodium: 103mg

Brown Rice Salad

Prep Time: 15 minutes, Cook Time: 5 minutes, Serves: 4

1 tsp. Dijon mustard
1 small shallot, minced
1 cup baby spinach
¼ cup Pecorino or mozzarella, low-salt, low-fat
¼ cup (60 ml) walnut oil
¼ cup (60 ml) red wine vinegar
2 cups cooked wild and brown rice blend
1 cup cooked butternut squash, cubed
½ cup dried cranberries
½ cup pecans, toasted
4 cups mixed baby salad greens

1.Combine together the vinegar, oil, and mustard in a small bowl. Add shallot and whisk to mix.2.Add rice, pecans, squash, spinach, cranberries, salad greens and cheese in a large salad bowl. Toss to mix.3.Divide salad evenly among four plates. Drizzle dressing on each portion. Serve.

Calories: 344, Fat: 3.7g, Carbs: 25.4g, Protein: 5.3g, Cholesterol: 6.3mg, Sodium: 195mg, Fiber: 5g

Savory Mexican Summer Salad

Prep Time: 20 minutes, Cook Time: 5 minutes, Serves: 6

3 heads romaine lettuce, chopped
⅛ cup extra virgin olive oil
1½ cups sliced unpeeled cucumber
¼ cup fresh lime juice
¼ cup very thinly sliced white onion
5 Roma tomatoes, chopped
Cracked black pepper
Sea salt

1.Add the lettuce, tomato, cucumber, and onion in a large bowl, then drizzle with the lime juice and oil, and mix together well. Sprinkle with salt and pepper to season.2.Transfer the mixture to a plate and enjoy.

Calories: 78, Fat: 5g, Protein: 2g, Carbs: 9g, Fiber: 2g, Sugar: 0.2g, Sodium: 61mg

Healthy Tuna Salad

Prep Time: 15 minutes, Cook Time: 10 minutes, Serves: 4 (1-cup) servings

2 (6-ounce (170g)) cans albacore tuna in water, no salt added, drained
3 tbsps. low-fat plain Greek yogurt
¼ cup chopped Roma tomato
⅛ tsp. cracked black pepper
½ jalapeño chile pepper, seeded and chopped
1 small avocado, thinly sliced
1 tsp. brown mustard
¼ cup chopped red onion
¼ cup chopped celery

1.In a medium bowl, combine the celery, chile pepper, tomato, and onion. Mix in the tuna, mustard, yogurt, and pepper until well combined.2.Top the salad with avocado slices, and serve.

Calories: 162, Fat: 7g, Protein: 21g, Carbs: 32g, Fiber: 6g, Sugar: 1g, Sodium: 241mg

Pepper and Tomato Salad

Prep Time: 10 minutes, Cook Time: 10 minutes, Serves: 6

2 cloves garlic, minced
4 large tomatoes, seeded and diced
3 large yellow peppers
¼ cup (60 ml) olive oil
1 small bunch fresh basil leaves
Sea salt and freshly ground pepper

CHAPTER 6 SALAD RECIPES

1. Preheat broiler to high heat and broil the peppers until blackened. 2. Remove from heat and place peppers in a paper bag. Seal and cool down peppers. 3. Peel the skins off the peppers, then seed and chop them. 4. Add half of the peppers to a food processor with olive oil, basil, and garlic, and pulse several times to make the dressing. 5. Mix the rest of the peppers with the tomatoes and toss with the dressing. 6. Season the salad with sea salt and freshly ground pepper. Serve with room temperature.

Calories: 113, Fat: 9.31g, Carbs: 7.43g, Protein: 1.62g, Cholesterol: 0mg, Sodium: 8mg, Fiber: 1.9g

Classic Blue Cheese Wedge Salad

Prep Time: 15 minutes, Cook Time: 0, Serves: 4

1 cup nonfat plain Greek yogurt	¼ tsp. freshly ground black pepper
2 heads romaine lettuce, stem end trimmed, halved lengthwise	¼ tsp. salt
	⅓ cup crumbled low-fat blue cheese
1 cup grape tomatoes, halved	½ cup slivered almonds
Juice of ½ large lemon	

1. In a small bowl, well combined the yogurt, lemon juice, pepper, salt, and blue cheese. Store the dressing in 4 condiment cups. 2. Divide the lettuce halves and tomatoes among 4 large storage containers. Store the almonds separately. 3. To serve, arrange a half-head of romaine on a plate and top with the grape tomatoes. Sprinkle with 2 tbsps. of almonds and drizzle with the salad dressing.

Calories: 216, Total Fat: 11g, Carbs: 20g, Fiber: 9g, Protein: 16g, Sodium: 329mg

Easy Crab Salad with Endive

Prep Time: 10 minutes, Cook Time: 10 minutes, Serves: 4

1 pound (454g) lump crab meat	Zest of 1 lemon
⅔ cup nonfat coconut yogurt	Juice of 1 lemon
3 tbsps. low-fat mayonnaise	½ tsp. kosher salt
3 tbsps. fresh chives, chopped, plus additional for garnish	¼ tsp. freshly ground black pepper
3 tbsps. fresh parsley, chopped, plus additional for garnish	4 endives, ends cut off and leaves separated
3 tbsps. fresh basil, chopped, plus additional for garnish	

1. Combine the crab, yogurt, mayonnaise, chives, parsley, basil, lemon zest, lemon juice, salt, and black pepper in a medium bowl, and mix until well combined. 2. Place the endive leaves on 4 salad plates. Divide the crab mixture evenly on top of the endive. Garnish with additional herbs if desired.

Calories: 200, Total Fat: 9g, Saturated Fat: 2g, Sodium: 570mg, Total Carbs: 44g, Fiber: 2g, Sugar: 2g, Protein: 25g

Healthy Southwestern Salad

Prep Time: 15 minutes, Cook Time: 20 minutes, Serves: 5

2 tbsps. olive oil	1 cup diced red peppers
1 can black beans	Black pepper and cumin
1 can red beans	2 tbsps. white wine vinegar
4 fresh tomatoes, sliced	1 tsp. hot sauce
½ cup chopped fresh cilantro	

1. Open the cans of beans and rinse them thoroughly with cool water. Combine the beans in a serving bowl. 2. Add the tomatoes, cilantro and red pepper to the beans. Sprinkle generously with pepper and cumin. Whisk together the oil, vinegar and hot sauce in a small bowl and drizzle over the salad. Toss gently, cover and chill. 3. Let the salad stand, covered at room temperature for 20 minutes before serving.

Calories: 138, Protein: 5.19g, Fat: 6.24g, Carbs: 16.84g, Fiber: 6g, Sugar: 4g, Sodium: 239mg

Classic Coleslaw

Prep Time: 15 minutes, Cook Time: 5 minutes, Serves: 4

⅓ cup (80 ml) white vinegar	3 tbsps. olive oil
2 carrots, julienned	1 tbsp. coconut sugar
2 scallions, minced	1 tsp. Dijon mustard
2 celery ribs, minced	1 tsp. celery seeds
4 cups thinly sliced cabbage	

1. In a salad bowl, stir the vinegar, sugar, oil, mustard, and celery seeds until well mixed. 2. Put in cabbage, scallions, celery and carrots. Toss to combine. 3. Refrigerate 1 hour or up to 4 hours. Serve.

Calories: 145, Fat: 10.8g, Carbs: 12.2g, Protein: 2.2g, Cholesterol: 0mg, Sodium: 75.1mg, Fiber: 3.8g

Fresh Raspberry Spinach Salad

Prep Time: 10 minutes, Cook Time: 30 minutes, Serves: 2

1 (6-ounce, 170g) bag baby spinach	½ cup whole walnuts
1 cup fresh red raspberries	¼ cup low-fat Italian dressing
1 Asian pear, cut into bite-sized pieces	¼ cup low-fat blue cheese crumbles

1. Toss all ingredients, let stand at room temperature for 30 minutes before serving. 2. Toss again right before plating.

Calories: 369, Protein: 9.39g, Fat: 20.84g, Carbs: 40.67g, Fiber: 7g, Sugar: 10g, Sodium: 468 mg

Rice Cauliflower Tabbouleh Salad

Prep Time: 15 minutes, Cook Time: 0, Serves: 4

¼ cup extra-virgin olive oil	¾ tsp. kosher salt
1 pound (454g) riced cauliflower	½ tsp. ground turmeric
1 English cucumber, diced	¼ tsp. ground coriander
12 cherry tomatoes, halved	¼ tsp. ground cumin
1 cup fresh parsley, chopped	¼ tsp. black pepper
¼ cup lemon juice	⅛ tsp. ground cinnamon
Zest of 1 lemon	½ cup fresh mint, chopped

1. In a large bowl, whisk together the olive oil, lemon juice, lemon zest, salt, turmeric, coriander, cumin, black pepper, and cinnamon. 2. Add the riced cauliflower to the bowl and mix well. Add in the cucumber, tomatoes, parsley, and mint and gently mix together.

Calories: 180, Total Fat: 15g, Saturated Fat: 2g, Sodium: 260mg, Total Carbs: 12g, Fiber: 5g, Sugar: 5g, Protein: 4g

Tomato and Peach Salad

Prep Time: 10 minutes, Cook Time: 5 minutes, Serves: 2

- 2 ripe peaches, pitted and sliced into wedges
- 2 ripe tomatoes, cut into wedges
- 3 tbsps. olive oil
- 1 tbsp. lemon juice
- ½ red onion, thinly sliced
- Sea salt and freshly ground pepper

1. Toss the peaches, red onion and tomatoes in a large bowl. Season to taste. 2. Put in the olive oil and lemon juice, and gently toss. Serve.

Calories: 275, Fat: 20.95g, Carbs: 22.9g, Protein: 2.9g, Cholesterol: 0mg, Sodium: 8mg, Fiber: 4.5g

Moroccan Roast Chili Salad

Prep Time: 10 minutes, Cook Time: 20 minutes, Serves: 6

- 2 large green bell peppers
- 1 hot red chili Fresno or jalapeño pepper
- Juice of 1 lemon
- Sea salt and freshly ground pepper
- 4 large tomatoes, peeled, seeded, and diced
- 4 tbsps. olive oil
- 1 large cucumber, peeled and diced
- 1 small bunch flat-leaf parsley, chopped
- 1 tsp. ground cumin

1. Preheat broiler on high. Broil all the peppers and chilies until the skin blackens and blisters. 2. Put the peppers and chilies in a paper bag. Seal and set aside to cool down. Mix the rest of the ingredients in a medium bowl. 3. Take peppers and chilies out from the bag and remove the skins and seeds. Chop the peppers and add them to the salad. 4. Season with sea salt and freshly ground pepper. 5. Toss to combine and set aside for 15–20 minutes before serving.

Calories: 124, Fat: 9.55g, Carbs: 9.44g, Protein: 2.2g, Cholesterol: 0mg, Sodium: 15mg, Fiber: 2.6g

Healthy Mediterranean Pasta Salad

Prep Time: 10 minutes, Cook Time: 15 minutes, Serves: 3

- 2 tbsps. extra-virgin olive oil
- 6 ounces (170g) whole wheat penne pasta
- 3 tbsps. grated low-fat Parmesan cheese
- 1 pint grape tomatoes, halved
- 2 garlic cloves, minced
- 2 tsps. dried oregano
- 1 tsp. dried basil
- 3 cups spinach leaves, stemmed
- 1 tbsp. balsamic vinegar
- ½ cup pitted Kalamata olives, sliced
- ¼ tsp. red pepper flakes (optional)

1. Bring a large pot of water to a boil. Add the pasta and cook until al dente according to the package directions. Drain well. 2. In a large skillet, heat the oil over medium heat. Add the garlic and cook, stirring for 30 seconds to 1 minute, or until fragrant. Add the oregano, basil, and spinach and sauté for about 3 minutes, or until the spinach is fully cooked. Remove from the heat and stir in the vinegar. 3. In a large bowl, combine the pasta, spinach mixture, tomatoes, and olives. Top with the Parmesan cheese and red pepper flakes (if using). 4. Divide evenly among 3 storage containers.

Calories: 435, Total Fat: 20g, Carbs: 61g, Fiber: 8.5g, Protein: 13g, Sodium: 546mg

Endive and Shrimp with Walnuts

Prep Time: 2 hours, Cook Time: 10 minutes, Serves: 4

- ¼ cup (60 ml) olive oil
- 1 small shallot, minced
- ½ cup tart green apple, diced
- 2 tbsps. toasted walnuts
- 1 tbsp. Dijon mustard
- Juice and zest of 1 lemon
- 14 shrimp, peeled and deveined
- 1 head endive
- Sea salt and freshly ground pepper
- 2 cups (480 ml) salted water

1. For the vinaigrette, whisk together the first five ingredients in a small bowl until creamy. 2. Refrigerate for at least 2 hours. 3. Boil salted water in a small pan. Put in the shrimp and cook for 1–2 minutes, or until the shrimp turns pink. Drain and cool down under cold water. 4. Wash and break the endive. Place on plates and top with the shrimp, toasted walnuts and green apple. 5. Drizzle with the vinaigrette before serving.

Calories: 195, Fat: 16.48g, Carbs: 8.38g, Protein: 5.71g, Cholesterol: 26mg, Sodium: 193mg, Fiber: 4.9g

Grilled Romaine Salad with Tomatoes and Walnuts

Prep Time: 5 minutes, Cook Time: 10 minutes, Serves: 4

- 2 tbsps. olive oil
- 1 head romaine lettuce (about 12 leaves)
- ¼ cup low-fat feta cheese
- ½ cup halved cherry tomatoes
- ¼ cup chopped walnuts
- Garlicky Balsamic Vinaigrette

1. Separate the leaves from the romaine head, and wash and dry them. 2. Heat a grill to medium-high, brush oil on both sides of each lettuce leaf, and place on the grill. Watch carefully and turn often, as the leaves can wilt quickly. 3. Once char marks are visible, remove the leaves and place three leaves on four individual plates. 4. Top the grilled lettuce with the cheese, tomatoes, and walnuts. Drizzle with 2 tbsps. balsamic vinaigrette, and serve.

Calories: 152, Protein: 3g, Fat: 14g, Carbs: 5g, Fiber: 1g, Sugar: 1g, Sodium: 109mg

Garden Salad with Sardine

Prep Time: 10 minutes, Cook Time: 10 minutes, Serves: 6

- ½ cup (120 ml) olive oil
- Juice of 1 medium lemon
- 1 tsp. Dijon mustard
- 4 medium tomatoes, diced
- 1 small red onion, thinly sliced
- 1 small bunch flat-leaf parsley, chopped
- 4 whole sardine filets packed in olive oil, drained and chopped
- Sea salt and freshly ground pepper
- 1 large cucumber, peeled and diced
- 1 pound (454 g) arugula, trimmed and chopped

1. For the dressing, mix the olive oil, mustard and lemon juice, and season with sea salt and pepper. Set aside. 2. Combine all the vegetables with the parsley in a large bowl, and toss. Put the sardine filets on top of the salad. 3. Drizzle the dressing over the salad and serve.

Calories: 227, Fat: 19.8g, Carbs: 9.53g, Protein: 5.44g, Cholesterol: 11mg, Sodium: 66mg, Fiber: 3.2g

Savory Greek Salad with Lemon Vinaigrette

Prep Time: 10 minutes, Cook Time: 5 minutes, Serves: 4

½ cup rinsed and drained, coarsely chopped canned artichoke hearts
¼ cup low-fat feta cheese
½ cup halved cherry tomatoes
10 black pitted olives, rinsed, drained, and chopped
4 cups chopped romaine leaves (about 2 large heads of lettuce)
8 tbsps. lemon vinaigrette
1 tsp. dried oregano

1. In a large salad bowl, add the cherry tomatoes, romaine leaves, artichoke hearts, cheese and olives, pour 1 tsp. oregano and combine thoroughly. 2. Divide the vegetable mixture into four portions and drizzle 2 tbsps. of lemon vinaigrette on each portion.

Calories: 69, Fat: 4g, Protein: 3g, Carbs: 7g, Fiber: 3g, Sugar: 0.8g, Sodium: 311mg

Carrot Salad with Nuts and Coconut Flakes

Prep Time: 15 minutes, Cook Time: 5 minutes, Serves: 2

2 tbsps. honey
¼ cup (60 ml) orange juice
2 cups carrots, grated or julienned
1 cup coconut flakes, unsweetened
½ cup unsalted pecans or cashews, toasted and chopped
1 tsp. ginger, minced
1 tsp. low-salt tamari
1 tbsp. orange-infused oil or olive oil

1. Combine honey, ginger, orange juice, tamari, and oil in a medium bowl. 2. Add nuts, carrots and coconut flakes. 3. Toss until dressing evenly coats salad. Serve.

Calories: 375, Fat: 25g, Carbs: 32.7g, Protein: 7g, Cholesterol: 0mg, Sodium: 74.6mg, Fiber: 3.2g

Pomegranate Salad with Avocado

Prep Time: 25 minutes, Cook Time: 5 minutes, Serves: 4

½ cup thinly sliced fennel
¼ cup pomegranate seeds
4 cups arugula
½ cup thinly sliced Anjou pears, thinly sliced
1 large avocado, pitted, peeled, and chopped

1. Add avocado, fennel, pear, and arugula in a large bowl, stirring constantly, to mix well. Then add pomegranate seeds and drizzle with your favorite oil and vinegar sauce. Enjoy it!

Calories: 106, Fat: 7g, Protein: 2g, Carbs: 12g, Fiber: 4g, Sugar: 4g, Sodium: 15mg

Apple Spinach Salad

Prep Time: 10 minutes, Cook Time: 5 minutes, Serves: 4

8 cups baby spinach
1 medium red apple, diced
½ cup toasted walnuts
1 medium Granny Smith apple, diced
3 tbsps. olive oil
1 tbsp. red wine vinegar or apple cider vinegar
2 ounces (57 g) low-fat, sharp white cheddar cheese, cubed

1. Toss the spinach, walnuts, apples, and cubed cheese together. Drizzle olive oil and vinegar over top and serve.

Calories: 249, Fat: 18g, Carbs: 17g, Protein: 7g, Cholesterol: 3mg, Sodium: 173mg, Fiber: 4.4g

Lemony Kale Salad

Prep Time: 10 minutes, Cook Time: 10 minutes, Serves: 4

2 heads kale
Sea salt and freshly ground pepper
Juice of 1 lemon
1+ ½ tbsp. olive oil
2 cloves garlic, minced
1 cup cherry tomatoes, sliced

1. Wash and dry kale. 2. Tear the kale into small pieces. 3. Heat olive oil in a large skillet, and add the garlic. Cook for 1 minute and then add the kale. 4. Add the tomatoes after kale wilted. 5. Cook until tomatoes are softened, then remove from heat. 6. Put tomatoes and kale together in a bowl, and season with sea salt and freshly ground pepper. 7. Drizzle with remaining olive oil and lemon juice, serve.

Calories: 59, Fat: 3.83g, Carbs: 5.95g, Protein: 2g, Cholesterol: 0mg, Sodium: 16mg, Fiber: 1.9g

Peppered Shredded Beef Salad

Prep Time: 10 minutes, Cook Time: 9 hours, Serves: 6

1 pound (454 g) grass-fed flank steak
2 red bell peppers, seeded and thinly sliced
1 cup (240 ml) beef broth
2 tsps. freshly ground black pepper
1 tsp. smoked paprika
1 tsp. garlic powder
½ tsp. ground coriander
8 cups shredded iceberg lettuce
½ tsp. sea salt
⅛ tsp. cayenne pepper

1. Mix the black pepper, garlic powder, paprika, coriander, salt, and cayenne in a small bowl. 2. Spread the mixture evenly over the flank steak, rubbing it in. 3. Combine the seasoned flank steak, bell peppers, and broth in the slow cooker. 4. Cover and cook on low for 8 hours. 5. Remove the beef from the sauce and shred it with forks. 6. Put the beef back to the sauce and mix well. 7. Serve the shredded beef on top of the shredded lettuce, with sauce drizzled on top.

Calories: 180, Total Fat: 7g, Saturated Fat: 3g, Carbs: 6g, Protein: 23g, Cholesterol: 42mg, Fiber: 2g, Sodium: 584mg

Zucchini and Cherry Tomato Salad

Prep Time: 10 minutes, Cook Time: 5 minutes, Serves: 2

1 medium zucchini, shredded or sliced paper thin
6 cherry tomatoes, halved
3–4 basil leaves, thinly sliced
2 tbsps. freshly grated, low-fat Parmesan cheese
3 tbsps. olive oil
Juice of 1 lemon
Sea salt and freshly ground pepper

1. Place the zucchini slices on 2 plates in even layers. Top with the tomatoes. 2. Drizzle with lemon juice and olive oil. Season to taste. 3. Top with the basil and sprinkle with cheese. Serve.

Calories: 211, Fat: 21.5g, Carbs: 4.63g, Protein: 1.82g, Cholesterol: 4mg, Sodium: 80mg, Fiber: 1g

CHAPTER 7　FISH AND SEAFOOD RECIPES

Tuna Salad with Lettuce 41	Thai Fish Curry 43
Spicy Cod 41	Salmon Tandoori 43
Veggie and Haddock Foil Packets 41	Amazing Salmon Fillets 43
Herbed Cod Steaks 41	Salmon with Basil Pesto 43
Dill-Lemon Salmon 41	Fish Fillets with Asparagus 44
Cod Cakes 41	Snapper with Spicy Tomato Sauce 44
Paprika Shrimp 42	Herbed Red Snapper 44
Halibut En Papillote 42	Mahi Mahi with Green Beans 44
Quick and Easy Shrimp 42	Salmon Cakes 44
Salmon with Lemon Mustard 42	Mahi-Mahi Fillets with Peppers 44
Spicy Shrimps 42	Curry Halibut 45
Simple Salmon 42	Chili-Rubbed Tilapia 45
Thyme-Sesame Crusted Halibut 42	Cod with Asparagus 45
Curried Salmon 42	Herbed Haddock 45
Lemon Pepper Salmon 43	Appetizing Tuna Patties 45
Lemony Salmon with Avocados 43	Crispy Baked Flounder with Green Beans 45
Shrimp Magic 43	

Tuna Salad with Lettuce

Prep Time: 12 minutes, Cook Time: 10 minutes, Serves: 4

- 2 tbsps. olive oil
- ½ lb. tuna, sliced
- 1 tbsp. fresh lemon juice
- 2 eggs
- 1 head lettuce
- Salt and pepper, to taste
- 1 cup water

1. In a large bowl, season the tuna with lemon juice, salt and pepper. Transfer the tuna to a baking dish. 2. Add the eggs, water, and steamer rack to the Instant Pot. Place the baking dish on the steamer rack. 3. Lock the lid. Select the Steam mode and set the cooking time for 10 minutes at Low Pressure. 4. Once cooking is complete, do a quick pressure release. Carefully open the lid. 5. Allow the eggs and tuna to cool. Peel the eggs and slice into wedges. Set aside. 6. Assemble the salad by shredding the lettuce in a salad bowl. Toss in the cooled tuna and eggs. 7. Sprinkle with olive oil, then serve.

Calories: 242, Fat: 17g, Protein: 16g, Carbs: 4g, Fiber: 2g, Sugar: 1g, Sodium: 182mg

Spicy Cod

Prep Time: 10 minutes, Cook Time: 11 minutes, Serves: 2

- 2 (6-ounces) (1½-inch thick) cod fillets
- 1 tsp. smoked paprika
- 1 tsp. cayenne pepper
- 1 tsp. onion powder
- 1 tsp. garlic powder
- Salt and ground black pepper, as required
- 2 tsps. olive oil

1. Preheat the Air fryer to 390°F (199°C) and grease an Air fryer basket. 2. Drizzle the cod fillets with olive oil and rub with the all the spices. 3. Arrange the cod fillets into the Air fryer basket and roast for about 11 minutes. 4. Dish out the cod fillets in the serving plates and serve hot.

Calories: 277, Fat: 15.4g, Carbs: 2.5g, Sugar: 0.9g, Protein: 33.5g, Sodium: 154mg

Veggie and Haddock Foil Packets

Prep Time: 5 minutes, Cook Time: 10 minutes, Serves: 4

- 1½ cups water
- 1 lemon, sliced
- 2 bell peppers, sliced
- 1 brown onion, sliced into rings
- 4 sprigs parsley
- 2 sprigs thyme
- 2 sprigs rosemary
- 4 haddock fillets
- Sea salt, to taste
- ⅓ tsp. ground black pepper, or more to taste
- 2 tbsps. extra-virgin olive oil

1. Pour the water and lemon into your Instant Pot and insert a steamer basket. 2. Assemble the packets with large sheets of heavy-duty foil. 3. Place the peppers, onion rings, parsley, thyme, and rosemary in the center of each foil. Place the fish fillets on top of the veggies. 4. Sprinkle with the salt and black pepper and drizzle the olive oil over the fillets. Place the packets in the steamer basket. 5. Lock the lid. Select the Manual mode and set the cooking time for 10 minutes at Low Pressure. 6. When the timer beeps, perform a quick pressure release. Carefully remove the lid. 7. Serve warm.

Calories: 216, Fat: 8g, Protein: 32g, Carbs: 9g, Fiber: 2g, Sugar: 3g, Sodium: 157mg

Herbed Cod Steaks

Prep Time: 5 minutes, Cook Time: 4 minutes, Serves: 4

- 1½ cups water
- 2 tbsps. garlic-infused oil
- 4 cod steaks, 1½-inch thick
- Sea salt, to taste
- ½ tsp. mixed peppercorns, crushed
- 2 sprigs thyme
- 1 sprig rosemary
- 1 yellow onion, sliced

1. Pour the water into your Instant Pot and insert a trivet. 2. Rub the garlic-infused oil into the cod steaks and season with the salt and crushed peppercorns. 3. Lower the cod steaks onto the trivet, skin-side down. Top with the thyme, rosemary, and onion. 4. Lock the lid. Select the Manual mode and set the cooking time for 4 minutes at High Pressure. 5. When the timer beeps, perform a quick pressure release. Carefully remove the lid. 6. Serve immediately.

Calories: 202, Fat: 9g, Protein: 26g, Carbs: 2g, Fiber: 0g, Sugar: 1g, Sodium: 340mg

Dill-Lemon Salmon

Prep Time: 3 minutes, Cook Time: 5 minutes, Serves: 2

- 2 (3-ounce / 85-g) salmon fillets, 1-inch thick
- 1 tsp. chopped fresh dill
- ½ tsp. salt
- ¼ tsp. pepper
- 1 cup water
- 2 tbsps. lemon juice
- ½ lemon, sliced

1. Season salmon with dill, salt, and pepper. 2. Pour the water into the Instant Pot and insert the trivet. Place the salmon on the trivet, skin-side down. Squeeze lemon juice over fillets and scatter the lemon slices on top. 3. Lock the lid. Select the Steam mode and set the cooking time for 5 minutes at High Pressure. 4. Once cooking is complete, do a quick pressure release. Carefully open the lid. 5. Serve warm.

Calories: 182, Fat: 8g, Protein: 22g, Carbs: 3g, Fiber: 1g, Sugar: 0g, Sodium: 663mg

Cod Cakes

Prep Time: 20 minutes, Cook Time: 14 minutes, Serves: 6

- 1 pound cod fillet
- 1 egg
- ⅓ cup coconut, grated and divided
- 1 scallion, finely chopped
- 2 tbsps. fresh parsley, chopped
- 1 tsp. fresh lime zest, finely grated
- 1 tsp. red chili paste
- Salt, as required
- 1 tbsp. fresh lime juice

1. Preheat the Air fryer to 375°F (191°C) and grease an Air fryer basket. 2. Put the cod fillet, lime zest, egg, chili paste, salt and lime juice in a food processor and pulse until smooth. 3. Transfer the cod mixture into a bowl and add scallion, parsley and 2 tbsps. of coconut. 4. Mix until well combined and make 12 equal-sized round cakes from the mixture. 5. Place the remaining coconut in a shallow bowl and coat the cod cakes with coconut. 6. Arrange cod cakes into the Air fryer basket in 2 batches and bake for about 7 minutes. 7. Dish out in 2 serving plates and serve warm.

Calories: 165, Fat: 4.5g, Carbs: 2.1g, Sugar: 1g, Protein: 27.7g, Sodium: 161mg

Paprika Shrimp

Prep Time: 10 minutes, Cook Time: 10 minutes, Serves: 2

1 pound tiger shrimp
2 tbsps. olive oil
½ tsp. smoked paprika
Salt, to taste

1. Preheat the Air fryer to 390°F (199°C) and grease an Air fryer basket. 2. Mix all the ingredients in a large bowl until well combined. 3. Place the shrimp in the Air fryer basket and air fry for about 10 minutes. 4. Dish out and serve warm.

Calories: 173, Fat: 8.3g, Carbs: 0.1g, Sugar: 0g, Protein: 23.8g, Sodium: 332mg

Halibut En Papillote

Prep Time: 12 minutes, Cook Time: 10 minutes, Serves: 4

1 cup water
1 cup chopped tomatoes
1 thinly sliced shallot
4 halibut fillets
½ tbsp. grated ginger
Salt and pepper, to taste

1. In the Instant Pot, set in a steamer basket and pour the water into the pot. 2. Get a large parchment paper and place the fillet in the middle. Season with salt and pepper. Add the grated ginger, tomatoes, and shallots. Fold the parchment paper to create a pouch and crimp the edges. 3. Place the parchment paper containing the fish. 4. Lock the lid. Select the Steam mode and cook for 10 minutes at Low Pressure. 5. Once cooking is complete, do a quick pressure release. Carefully open the lid. 6. Serve warm.

Calories: 145, Fat: 2g, Protein: 28g, Carbs: 4g, Fiber: 1g, Sugar: 2g, Sodium: 168mg

Quick and Easy Shrimp

Prep Time: 10 minutes, Cook Time: 5 minutes, Serves: 2

½ pound tiger shrimp
1 tbsp. olive oil
½ tsp. old bay seasoning
¼ tsp. smoked paprika
¼ tsp. cayenne pepper
Salt, to taste

1. Preheat the Air fryer to 390°F (199°C) and grease an Air fryer basket. 2. Mix all the ingredients in a large bowl until well combined. 3. Place the shrimps in the Air fryer basket and air fry for about 5 minutes. 4. Dish out and serve warm.

Calories: 174, Fat: 8.3g, Carbs: 0.3g, Sugar: 0g, Protein: 23.8g, Sodium: 492mg

Salmon with Lemon Mustard

Prep Time: 8 minutes, Cook Time: 10 minutes, Serves: 4

1 cup water
1 garlic clove, minced
4 skinless salmon fillets
2 tbsps. Dijon mustard
Salt and pepper, to taste
2 tbsps. freshly squeezed lemon juice

1. Set a trivet in the Instant Pot and pour the water into the pot. 2. In a bowl, mix lemon juice, mustard, and garlic. Sprinkle salt and pepper for seasoning. 3. Top the salmon fillets with the mustard mixture. Place the fish fillets on the trivet. 4. Lock the lid. Select the Steam mode and cook for 10 minutes at Low Pressure. 5. Once cooking is complete, do a quick pressure release. Carefully open the lid. 6. Serve warm.

Calories: 230, Fat: 12g, Protein: 29g, Carbs: 2g, Fiber: 0g, Sugar: 0g, Sodium: 296mg

Spicy Shrimps

Prep Time: 15 minutes, Cook Time: 5 minutes, Serves: 3

1 pound shrimps, peeled and deveined
2 tbsps. olive oil
1 tsp. old bay seasoning
½ tsp. red chili flakes
½ tsp. smoked paprika
½ tsp. cayenne pepper
Salt, as required

1. Preheat the Air fryer to 390°F (199°C) and grease an Air fryer basket. 2. Mix shrimp with olive oil and other seasonings in a large bowl. 3. Arrange the shrimp into the Air fryer basket in a single layer and roast for about 5 minutes. 4. Dish out the shrimp onto serving plates and serve hot.

Calories: 262, Fat: 12g, Carbs: 2.7g, Sugar: 0.1g, Protein: 34.5g, Sodium: 633mg

Simple Salmon

Prep Time: 5 minutes, Cook Time: 10 minutes, Serves: 2

2 (6-ounces) salmon fillets
Salt and black pepper, as required
1 tbsp. olive oil

1. Preheat the Air fryer to 390°F (199°C) and grease an Air fryer basket. 2. Season each salmon fillet with salt and black pepper and drizzle with olive oil. 3. Arrange salmon fillets into the Air fryer basket and roast for about 10 minutes. 4. Remove from the Air fryer and dish out the salmon fillets onto the serving plates.

Calories: 285, Fat: 17.5g, Carbs: 0g, Sugar: 0g, Protein: 33g, Sodium: 153mg

Thyme-Sesame Crusted Halibut

Prep Time: 6 minutes, Cook Time: 8 minutes, Serves: 4

1 cup water
1 tsp. dried thyme leaves
1 tbsp. toasted sesame seeds
8 oz. halibut, sliced
Salt and pepper, to taste
1 tbsp. freshly squeezed lemon juice

1. Set a trivet in the Instant Pot and pour the water into the pot. 2. Season the halibut with lemon juice, salt, and pepper. Sprinkle with dried thyme leaves and sesame seeds. 3. Place the fish on the trivet. 4. Lock the lid. Select the Steam mode and cook for 8 minutes at Low Pressure. 5. Once cooking is complete, do a quick pressure release. Carefully open the lid. 6. Serve warm.

Calories: 103, Fat: 3g, Protein: 17g, Carbs: 1g, Fiber: 0g, Sugar: 0g, Sodium: 159mg

Curried Salmon

Prep Time: 6 minutes, Cook Time: 8 minutes, Serves: 4

2 cups unsweetened coconut milk
2 tbsps. coconut oil
1 onion, chopped
1 lb. raw salmon, diced
1½ tbsps. minced garlic

1. Press the Sauté button on the Instant Pot and heat the oil. 2. Sauté the garlic and onions until fragrant, about 2 minutes. 3. Add the diced salmon and stir for 1 minute. 4. Pour in the coconut milk. 5. Lock the lid. Select the Manual mode and cook for 4 minutes at Low Pressure. 6. Once cooking is complete, do a quick pressure release. Carefully open the lid. 7. Let the salmon cool for 5 minutes before serving.

Calories: 374, Fat: 29g, Protein: 22g, Carbs: 7g, Fiber: 1g, Sugar: 2g, Sodium: 54mg

Lemon Pepper Salmon

Prep Time: 15 minutes, Cook Time: 5 minutes, Serves: 4

1 cup water	2 tbsps. olive oil
1 tsp. ground dill	Salt, to taste
1 tsp. ground tarragon	4 lemon slices
1 tsp. ground basil	1 carrot, sliced
4 salmon fillets	1 zucchini, sliced

1. In the Instant Pot, add the water, dill, tarragon, and basil. 2. Place the steamer basket inside. 3. Set in the salmon. Drizzle with a tbsp. of olive oil, pepper and salt. Top with lemon slices. 4. Lock the lid. Select the Steam mode and cook for 3 minutes at Low Pressure. 5. Once cooking is complete, do a quick pressure release. Carefully open the lid. 6. Transfer the fish to a plate and discard the lemon slices. 7. Drizzle the Instant Pot with remaining olive oil. Add the carrot and zucchini to the Instant Pot. Set to Sauté mode, then sauté for 2 minutes or until the vegetables are tender. 8. Serve the salmon with the veggies. 9. Garnish with fresh lemon wedges.

Calories: 283, Fat: 16g, Protein: 29g, Carbs: 6g, Fiber: 2g, Sugar: 2g, Sodium: 187mg

Lemony Salmon with Avocados

Prep Time: 10 minutes, Cook Time: 7 minutes, Serves: 2

2 (3-ounce / 85-g) salmon fillets	⅓ cup low-fat mayonnaise
½ tsp. salt	Juice of ½ lemon
¼ tsp. pepper	2 avocados
1 cup water	½ tsp. chopped fresh dill

1. Season the salmon fillets on all sides with the salt and pepper. Add the water to the Instant Pot and insert a trivet. 2. Arrange the salmon fillets on the trivet, skin-side down. 3. Secure the lid. Select the Steam mode and set the cooking time for 7 minutes at Low Pressure. 4. Once cooking is complete, do a quick pressure release. Carefully open the lid. Set aside to cool. 5. Mix together the mayonnaise and lemon juice in a large bowl. Cut the avocados in half. Remove the pits and dice the avocados. Add the avocados to the large bowl and gently fold into the mixture. 6. Flake the salmon into bite-sized pieces with a fork and gently fold into the mixture. 7. Serve garnished with the fresh dill.

Calories: 413, Fat: 31g, Protein: 17g, Carbs: 17g, Fiber: 10g, Sugar: 2g, Sodium: 689mg

Shrimp Magic

Prep Time: 20 minutes, Cook Time: 5 minutes, Serves: 3

1½ pounds shrimps, peeled and deveined	1 red chili pepper, seeded and chopped
Lemongrass stalks	2 tbsps. olive oil
4 garlic cloves, minced	½ tsp. smoked paprika

1. Preheat the Air fryer to 390ºF (199ºC) and grease an Air fryer basket. 2. Mix all the ingredients in a large bowl and refrigerate to marinate for about 2 hours. 3. Thread the shrimps onto lemongrass stalks and transfer into the Air fryer basket. 4. Air fry for about 5 minutes and dish out to serve warm.

Calories: 367, Fat: 13.3g, Carbs: 7.5g, Sugar: 0.2g, Protein: 52.2g, Sodium: 555mg

Thai Fish Curry

Prep Time: 6 minutes, Cook Time: 6 minutes, Serves: 6

1½ lbs. salmon fillets	⅓ cup olive oil
2 cups unsweetened coconut milk	2 tbsps. curry powder
¼ cup chopped cilantro	Salt and pepper, to taste

1. In the Instant Pot, add all the ingredients. Give a good stir. 2. Lock the lid. Select the Manual mode and set the cooking time for 6 minutes at Low Pressure. 3. Once cooking is complete, do a quick pressure release. Carefully open the lid. Set warm.

Calories: 468, Fat: 36g, Protein: 24g, Carbs: 8g, Fiber: 2g, Sugar: 2g, Sodium: 85mg

Salmon Tandoori

Prep Time: 2 hours, Cook Time: 6 minutes, Serves: 4

1½ lbs. salmon fillets	Salt and pepper, to taste
3 tbsps. coconut oil	1 tbsp. tandoori spice mix

1. In a bowl, add all the ingredients. Toss well until the fish is fully coated. Allow the fish to marinate for 2 hours in the fridge. 2. Place the marinated salmon in the Instant Pot. 3. Lock the lid. Select the Manual mode and cook for 6 minutes at Low Pressure. Flip the fish halfway through the cooking time. 4. Once cooking is complete, do a quick pressure release. Carefully open the lid. 5. Remove from the pot and serve on a plate.

Calories: 321, Fat: 20g, Protein: 32g, Carbs: 1g, Fiber: 0g, Sugar: 0g, Sodium: 90mg

Amazing Salmon Fillets

Prep Time: 5 minutes, Cook Time: 7 minutes, Serves: 2

2 (7-ounce) (¾-inch thick) salmon fillets	1 tbsp. Italian seasoning
	1 tbsp. fresh lemon juice

1. Preheat the Air fryer to 355ºF (179ºC) and grease an Air fryer grill pan. 2. Rub the salmon evenly with Italian seasoning and transfer into the Air fryer grill pan, skin-side up. 3. Grill for about 7 minutes and squeeze lemon juice on it to serve.

Calories: 88, Fat: 4.1g, Carbs: 0.1g, Sugar: 0g, Protein: 12.9g, Sodium: 55mg

Salmon with Basil Pesto

Prep Time: 6 minutes, Cook Time: 6 minutes, Serves: 6

3 garlic cloves, minced	2 tbsps. freshly squeezed lemon juice
1½ lbs. salmon fillets	½ cup olive oil
2 cups basil leaves	Salt and pepper, to taste

1. Make the pesto sauce: Put the basil leaves, olive oil, lemon juice, and garlic in a food processor, and pulse until smooth. 2. Season with salt and pepper. 3. Place the salmon fillets in the Instant Pot and add the pesto sauce. 4. Lock the lid. Select the Manual mode and set the cooking time for 6 minutes at Low Pressure. 5. Once cooking is complete, do a quick pressure release. Carefully open the lid. 6. Divide the salmon among six plates and serve.

Calories: 283, Fat: 29g, Protein: 27g, Carbs: 2g, Fiber: 1g, Sugar: 0g, Sodium: 140mg

Fish Fillets with Asparagus

Prep Time: 5 minutes, Cook Time: 3 minutes, Serves: 4

2 lemons	1 tsp. ground black pepper
2 cups cold water	1 bundle asparagus, ends trimmed
2 tbsps. extra-virgin olive oil	2 tbsps. lemon juice
4 (4-ounce / 113-g) white fish fillets, such as cod or haddock	Fresh dill, for garnish
1 tsp. fine sea salt	

1. Grate the zest off the lemons until you have about 1 tbsp. and set the zest aside. Slice the lemons into ⅛-inch slices. 2. Pour the water into the Instant Pot. Add 1 tbsp. of the olive oil to each of two stackable steamer pans. 3. Sprinkle the fish on all sides with the lemon zest, salt, and pepper. 4. Arrange two fillets in each steamer pan and top each with the lemon slices and then the asparagus. Sprinkle the asparagus with the salt and drizzle the lemon juice over the top. 5. Stack the steamer pans in the Instant Pot. Cover the top steamer pan with its lid. 6. Lock the lid. Select the Manual mode and set the cooking time for 3 minutes at High Pressure. 7. Once cooking is complete, do a natural pressure release for 7 minutes, then release any remaining pressure. Carefully open the lid. 8. Lift the steamer pans out of the Instant Pot. 9. Transfer the fish and asparagus to a serving plate. Garnish with the lemon slices and dill. 10. Serve immediately.

Calories: 204, Fat: 9g, Protein: 25g, Carbs: 7g, Fiber: 3g, Sugar: 2g, Sodium: 653mg

Snapper with Spicy Tomato Sauce

Prep Time: 5 minutes, Cook Time: 5 minutes, Serves: 6

2 tsps. coconut oil, melted	1 (14-ounce / 113-g) can fire-roasted diced tomatoes
1 tsp. celery seeds	1 bell pepper, sliced
½ tsp. fresh grated ginger	1 jalapeño pepper, minced
½ tsp. cumin seeds	Sea salt and ground black pepper, to taste
1 yellow onion, chopped	¼ tsp. chili flakes
2 cloves garlic, minced	½ tsp. turmeric powder
1½ pounds (680 g) snapper fillets	
¾ cup vegetable broth	

1. Set the Instant Pot to Sauté. Add and heat the sesame oil until hot. Sauté the celery seeds, fresh ginger, and cumin seeds. 2. Add the onion and continue to sauté until softened and fragrant. 3. Mix in the minced garlic and continue to cook for 30 seconds. Add the remaining ingredients and stir well. 4. Lock the lid. Select the Manual mode and set the cooking time for 3 minutes at Low Pressure. 5. When the timer beeps, perform a quick pressure release. Carefully remove the lid. 6. Serve warm.

Calories: 169, Fat: 4g, Protein: 28g, Carbs: 6g, Fiber: 2g, Sugar: 3g, Sodium: 481mg

Herbed Red Snapper

Prep Time: 3 minutes, Cook Time: 12 minutes, Serves: 4

1 cup water	3 tbsps. freshly squeezed lemon juice
4 red snapper fillets	Salt and pepper, to taste
1½ tsps. chopped fresh herbs	
¼ tsp. paprika	

1. Set a trivet in the Instant Pot and pour the water into the pot. 2. Mix all ingredients in a heat-proof dish that will fit in the Instant Pot. Combine to coat the fish with all ingredients. 3. Place the heat-proof dish on the trivet. 4. Lock the lid. Select the Manual mode and cook for 12 minutes at Low Pressure. 5. Once cooking is complete, do a quick pressure release. Carefully open the lid. 6. Serve warm.

Calories: 139, Fat: 2g, Protein: 26g, Carbs: 1g, Fiber: 0g, Sugar: 0g, Sodium: 99mg

Mahi Mahi with Green Beans

Prep Time: 15 minutes, Cook Time: 12 minutes, Serves: 4

5 cups green beans	Salt, as required
2 tbsps. fresh dill, chopped	2 garlic cloves, minced
4 (6-ounces) Mahi Mahi fillets	2 tbsps. fresh lemon juice
1 tbsp. avocado oil	1 tbsp. olive oil

1. Preheat the Air fryer to 375ºF (191ºC) and grease an Air fryer basket. 2. Mix the green beans, avocado oil and salt in a large bowl. 3. Arrange green beans into the Air fryer basket and air fry for about 6 minutes. 4. Combine garlic, dill, lemon juice, salt and olive oil in a bowl. 5. Coat Mahi Mahi in this garlic mixture and place on the top of green beans. 6. Air fry for 6 more minutes and dish out to serve warm.

Calories: 310, Fat: 14.8g, Carbs: 11.5g, Sugar: 2.1g, Protein: 32.6g, Sodium: 127mg

Salmon Cakes

Prep Time: 15 minutes, Cook Time: 9 minutes, Serves: 4

½ pound (227 g) cooked salmon, shredded	1 tbsp. Worcestershire sauce
2 medium green onions, sliced	1 tsp. salt
2 large eggs, lightly beaten	½ tbsp. garlic powder
1 cup bread crumbs	½ tsp. cayenne pepper
½ cup chopped flat leaf parsley	¼ tsp. celery seed
¼ cup soy sauce	4 tbsps. olive oil, divided

1. Stir together all the ingredients except the olive oil in a large mixing bowl until combined. 2. Set your Instant Pot to Sauté and heat 2 tbsps. of olive oil. 3. Scoop out golf ball-sized clumps of the salmon mixture and roll them into balls, then flatten to form cakes. 4. Working in batches, arrange the salmon cakes in an even layer in the Instant Pot. 5. Cook each side for 2 minutes until golden brown. Transfer to a paper towel-lined plate. Repeat with the remaining 2 tbsps. of olive oil and salmon cakes. 6. Serve immediately.

Calories: 358, Fat: 20g, Protein: 20g, Carbs: 25g, Fiber: 2g, Sugar: 2g, Sodium: 753mg

Mahi-Mahi Fillets with Peppers

Prep Time: 10 minutes, Cook Time: 3 minutes, Serves: 3

2 sprigs fresh rosemary	Sea salt and ground black pepper, to taste
2 sprigs dill, tarragon	1 serrano pepper, seeded and sliced
1 sprig fresh thyme	
1 cup water	1 green bell pepper, sliced
1 lemon, sliced	1 red bell pepper, sliced
3 mahi-mahi fillets	
2 tbsps. coconut oil, melted	

1. Add the herbs, water, and lemon slices to the Instant Pot and insert a steamer basket. 2. Arrange the mahi-mahi fillets in the

steamer basket.3.Drizzle the melted coconut oil over the top and season with the salt and black pepper.4.Lock the lid. Select the Manual mode and set the cooking time for 3 minutes at Low Pressure.5.When the timer beeps, perform a natural pressure release for 10 minutes, then release any remaining pressure. Carefully remove the lid.6.Place the peppers on top. Select the Sauté mode and let it simmer for another 1 minute.7.Serve immediately.

Calories: 272, Fat: 12g, Protein: 34g, Carbs: 10g, Fiber: 3g, Sugar: 3g, Sodium: 86mg

Curry Halibut

Prep Time: 3 minutes, Cook Time: 10 minutes, Serves: 4

2 tbsps. chopped cilantro
4 skinless halibut fillets
3 green curry leaves
1 cup chopped tomatoes
1 tbsp. freshly squeezed lime juice
Salt and pepper, to taste

1.Place all ingredients in the Instant Pot. Give a good stir to combine the ingredients.2.Lock the lid. Select the Manual mode and cook for 10 minutes at Low Pressure.3.Do a quick pressure release.

Calories: 121, Fat: 3g, Protein: 20g, Carbs: 6g, Fiber: 2g, Sugar: 3g, Sodium: 52mg

Chili-Rubbed Tilapia

Prep Time: 6 minutes, Cook Time: 10 minutes, Serves: 4

1 cup water
½ tsp. garlic powder
1 lb. skinless tilapia fillet
2 tbsps. extra virgin olive oil
Salt and pepper, to taste
2 tbsps. chili powder

1.Set a trivet in the Instant Pot and pour the water into the pot. 2.Season the tilapia fillets with salt, pepper, chili powder, and garlic powder. Drizzle with olive oil on top.3.Place in the steamer basket.4.Lock the lid. Select the Steam mode and cook for 10 minutes at Low Pressure.5.Once cooking is complete, do a quick pressure release. Carefully open the lid.6.Serve warm.

Calories: 195, Fat: 9g, Protein: 24g, Carbs: 2g, Fiber: 1g, Sugar: 0g, Sodium: 121mg

Cod with Asparagus

Prep Time: 15 minutes, Cook Time: 11 minutes, Serves: 2

2 (6-ounces) boneless cod fillets
2 tbsps. fresh parsley, roughly chopped
2 tbsps. fresh dill, roughly chopped
1 bunch asparagus
1 tsp. dried basil
1½ tbsps. fresh lemon juice
1 tbsp. olive oil
Salt and black pepper, to taste

1.Preheat the Air fryer to 400ºF (204ºC) and grease an Air fryer basket.2.Mix lemon juice, oil, basil, salt, and black pepper in a small bowl.3.Combine the cod and ¾ of the oil mixture in another bowl.4.Coat asparagus with remaining oil mixture and transfer to the Air fryer basket.5.Roast for about 3 minutes and arrange cod fillets on top of asparagus.6.Roast for about 8 minutes and dish out in serving plates.

Calories: 331, Fat: 18g, Carbs: 8.8g, Sugar: 3.5g, Protein: 37.6g, Sodium: 167mg

Herbed Haddock

Prep Time: 10 minutes, Cook Time: 8 minutes, Serves: 2

2 (6-ounce) haddock fillets
2 tbsps. pine nuts
3 tbsps. fresh basil, chopped
1 tbsp. low-fat Parmesan cheese, grated
½ cup extra-virgin olive oil
Salt and black pepper, to taste

1.Preheat the Air fryer to 355ºF (179ºC) and grease an Air fryer basket.2.Coat the haddock fillets evenly with olive oil and season with salt and black pepper.3.Place the haddock fillets in the Air fryer basket and roast for about 8 minutes.4.Dish out the haddock fillets in serving plates.5.Meanwhile, put remaining ingredients in a food processor and pulse until smooth.6.Top this cheese sauce over the haddock fillets and serve hot.

Calories: 751, Fat: 65.5g, Carbs: 1.3g, Sugar: 0g, Protein: 43.5g, Sodium: 176mg

Appetizing Tuna Patties

Prep Time: 15 minutes, Cook Time: 10 minutes, Serves: 6

2 (6-ounce) cans tuna, drained
½ cup panko bread crumbs
1 egg
2 tbsps. fresh parsley, chopped
2 tsps. Dijon mustard
Dash of Tabasco sauce
Salt and black pepper, to taste
1 tbsp. fresh lemon juice
1 tbsp. olive oil

1.Preheat the Air fryer to 355ºF (179ºC) and line a baking tray with foil paper.2.Mix all the ingredients in a large bowl until well combined.3.Make equal sized patties from the mixture and refrigerate overnight.4.Arrange the patties on the baking tray and transfer to an Air fryer basket.5.Bake for about 10 minutes and dish out to serve warm.

Calories: 130, Fat: 6.2g, Carbs: 5.1g, Sugar: 0.5g, Protein: 13g, Sodium: 94mg

Crispy Baked Flounder with Green Beans

Prep Time: 10 minutes, Cook Time: 20 minutes, Serves: 4

1 pound (454 g) flounder
2 cups green beans
4 tbsps. almond butter
8 basil leaves
1.75 ounces (50 g) pork rinds
½ cup reduced fat Parmesan cheese
3 cloves garlic
Salt and ground black pepper, to taste
Nonstick cooking spray

1.Heat oven to 350ºF (180ºC). Spray a baking dish with cooking spray.2.Steam green beans until they are almost tender, about 15 minutes, less if you use frozen or canned beans. Lay green beans in the prepared dish.3.Place the fish fillets over the green beans and season with salt and pepper.4.Place the garlic, basil, pork rinds, and Parmesan in a food processor and pulse until mixture resembles crumbs. Sprinkle over fish. Cut almond butter into small pieces and place on top.5.Bake for 15 to 20 minutes or until fish flakes easily with a fork. Serve.

Calories: 360, Fat: 20g, Protein: 39.1g, Carbs: 5.1g, Fiber: 2g, Sugar: 1g, Sodium: 322mg

CHAPTER 8

POULTRY RECIPES

Sunflower Seed Encrusted Turkey Cutlets ········47
Broiled Curried Chicken Tenders ················47
Simple Oatmeal Chicken Tenders ················47
Easy Sumac Chicken with Cauliflower and Carrots ··47
Herb Turkey Cutlets ····························47
Healthy Grilled Chicken and Black Bean Salsa ·48
Healthy Turkey Chili ···························48
Chicken Cacciatore ····························48
Tasty Pita Sandwich with Curried Chicken Salad ·48
Turkey Scallopini with Creamy Lemon Sauce ··48
Easy Quick Greek Turkey Burger ················49
White Beans Chicken Chili ·····················49
Spinach and Mushroom Stuffed Chicken ········49
Chicken with Peanut Sauce ·····················49
Chicken and Apple Sandwich ···················49
Crispy Apricot Chicken with Steamed Baby Greens ·50

Traditional Open Face Turkey Burger ············50
Chili Turkey with Beans ·························50
Harissa Chicken Thighs with Yogurt ·············50
Sauté Turkey Cutlets ···························50
Chicken Stew with Olives and Lemon ············51
Italian Chicken Cacciatore ······················51
Stir-Fried Chicken and Broccoli ·················51
Tender Turkey Meatballs with Marinara Sauce ··51
Savory Orange Chicken with Brown Rice ········52
Curry Chicken with Lemongrass and Coconut ··52
One-Pot Creamy Tuscan Chicken ················52
Crispy Za'atar Chicken Tenders ·················52
Ground Turkey Spinach Stir-Fry ·················52
Chicken with Crispy Kale and Artichokes ········53
Slaw and Chicken Stir-Fry ······················53

Easy Quick Greek Turkey Burger

Prep Time: 10 minutes, Cook Time: 10 minutes, Serves: 4

1 pound (454g) ground turkey
1 medium zucchini, grated
¼ cup crumbled low-fat feta cheese
1 tbsp. extra-virgin olive oil
1 large egg, beaten
¼ cup whole-wheat bread crumbs
¼ cup red onion, minced
1 tbsp. fresh oregano, chopped
1 tsp. kosher salt
1 garlic clove, minced
¼ tsp. freshly ground black pepper

1. Add the turkey, zucchini, onion, bread crumbs, egg, garlic, oregano, feta cheese, salt, and black pepper in a large bowl, and mix well. Using your hands to shape the mixture into 4 equal patties. 2. In a large nonstick grill pan or skillet, heat 1 tbsp. olive oil over medium-high heat. Place the burgers on the pan and change the heat to medium. Fried one side for 5 minutes, then turn over and cook the other side for 5 minutes more. 3. Transfer the burgers to a plate or dish and serve warm.

Calories: 285, Total Fat: 16g, Saturated Fat: 5g, Protein: 26g, Total Carbs: 9g, Fiber: 2g, Sugar: 2g, Sodium: 465mg

White Beans Chicken Chili

Prep Time: 5 minutes, Cook Time: 25 minutes, Serves: 4

three (15-ounce, 425 g) cans white beans
1 tbsp. canola oil
1 onion, chopped
3 garlic cloves, minced
1 to 3 jalapeños, seeded and diced
2 tsps. ground cumin
1½ tsp. ground coriander
1 tsp. chili powder
1 tsp. dried oregano
¼ to ½ tsp. cayenne
4 cups low-sodium chicken broth
3 cups chopped cooked chicken breast
¼ cup chopped cilantro, for garnish

1. In a large stockpot, heat the canola oil over medium heat. Add the garlic, onion and cook about 5 minutes, stirring frequently, until the onion is soft. Add the jalapeño, coriander, cumin, oregano, chili powder, and cayenne. Cook for 2 to 3 minutes, stirring frequently, until the jalapeño begins to soften. 2. Add the chicken, broth, and beans, and bring to a boil over medium-high heat. Reduce the heat to medium-low and simmer for about 15 minutes, uncovered, stirring occasionally. Serve, garnished with cilantro.

Calories: 627, Protein: 63.4g, Fat: 10g, Carbs: 73.5g, Fiber: 17.5g, Sodium: 192mg

Spinach and Mushroom Stuffed Chicken

Prep Time: 15 minutes, Cook Time: 35 minutes, Serves: 4

Nonstick cooking spray (optional)
3 tbsps. extra-virgin olive oil, divided
2 (8-ounce, 227g) boneless, skinless chicken breasts
2 garlic cloves, chopped
12 small cremini mushrooms, sliced
2 cups baby spinach, chopped
¼ tsp. freshly ground black pepper
¼ cup grated low-fat Parmesan cheese
Zest of 1 large lemon, divided
3 tsps. fresh lemon juice, divided

1. Preheat the oven to 375°F(190°C). Line a sheet pan with aluminum foil or coat with nonstick cooking spray. 2. From the thickest part of each breast, cut an opening about 3 inches wide, then cut three-quarters of the way through the breast to create a pocket. Do not cut all the way through the chicken or the stuffing will spill out. 3. In a skillet, heat 2 tbsps. of oil over medium-high heat. Add the garlic and stir frequently for 30 seconds to 1 minute. Add the mushrooms and cook for about 2 minutes, or until tender. Add the spinach and stir for about 1 minute, or until wilted. Season with the pepper. 4. Transfer the cooked vegetables to a medium bowl. Add the Parmesan cheese, half of the lemon zest, and 1½ tsps. of lemon juice. Divide the filling into 2 portions and stuff each chicken breast. 5. Stir together the remaining 1 tbsp. of oil and the remaining 1½ tsps. of lemon juice in a small bowl. Brush on top of each chicken breast. 6. Bake for about 35 minutes, or until the internal temperature of the chicken reaches 165°F(74°C). Let cool, top with remaining lemon zest, then cut each stuffed breast in half and divide into 4 storage containers.

Calories: 254, Total Fat: 14g, Carbs: 5g, Fiber: 1g, Protein: 27g, Sodium: 170mg

Chicken with Peanut Sauce

Prep Time: 15 minutes, Cook Time: 8 minutes, Serves: 4

3 tsps. low-salt soy sauce
3 tbsps. lime juice
3 tbsps. canola oil
1 pound (454 g) boneless chicken strips
2 tsps. honey
¼ tsp. cayenne pepper
Peanut Sauce
2 tbsps. smooth peanut butter
1 tsp. low-salt fish sauce
1 tbsp. lime juice
2 tbsps. low-fat coconut milk

1. Preheat a grill. Whisk together lime juice, oil, honey, soy sauce, and cayenne in a pie plate. Add the chicken and marinate 15 minutes. 2. To make peanut sauce: Mix together peanut butter, coconut milk, lime juice, fish sauce and 1 tsp. soy sauce in a medium bowl. Set aside. 3. Grill chicken about 3 minutes per side until cooked through. Serve with peanut sauce.

Calories: 204, Fat: 8.9g, Carbs: 2.2g, Protein: 28g, Sodium: 175.3mg, Fiber: 0.8g

Chicken and Apple Sandwich

Prep Time: 10 minutes, Cook Time: 2 minutes, Serves: 2

4 slices multigrain bread, low-sodium
2 slices low-sodium Cheddar cheese, about ¼ inch thick
1 tart apple, cored and cut into thin slices
4 ounces (113 g) cooked chicken breast, cut into 4 thin slices
1 cup gently packed shredded arugula
2 tbsps. mayonnaise, low-fat

1. Toast bread until golden brown, and spread bread slices with mayonnaise. 2. Place chicken, apple and Cheddar cheese evenly on two slices of bread. 3. Top with arugula and a second slice of bread. 4. Cut them in half and serve.

Calories: 432, Fat: 17.6g, Carbs: 40g, Protein: 30.4g, Sodium: 184mg, Fiber: 4.4g

Crispy Apricot Chicken with Steamed Baby Greens

Prep Time: 10 minutes, Cook Time: 25 minutes, Serves: 4

½ cup chopped apricots
½ cup flaxseed meal
1 tsp. allspice
½ tsp. freshly ground black pepper
⅛ tsp. salt
4 boneless, skinless chicken breasts (4 ounces each)
4 cups baby greens
1 avocado, seeded and diced

1. Preheat the oven to 350°F (180ºC). Lightly grease a baking dish with oil spray. 2. Process the walnuts into a meal in a food processor or blender. 3. Stir together the apricot meal, flaxseed meal, allspice, black pepper, and salt in a resealable plastic bag. One at a time, place a chicken breast in the bag, seal the bag, and shake until evenly coated. Place the coated chicken breast to the prepared baking dish and spread with any reserving apricot/flaxseed meal. (Do not keep the apricot/flaxseed mixture for another purpose as it has touched the raw chicken and you want to avoid cross-contamination.) 4. Place the chicken to the oven and bake until no longer pink in the center, the juices run clear, and an instant-read thermometer inserted in the center reads 165°F (74ºC), 25 to 30 minutes. 5. In the meantime, about 5 minutes before the chicken is done, place the baby greens in a microwave-safe dish and add about 4 tbsps. water over the top. Seal with a microwave lid or cover with a paper towel and cook on high for 3 minutes. Remove the lid carefully and check to see if the baby greens are softened. If not, microwave in a further 1-minute increment. Carefully remove the baby greens from the microwave and drain. 6. Serve the chicken along with the baby greens, with avocado for squeezing. If desired, season the dish with a pinch of salt, pepper, and allspice.

Calories: 310, Total Fat: 18g, Saturated Fat: 1g, Total Carbs: 14g, Protein: 31g, Sodium: 308mg, Fiber: 8g, Sugar: 2g

Traditional Open Face Turkey Burger

Prep Time: 10 minutes, Cook Time: 25 minutes, Serves: 4

1 tbsp. olive oil
1 pound (454g) lean ground white meat turkey
1 cup mushrooms, finely chopped
2 tomatoes, sliced
1 clove garlic, minced
½ tsp. freshly ground black pepper
⅛ tsp. salt
Cooking spray
4 cups baby spinach

1. In a large skillet, heat the olive oil over medium-low heat. Add the mushrooms and cook for about 5 minutes, until soft and browned. Stir in the garlic and cook for 1 minute. Remove from heat and allow to cool. 2. Combine the turkey, pepper, salt, and mushroom garlic mixture in a large bowl. Mix until well combined, then form into 8 small patties. 3. Prepare a grill for medium-high heat. Apply cooking spray to the grill rack. Grill the burgers until cooked through, 6 to 8 minutes per side and until an instant-read thermometer registers 165°F(74°C). If you don't have a grill, you can broil the burgers in an oven-safe skillet under the broiler element for about 10 minutes per side, or until an instant-read thermometer registers 165°F(74°C). 4. Divide the spinach among 4 serving plates, top with 2 patties per plate. Top each stack with tomato slices and serve immediately.

Calories: 179, Total Fat: 5g, Saturated Fat: 1g, Sodium: 135mg, Total Carbs: 6g, Fiber: 2g, Sugar: 1g, Protein: 28g

Chili Turkey with Beans

Prep Time: 5 minutes, Cook Time: 35 minutes, Serves: 6

One (16-ounce, 454 g) can low-salt navy beans, rinsed and drained
One (16-ounce, 454 g) can low-salt black beans, rinsed and drained
One (16-ounce, 454 g) can low-salt red kidney beans, rinsed and drained
One (16-ounce, 454 g) can low-salt chickpeas, rinsed and drained
4 large tomatoes, diced
1 tsp. olive oil
1 tsp. minced garlic
½ pound (227 g) lean ground turkey
1 small sweet onion, chopped
3 tbsps. chili powder
1 tsp. ground cumin

1. Add olive oil in a large pot over medium-high heat. Sauté turkey meat in oil about 6 minutes until completely cooked through. 2. Add onion and garlic and cook about 3 minutes, stirring frequently, until translucent. 3. Put in kidney beans, navy beans, black beans, chickpeas, tomatoes, chili powder, and cumin. Boil, then reduce heat to a simmer. Stir occasionally for 20 to 25 minutes. 4. Remove from heat and serve hot.

Calories: 383, Fat: 6.1g, Carbs: 55.5g, Protein: 28.6g, Sodium: 109mg, Fiber: 21.9g

Harissa Chicken Thighs with Yogurt

Prep Time: 5 minutes, plus 15 minutes to marinate, Cook Time: 25 minutes, Serves: 4

1½ pounds (680g) boneless, skinless chicken thighs
½ cup nonfat coconut yogurt
½ tsp. kosher salt
¼ tsp. freshly ground black pepper
2 tbsps. harissa
1 tbsp. lemon juice

1. Put lemon juice, the yogurt, salt, harissa, and black pepper in a bowl, stir completely, and then add the chicken and mix together. Marinate for at least 15 minutes, and put it in the refrigerator for 4 hours. 2. Preheat the oven to 425°F before toasting. Transfer the chicken thighs from the marinade and place in a single layer on the baking sheet lined with parchment paper or foil. Roast for 20 minutes, turning over the chicken halfway through the baking time. 3. Set the oven temperature to broil. Broiling until the chicken is golden brown spots, about 2 to 3 minutes.

Calories: 190, Total Fat: 10g, Saturated Fat: 2g, Protein: 24g, Total Carbs: 1g, Fiber: 0g, Sugar: 1g, Sodium: 230mg

Sauté Turkey Cutlets

Prep Time: 5 minutes, Cook Time: 20 minutes, Serves: 4

Salt and freshly ground black pepper
1 pound (454 g) turkey breast cutlets
2 tbsps. extra-virgin olive oil
2 cloves garlic, minced
1 large yellow bell pepper, cut into strips
1 large red bell pepper, cut into strips
1 (14.5-ounce, 410 g) can no-salt-added diced tomatoes, undrained
1 cup button mushrooms, sliced
1 tbsp. dried tarragon

1. Sprinkle salt and pepper over the turkey cutlets. Heat 1 tbsp. of the olive oil in a large skillet over medium-high heat. Add the turkey cutlets to the skillet and cook for 1 to 3 minutes until browned on the bottom. Flip and continue cooking for 1 to 3 minutes more until cooked all the way through. The outside

should be nicely browned and the inside fully cooked. Remove the turkey to a plate and cover with foil to keep warm.2.Add the remaining olive oil to the skillet, then add the garlic and sauté for 1 minute, until sizzling. Put in bell peppers and mushrooms and continue cooking 5 to 7 minutes until starting to soften.3.Add the tarragon and tomatoes and their juices, cover, and bring to a simmer for 3 to 5 minutes, stirring often, until slightly reduced.4.Return the turkey cutlets to the skillet. Reduce the heat to medium-low and cook for 2 to 3 minutes to warm the turkey through.

Calories: 225, Total Fat: 8g, Saturated Fat: 1g, Total Carbs: 10g, Protein: 30g, Sodium: 67mg, Fiber: 2g, Sugar: 3g

Chicken Stew with Olives and Lemon

Prep Time: 20 minutes, Cook Time: 35 minutes, Serves: 4

- 1½ pounds (680g) boneless, skinless chicken thighs
- ¼ tsp. freshly ground black pepper
- 2 tbsps. olive oil
- 1¼ cups no-salt-added chicken stock
- 1 onion, julienned
- 4 garlic cloves, sliced
- 1 tsp. ground turmeric
- 1 tsp. ground cumin
- ½ tsp. ground coriander
- ½ tsp. ground cinnamon
- ¼ tsp. red pepper flakes
- 1 dried bay leaf
- ¼ cup white wine vinegar
- 2 tbsps. lemon juice
- 1 tbsp. lemon zest
- 1 (14-ounce) can artichoke hearts, drained
- ¼ cup olives, pitted and chopped
- 1 tsp. capers, rinsed and chopped
- 1 tbsp. fresh mint, chopped
- 1 tbsp. fresh parsley, chopped
- 1 tsp. kosher salt, divided

1.Season the chicken with ½ tsp. of salt and pepper.2.Heat the olive oil in a large skillet or sauté pan over medium heat. Add the chicken and sauté 2 to 3 minutes per side, until browned. Transfer to a plate and set aside.3.Add the onion to the same pan and sauté until translucent, about 5 minutes. Add the garlic and sauté 30 seconds. Add the remaining ½ tsp. salt, the turmeric, cumin, coriander, cinnamon, red pepper flakes, and bay leaf and sauté 30 seconds.4.Add ¼ cup of the chicken stock and increase the heat to medium-high to deglaze the pan, scraping up any brown bits on the bottom. Add the remaining 1 cup stock, the lemon juice, and lemon zest. Cover, reduce the heat to low, and simmer for 10 minutes.5.Add the artichokes, olives, and capers and mix well. Add the reserved chicken and nestle it into the mixture. Simmer, uncovered, until the chicken fully cooks through, about 10 to 15 minutes. Garnish with the mint and parsley.

Calories: 500, Total Fat: 36g, Saturated Fat: 9g, Sodium: 570mg, Total Carbs: 11g, Fiber: 3g, Sugar: 3g, Protein: 30g

Italian Chicken Cacciatore

Prep Time: 10 minutes, Cook Time: 8 hours, Serves: 6

- 1 pound (454 g) boneless, skinless chicken thighs, cut into 1-inch pieces
- 1 pound (454 g) fresh mushrooms, halved
- 2 onions, sliced
- 2 green bell peppers, seeded and sliced
- 1 (14-ounce, 397 g) can diced tomatoes, with their juice
- 1½ tsp. garlic powder
- 1 tsp. dried Italian seasoning
- ¼ tsp. red pepper flakes
- ¼ tsp. sea salt
- ¼ tsp. freshly ground black pepper

1.Mix all the ingredients in the slow cooker.2.Cover and cook on low for 8 hours.3.Serve the chicken with sauce spooned over the top.

Calories: 204, Total Fat: 6g, Saturated Fat: 2g, Carbs: 12g, Protein: 26g, Fiber: 3g, Sodium: 363mg

Stir-Fried Chicken and Broccoli

Prep Time: 15 minutes, Cook Time: 15 minutes, Serves: 4 to 6

- 2 tbsps. coconut oil
- 1 pound (454 g) boneless, skinless chicken thighs, cut into thin strips
- 2 garlic cloves, thinly sliced
- 1 tsp. minced fresh ginger root
- 2 cups broccoli florets
- ¼ tsp. red pepper flakes
- ½ tsp. salt
- ¾ cup chicken broth
- 1 tsp. toasted sesame oil (optional)
- 1 tbsp. sesame seeds (optional)

1.Heat the coconut oil in a Dutch oven over high heat.2.Place the chicken in the oven and sauté for 5 to 8 minutes, until it starts to brown.3.Stir in the garlic, ginger, broccoli florets, red pepper flakes, salt and broth.4.Cover the pot, reduce the heat to medium, and allow the mixture to steam for about 5 minutes, until the broccoli turns bright green.5.Remove from the heat, sprinkle with the sesame oil and sesame seeds (if using), and serve.

Calories: 250, Total Fat: 14 g, Total Carbs: 5g, Sugar: <1g, Fiber: 1g, Protein: 27g, Sodium: 597mg

Tender Turkey Meatballs with Marinara Sauce

Prep Time: 10 minutes, Cook Time: 40 minutes, Serves: 4 (16 meatballs)

- 4 tbsps. extra virgin olive oil
- 1 pound (454g) lean ground turkey
- 1 (16-ounce, 454g) jar low-sodium marinara sauce
- ½ cup low-fat feta cheese
- ½ small red onion, finely chopped
- 2 large cloves garlic, minced
- ¼ cup red bell pepper, finely chopped
- 3 tbsps. finely chopped fresh parsley
- ½ tsp. chile pepper flakes
- ⅛ tsp. ground cumin
- ½ tsp. dried Italian herbs (premixed, or use thyme, rosemary, oregano, parsley, and basil)
- ⅛ tsp. cracked black pepper
- 1 large egg
- ¼ cup whole wheat bread crumbs
- ⅛ tsp. sea salt

1.Preheat the oven to 375°F(190°C).2.In a large bowl, combine all ingredients except the oil, marinara, and feta. Mix well by hand until ingredients are incorporated into the meat, being careful not to overmix. Roll the meat mixture into meatballs(size of golf balls).3.Heat a large nonstick skillet over medium-high heat. Once the pan is hot, add the oil and then the meatballs in batches of five. Sear on each side (do not cook all the way through), and place in an ovenproof dish.4.Once all the meatballs have been seared and placed in the dish, top with the marinara sauce, and cover with foil. Bake for 20 to 25 minutes. 5.Remove from the oven, and raise the temperature to 400°F(205°C). Remove the foil from the dish, top the meatballs with the feta, and bake for 4 minutes. Remove and serve immediately.

Calories: 546, Protein: 32g, Fat: 33g, Carbs: 32g, Fiber: 6g, Sugar: 2g, Sodium: 508mg

Savory Orange Chicken with Brown Rice

Prep Time: 15 minutes, Cook Time: 10 minutes, Serves: 2

2 (4-ounce (113g)) boneless, skinless chicken breasts
½ cup coarsely chopped shiitake mushroom
1 tbsp. sesame oil
1 tbsp. extra virgin olive oil
½ tsp. grated orange zest
1 large clove garlic, minced
¼ tsp. ground ginger
¼ cup chopped white onion
¼ tsp. grated lemon zest
¼ tsp. cracked black pepper
Juice of ½ orange
4 cups spinach
1 cup cooked brown rice

1. Before cooking, remove the fat from the chicken breast, then cut the chicken breast into small cubes. 2. In a medium saucepan, add sesame oil and olive oil and heat over medium heat. Put the mushrooms, onions and garlic in the same pan, stir fry for a minute, then add the chicken, sprinkle with pepper, ginger, orange zest and lemon zest to taste, cook for about 4 to 5 minutes, until the chicken is browned. Then pour the orange juice, stir the chicken and scrape off the bottom of the pan to add flavor. Put the spinach, then remove the pot from the heat, immediately cover the pot and steam the spinach, 3 to 4 minutes. 3. Divide the cooked brown rice into two portions, put orange chicken on top, and enjoy.

Calories: 334, Fat: 15g, Protein: 27g, Carbs: 25g, Fiber: 4g, Sugar: 5g, Sodium: 282mg

Curry Chicken with Lemongrass and Coconut

Prep Time: 10 minutes, Cook Time: 45 minutes, Serves: 4

1 pound (454 g) boneless, skinless chicken breasts, cut into bite-size cubes
¼ cup chopped unsalted cashews
1 cup brown jasmine rice
1 medium red bell pepper, sliced
3 tbsps. minced fresh ginger
1½ tbsp. curry powder
2 tsps. extra-virgin olive oil
3 cloves garlic, minced
1 stalk lemongrass, bottom 6 inches only, outer leaves peeled
1 tbsp. honey
⅔ cup (160 ml) canned unsweetened coconut milk
¾ cup (180 ml) low-sodium chicken broth
2 tbsps. unsweetened shredded coconut (optional)
2 tbsps. golden raisins
4 tbsps. chopped fresh cilantro leaves

1. Combine the rice and 2 cups water in a medium saucepan with a tight-fitting lid, bring to a boil, stir once, cover and turn down the heat. Simmer for 30 to 35 minutes until all of the liquid is absorbed. Do not lift the lid or stir during cooking. 2. Meanwhile, heat the olive oil over medium-high heat in a large skillet. Add the garlic and sauté for 1 minute. Put in the bell pepper and continue cooking for 2 minutes. Mix the ginger and curry powder well, cooking for 1 minute. 3. Mash the lemongrass lightly with a kitchen mallet to release the flavors. Add the lemongrass, coconut milk, honey, and broth to the skillet. reduce the heat to medium, and cook for 3 minutes. 4. Put the chicken to the pan, stir all of the ingredients, and cover the pan. Simmer over medium-low heat about 25 to 30 minutes until the chicken is cooked through. 5. Remove and discard the lemongrass stalk and stir in the cashews, raisins, shredded coconut, and cilantro. 6. Fluff the rice with a fork and divide onto 4 serving plates. Serve the chicken over the rice.

Calories: 426, Total Fat: 12g, Saturated Fat: 5g, Total Carbs: 52g, Protein: 29g, Sodium: 229mg, Fiber: 5g, Sugar: 8g

One-Pot Creamy Tuscan Chicken

Prep Time: 5 minutes, Cook Time: 20 minutes, Serves: 4

⅛ tsp. freshly ground black pepper
½ tsp. sea salt
1 tsp. garlic powder
4 boneless, skinless chicken breast halves, pounded to ½- to ¾-inch thickness
2 tbsps. extra-virgin olive oil
2 cups cherry tomatoes
½ cup sliced green olives
1 zucchini, chopped
¼ cup dry white wine

1. Use the pepper, salt and garlic powder to season the chicken breasts. 2. Heat the olive oil in a large nonstick skillet over medium-high heat, until it shimmers. Place the chicken into the skillet and cook for 7 to 10 minutes per side, until it reaches an internal temperature of 165°F(74°C). Transfer the chicken onto a platter, and set aside, use foil to tent. 3. Place the tomatoes, olives and zucchini into the same skillet. Cook until the zucchini is tender, about 4 minutes, stirring occasionally. 4. Pour in the white wine and scrape any browned bits from the bottom of the pan with a wooden spoon. Simmer for 1 minute. Place the chicken and any juices that have collected on the platter back to the pan and stir to coat with the sauce and vegetables.

Calories: 171, Total Fat: 11g, Total Carbs: 8g, Sugar: 4g, Fiber: 2g, Protein: 8g, Sodium: 743mg

Crispy Za'atar Chicken Tenders

Prep Time: 5 minutes, Cook Time: 15 minutes, Serves: 4

Olive oil cooking spray
1 pound (454g) chicken tenders
1½ tbsps. za'atar
½ tsp. kosher salt
¼ tsp. freshly ground black pepper

1. Preheat the oven to 450°F(235°C). Line a baking sheet with parchment paper or foil and lightly spray with olive oil cooking spray. 2. In a large bowl, mix together the chicken, za'atar, salt, and black pepper well, covering the chicken tenders fully. Arrange in a single layer on the baking sheet and bake for 15 minutes, turning the chicken over once halfway through the cooking time.

Calories: 145, Total Fat: 4g, Saturated Fat: 1g, Sodium: 190mg, Total Carbs: 0g, Fiber: 0g, Sugar: 0g, Protein: 26g

Ground Turkey Spinach Stir-Fry

Prep Time: 10 minutes, Cook Time: 10 minutes, Serves: 4

2 tbsps. extra-virgin olive oil
1 onion, chopped
1½ pounds (670 g) ground turkey breast
4 cups fresh baby spinach
1 oz. stir-fry sauce

1. Heat the olive oil in a large nonstick skillet over medium-high heat, until it shimmers. 2. Stir in the onion, turkey and spinach. Cook for about 5 minutes, use a spoon to break up the turkey, until the meat is browned. 3. Pour in the stir-fry sauce. Cook until it thickens, about 3 to 4 minutes, stirring constantly.

Calories: 424, Total Fat: 20 g, Total Carbs: 9g, Sugar: 3g, Fiber: 2g, Protein: 51g, Sodium: 270mg

Chicken with Crispy Kale and Artichokes

Prep Time: 5 minutes, plus 30 minutes to marinate, Cook Time: 35 minutes, Serves: 4

- 3 tbsps. extra-virgin olive oil, divided
- 1½ pounds (680g) boneless, skinless chicken breast
- 2 tbsps. lemon juice
- Zest of 1 lemon
- 2 garlic cloves, minced
- 2 tsps. dried rosemary
- ¼ tsp. freshly ground black pepper
- 2 (14-ounce, 397g) cans artichoke hearts, drained
- 1 bunch (about 6 ounces, 170g) Lacinato kale, stemmed and torn or chopped into pieces
- ½ tsp. kosher salt

1. In a large bowl or zip-top bag, combine 2 tbsps. of the olive oil, the lemon juice, lemon zest, garlic, rosemary, salt, and black pepper. Mix well and then add the chicken and artichokes. Marinate for at least 30 minutes, and up to 4 hours in the refrigerator. 2. Preheat the oven to 350°F(180°C). Line a baking sheet with parchment paper or foil. Remove the chicken and artichokes from the marinade and spread them in a single layer on the baking sheet. Roast for 15 minutes, turn the chicken over, and roast another 15 minutes. Remove the baking sheet and put the chicken, artichokes, and juices on a platter or large plate. Tent with foil to keep warm. 3. Change the oven temperature to broil. In a large bowl, combine the kale with the remaining 1 tbsp. of the olive oil. Arrange the kale on the baking sheet and broil until golden brown in spots and as crispy as you like, about 3 to 5 minutes. 4. Place the kale on top of the chicken and artichokes.

Calories: 430, Total Fat: 16g, Saturated Fat: 3g, Sodium: 350mg, Total Carbs: 29g, Fiber: 19g, Sugar: 3g, Protein: 46g

Slaw and Chicken Stir-Fry

Prep Time: 10 minutes, Cook Time: 20 minutes, Serves: 4

- 1 pound (454 g) boneless, skinless chicken breasts, cut into ½" x 2" strips
- ½ bag broccoli slaw
- ½ bag frozen onion and pepper mixture
- 2 tbsps. canola oil
- low-sodium stir-fry sauce

1. In a large skillet over medium-high heat, heat the canola oil. 2. When oil is hot (without smoking), add half of chicken strips to oil, and sauté 1 - 2 minutes, stirring with spatula until cooked on all sides. 3. Remove chicken and put on warm plate. Cover plate with pot lid or aluminum foil to keep warm. 4. Add pepper and onion mixture to pan. Stir-fry 3 - 4 minutes. Add broccoli slaw, and sauté until tender. 5. Add ¼ cup stir-fry sauce, and place chicken back into pan. Stir well to mix sauce and reheat chicken.

Calories: 235, Protein: 29 g, Carbs:10 g, Fat:9g, Fiber:3g, Sodium: 184mg, Potassium: 610mg

CHAPTER 9 — VEGETABLE RECIPES

Cauliflower and Cashew Gratin 55	Tomato-Topped Spaghetti Squash 58
Cauliflower Tater Tots 55	Italian Eggplant Parmesan 58
Crispy Jicama Fries 55	Braised Green Cabbage and Onion 58
Saltine Wax Beans 55	Green Beans with Shallot 58
Classic Spaghetti Squash 55	Italian Beets and Tomato 58
Zucchini Balls 55	Balsamic Brussels Sprouts 58
Vegetable Chili 56	Sesame Taj Tofu 59
Simple Curried Squash 56	Turmeric Cauliflower and Chickpea Stew 59
Bean Tostadas 56	Honey Roasted Carrots and Parsnips 59
Spicy Cannellini Bean Ratatouille 56	Spicy Cauliflower Roast 59
Delicious Baked Broccoli Rice Cakes 56	Asparagus, Mushroom and Tomato Frittata 59
Healthy Mushroom Cashew Rice 57	Quick Quinoa Tabbouleh 59
Chermoula Beet Roast 57	Roasted Colorful Bell Peppers 59
Black Bean and Tomato Chili 57	Ratatouille 60
Tandoori Zucchini Cauliflower Curry 57	Cauliflower, Chickpea, and Avocado Mash 60
Shakshuka with Red Peppers 57	Roasted Eggplant Slices 60
Mediterranean Air Fried Veggies 58	

Cauliflower and Cashew Gratin

Prep Time: 6 minutes, Cook Time: 30 minutes, Serves: 4

Nonstick cooking spray	3 tbsps. almond flour
3 cups bite-size cauliflower florets	1¼ tsps. garlic powder, divided
1¾ cups raw cashews, divided	1¼ tsps. onion powder, divided
¾ cup unsweetened almond milk	1 tsp. cumin
¼ cup nutritional yeast, plus 1 tbsp.	¼ tsp. dried parsley
1 cup vegetable broth	¼ tsp. sea salt, divided
3 tbsps. hemp seeds	

1. Preheat the oven to 400ºF (205ºC) and line a 9-inch square baking dish with nonstick cooking spray. 2. In a medium saucepan, cover the cauliflower florets with water and bring to a boil over high heat. Lower the heat and simmer for about 5 minutes. Drain the water and keep the cauliflower aside in a large bowl. 3. To make the topping: When the cauliflower is cooking, place 1 cup cashews, ⅛ tsp. of salt, hemp seeds, parsley, 1 tbsp. of nutritional yeast, ¼ tsp. of onion powder and ¼ tsp. of garlic powder to a food processor or high-speed blender and blend until finely chopped. Keep aside. 4. To make the cashew cheese: Add the remaining ¾ cup cashews, ¼ cup nutritional yeast, 1 tsp. garlic powder, 1 tsp. onion powder, almond milk, vegetable broth, almond flour, and cumin in the food processor or high-speed blender. Blend until smooth. 5. Place the cashew cheese over the cauliflower and mix well. Pour the cauliflower into the sprayed baking dish and cover with the topping. Put in the oven and bake for about 20 minutes. Divide among 4 bowls evenly and serve immediately.

Calories: 429, Fat: 32g, Protein: 17g, Carbs: 26g, Fiber: 5g, Sugar: 8g, Sodium: 357mg

Cauliflower Tater Tots

Prep Time: 15 minutes, Cook Time: 16 minutes, Serves: 12

1 pound (454 g) cauliflower, steamed and chopped	1 tsp. minced garlic
½ cup nutritional yeast	1 tsp. chopped parsley
1 tbsp. oats	1 tsp. chopped oregano
1 tbsp. desiccated coconuts	1 tsp. chopped chives
3 tbsps. flaxseed meal	Salt and ground black pepper, to taste
3 tbsps. water	½ cup bread crumbs
1 onion, chopped	

1. Preheat the air fryer to 390ºF (199ºC). 2. Drain any excess water out of the cauliflower by wringing it with a paper towel. 3. In a bowl, combine the cauliflower with the remaining ingredients, save the bread crumbs. Using the hands, shape the mixture into several small balls. 4. Coat the balls in the bread crumbs and transfer to the air fryer basket. Air fry for 6 minutes, then raise the temperature to 400ºF (204ºC) and then air fry for an additional 10 minutes. 5. Serve immediately.

Calories: 45, Fat: 1g, Protein: 2g, Carbs: 7g, Fiber: 2g, Sugar: 1g, Sodium: 56mg

Crispy Jicama Fries

Prep Time: 5 minutes, Cook Time: 20 minutes, Serves: 1

1 small jicama, peeled	¼ tsp. garlic powder
¼ tsp. onion powder	¼ tsp. ground black pepper
¾ tsp. chili powder	

1. Preheat the air fryer to 350ºF (177ºC). 2. To make the fries, cut the jicama into matchsticks of the desired thickness. 3. In a bowl, toss them with the onion powder, chili powder, garlic powder, and black pepper to coat. Transfer the fries into the air fryer basket. 4. Air fry for 20 minutes, giving the basket an occasional shake throughout the cooking process. The fries are ready when they are hot and golden. 5. Serve immediately.

Calories: 80, Fat: 0.3g, Protein: 1g, Carbs: 19g, Fiber: 10g, Sugar: 5g, Sodium: 10mg

Saltine Wax Beans

Prep Time: 10 minutes, Cook Time: 7 minutes, Serves: 4

½ cup whole wheat flour	2 eggs, beaten
1 tsp. smoky chipotle powder	½ cup crushed saltines
½ tsp. ground black pepper	10 ounces (283 g) wax beans
1 tsp. sea salt flakes	Cooking spray

1. Preheat the air fryer to 360ºF (182ºC). 2. Combine the whole wheat flour, chipotle powder, black pepper, and salt in a bowl. Put the eggs in a second bowl. Put the crushed saltines in a third bowl. 3. Wash the beans with cold water and discard any tough strings. 4. Coat the beans with the flour mixture, before dipping them into the beaten egg. Cover them with the crushed saltines. 5. Spritz the beans with cooking spray. 6. Air fry for 4 minutes. Give the air fryer basket a good shake and continue to air fry for 3 minutes. Serve hot.

Calories: 150, Fat: 5g, Protein: 6g, Carbs: 21g, Fiber: 3g, Sugar: 1g, Sodium: 680mg

Classic Spaghetti Squash

Prep Time: 2 minutes, Cook Time: 45 minutes, Makes: 1 spaghetti squash

1 (2- to 3-pound / 907-g to 1.4-kg) spaghetti squash

1. Preheat the oven to 400ºF (205ºC). Line a baking sheet with foil. 2. Cut the spaghetti squash in half lengthwise and scoop the seeds out. 3. Place the spaghetti squash cut-sides down. Bake for 45 minutes or until the skin is easy to push in and the inserted strands of a fork pull out easily.

Calories: 107, Fat: 1.1g, Protein: 4g, Carbs: 24g, Fiber: 5.2g, Sugar: 0.4g, Sodium: 68mg

Zucchini Balls

Prep Time: 5 minutes, Cook Time: 10 minutes, Serves: 4

4 zucchinis	1 tbsp. Italian herbs
1 egg	1 cup grated coconut
½ cup grated low-fat Parmesan cheese	

1. Thinly grate the zucchinis and dry with a cheesecloth, ensuring to remove all the moisture. 2. In a bowl, combine the zucchinis with the egg, Parmesan, Italian herbs, and grated coconut, mixing well to incorporate everything. Using the hands, mold the mixture into balls. 3. Preheat the air fryer to 400ºF (204ºC). 4. Lay the zucchini balls in the air fryer basket and air fry for 10 minutes. 5. Serve hot.

Calories: 100, Fat: 6g, Protein: 6g, Carbs: 7g, Fiber: 3g, Sugar: 3g, Sodium: 220mg

Vegetable Chili

Prep Time: 14 minutes, Cook Time: 1 hour, Serves: 12

2 tbsps. olive oil
1 large sweet onion, peeled and finely chopped
3 tsps. garlic, minced
2 cups button mushrooms, chopped
2 large carrots, peeled and diced
1 large red bell pepper, seeded and diced
1 large zucchini, diced
1 jalapeño pepper, seeded and chopped
¼ cup chili powder
1 tbsp. cumin, ground
1 tbsp. dried oregano
1 tsp. red pepper flakes,
4 large tomatoes, chopped
1 (6-ounce / 170-g) can sodium-free tomato paste
1 cup fat-free, low-sodium vegetable stock
2 cups black beans, rinsed and drained
2 cups red kidney beans, rinsed and drained
2 cups navy beans, rinsed and drained

1. In a large pot, heat the olive oil over medium-high heat and sauté the onion, garlic, and mushrooms until softened, about 3 minutes. 2. Add the carrots, red bell pepper, and zucchini and sauté for 8 minutes. 3. Add the remaining ingredients and stir. 4. Bring the chili to a boil and then lower the heat. 5. Simmer the vegetables until they are fork-tender and the flavors have mellowed, about 45 minutes. 6. Remove the chili from the heat. Rest for about 10 minutes before serving.

Calories: 408, Fat: 6g, Protein: 24g, Carbs: 69g, Fiber: 14g, Sugar: 7g, Sodium: 54mg

Simple Curried Squash

Prep Time: 17 minutes, Cook Time: 7 hours, Serves: 6 to 8

3 acorn squashes, peeled, seeded, and cut into 1-inch pieces
1 large butternut squash, peeled, seeded, and cut into 1-inch pieces
⅓ cup freshly squeezed orange juice
2 onions, finely chopped
5 garlic cloves, minced
1 tbsp. curry powder
½ tsp. salt

1. Mix all of the ingredients in a 6-quart slow cooker. Cover the slow cooker and cook on low for 6 to 7 hours, or until the squash is tender when pierced with a fork. Serve warm.

Calories: 88, Fat: 0g, Protein: 2g, Carbs: 24g, Fiber: 3g, Sugar: 4g, Sodium: 169mg

Bean Tostadas

Prep Time: 12 minutes, Cook Time: 15 minutes, Serves: 4

8 (6-inch) whole-wheat tortillas
Nonstick cooking spray
3 cups canned sodium-free black beans, drained and rinsed
1 small sweet onion, peeled and coarsely chopped
1 red bell pepper, seeded and diced
2 jalapeño peppers, seeded and coarsely chopped
1 tsp. cumin, ground
4 tbsps. water
4 tsps. fresh cilantro, chopped
¼ cup crumbled low-sodium feta
1 large tomato, diced
1 cup romaine lettuce, shredded

1. Preheat the oven to 400°F (205°C). 2. On two baking sheets, toast the tortillas in the oven until crisp, about 5 minutes. 3. Remove the tortillas from the baking sheets. 4. Lightly coat the baking sheets with cooking spray. Spread the beans, onion, red pepper, and jalapeño peppers evenly on the sheets. Roast the mixture for about 10 minutes. 5. In a food processor, combine the roasted beans and vegetables with the cumin and water. Process until coarsely chopped. 6. On each tortilla, spread an equal amount of the bean mixture. Sprinkle with the cilantro and feta. 7. Top each with the tomato and shredded lettuce. 8. Serve two tostadas per person.

Calories: 250, Fat: 3g, Protein: 11g, Carbs: 55g, Fiber: 23g, Sugar: 2g, Sodium: 554mg

Spicy Cannellini Bean Ratatouille

Prep Time: 18 minutes, Cook Time: 20 minutes, Serves: 4

2 tbsps. extra-virgin olive oil
1 (15-ounce / 425-g) can cannellini beans, drained and rinsed
1 (15-ounce / 425-g) can fire-roasted diced tomatoes
1 zucchini, cut into 1-inch cubes
1 small yellow squash, cut into 1-inch cubes
1 small eggplant, cut into 1-inch cubes
½ yellow onion, chopped
¼ cup chopped fresh basil
3 garlic cloves, minced
2 tbsps. tomato paste
½ tsp. sea salt
⅛ tsp. freshly ground black pepper
Optional Toppings:
¼ cup olives
¼ cup pine nuts

1. In a large, deep skillet over medium heat, heat the olive oil. Place the onion, garlic, and tomato paste and cook for 2 minutes, or until the onions are tender. Add the yellow squash, zucchini, and eggplant and cook for 8 minutes. Halfway through the cooking time, pour in ¼ cup water and mix well, scraping the bottom of the skillet. 2. Place the salt, pepper, diced tomatoes, and beans. Cook for an additional 10 minutes and stir in the basil. 3. Serve in 4 bowls. Place optional toppings of pine nuts and olives. Store in an airtight container in the refrigerator up to 5 days.

Calories: 302, Fat: 15g, Protein: 10g, Carbs: 35g, Fiber: 12g, Sugar: 12g, Sodium: 662mg

Delicious Baked Broccoli Rice Cakes

Prep Time: 13 minutes, Cook Time: 25 minutes, Serves: 4

Nonstick cooking spray
2 cups broccoli florets, chopped
2 cups cooked brown rice
¼ cup nonfat plain Greek yogurt
2 eggs, lightly beaten
½ cup low-fat Cheddar cheese, grated
¼ tsp. nutmeg, ground
Black pepper, freshly ground

1. Preheat the oven to 350°F (180°C). Lightly coat 8 muffin cups with cooking spray. 2. Fill a medium saucepan with water. Bring to a boil over medium-high heat. 3. Add the broccoli to the boiling water and blanch until tender-crisp, about 3 minutes. Drain the water. 4. In a large bowl, combine the broccoli with the rice, yogurt, eggs, cheese, and nutmeg. Season with pepper to taste. 5. Evenly portion the broccoli mixture among the muffin cups and bake until golden, about 20 minutes. 6. Remove the cakes from the oven and rest for 5 minutes. Run a knife around the edges to loosen. 7. Serve two cakes per person with a green salad.

Calories: 461, Fat: 10g, Protein: 16g, Carbs: 76g, Fiber: 6g, Sugar: 2g, Sodium: 142mg

Healthy Mushroom Cashew Rice

Prep Time: 9 minutes, Cook Time: 50 minutes, Serves: 6

1 tbsp. olive oil
3 celery stalks, chopped
½ small sweet onion, peeled and chopped
2 tsps. garlic, minced
1 cup sliced button mushrooms
2 cups uncooked brown basmati rice
3½ cups fat-free, low-sodium vegetable stock
Black pepper, freshly ground
½ cup cashews, chopped

1. In a large saucepan, heat the oil over medium-high heat and sauté the celery, onion, garlic, and mushrooms until they are softened. 2. Add the rice and sauté for 1 minute. 3. Add the stock and bring to a boil, then lower the heat and cover the pot. 4. Simmer the rice until the liquid is absorbed and the rice is tender, about 35 to 40 minutes. 5. Season with pepper to taste. Top with cashews and serve.

Calories: 341, Fat: 9g, Protein: 10g, Carbs: 51g, Fiber: 9g, Sugar: 2g, Sodium: 458mg

Chermoula Beet Roast

Prep Time: 15 minutes, Cook Time: 25 minutes, Serves: 4

For the Chermoula:
1 cup packed fresh cilantro leaves
½ cup packed fresh parsley leaves
6 cloves garlic, peeled
2 tsps. smoked paprika
2 tsps. ground cumin
1 tsp. ground coriander
½ to 1 tsp. cayenne pepper
Pinch of crushed saffron (optional)
½ cup extra-virgin olive oil
Kosher salt, to taste
For the Beets:
3 medium beets, trimmed, peeled, and cut into 1-inch chunks
2 tbsps. chopped fresh cilantro
2 tbsps. chopped fresh parsley

1. In a food processor, combine the cilantro, parsley, garlic, paprika, cumin, coriander, and cayenne. Pulse until coarsely chopped. Add the saffron, if using, and process until combined. With the food processor running, slowly add the olive oil in a steady stream; process until the sauce is uniform. Season with salt. 2. Preheat the air fryer to 375°F (191°C). 3. In a large bowl, drizzle the beets with ½ cup of the chermoula to coat. Arrange the beets in the air fryer basket. Roast for 25 to minutes, or until the beets are tender. 4. Transfer the beets to a serving platter. Sprinkle with the chopped cilantro and parsley and serve.

Calories: 230, Fat: 19g, Protein: 2g, Carbs: 13g, Fiber: 3g, Sugar: 6g, Sodium: 60mg

Black Bean and Tomato Chili

Prep Time: 15 minutes, Cook Time: 23 minutes, Serves: 6

1 tbsp. olive oil
1 medium onion, diced
3 garlic cloves, minced
1 cup vegetable broth
3 cans black beans, drained and rinsed
2 cans diced tomatoes
2 chipotle peppers, chopped
2 tsps. cumin
2 tsps. chili powder
1 tsp. dried oregano
½ tsp. salt

1. Over a medium heat, fry the garlic and onions in the olive oil for 3 minutes. 2. Add the remaining ingredients, stirring constantly and scraping the bottom to prevent sticking. 3. Preheat the air fryer to 400°F (204°C). 4. Take a dish and place the mixture inside. Put a sheet of aluminum foil on top. 5. Transfer to the air fryer and bake for 20 minutes. 6. When ready, plate up and serve immediately.

Calories: 236, Fat: 3g, Protein: 11g, Carbs: 43g, Fiber: 14g, Sugar: 5g, Sodium: 700mg

Tandoori Zucchini Cauliflower Curry

Prep Time: 6 minutes, Cook Time: 25 minutes, Serves: 2

1 tbsp. extra-virgin olive oil
½ head cauliflower, broken into small florets
1 zucchini, cubed
1 yellow onion, sliced
2 garlic cloves, minced
2 to 3 tbsps. tandoori curry paste
¼ tsp. Himalayan salt
Spice it up:
¼ cup fresh coriander

1. In a pot of water, cook the cauliflower florets for about 5 minutes, until tender. Reserve about 2 cups of the cooking liquid. 2. In a large saucepan, heat the olive oil over medium heat. Place the onion and garlic. Cook for 2 minutes. 3. Add the zucchini and cook for an additional 3 minutes. 4. Place the cauliflower, reserved liquid, curry paste, and salt. Stir, cover, and cook for 15 minutes more. 5. Garnish with fresh coriander, if desired. Serve hot.

Calories: 66, Fat: 4g, Protein: 2g, Carbs: 7g, Fiber: 3g, Sugar: 1g, Sodium: 94mg

Shakshuka with Red Peppers

Prep Time: 8 minutes, Cook Time: 23 minutes, Serves: 4

1 tbsp. extra-virgin olive oil
1 small yellow onion, diced
1 medium red bell pepper, cut into thin strips
2 garlic cloves, minced
2 cups kale, chopped
1 tbsp. red wine vinegar
1 tsp. Italian seasoning
½ tsp. black pepper, freshly ground
¼ tsp. red pepper flakes (optional)
¼ tsp. salt
1 (28-ounce / 794-g) can no-salt-added diced tomatoes with juice
8 large eggs

1. Heat the oil in a large cast-iron or nonstick skillet over medium heat. Add the onion and cook for 2 to 3 minutes, stirring frequently, until translucent. 2. Add the red bell pepper and cook for 5 minutes, stirring frequently, until the vegetables are soft. 3. Stir in the garlic. 4. Add the kale one handful a time. Cook, stirring continuously, adding more kale as it wilts. 5. Pour in the vinegar, stirring constantly for 1 minute to remove any stuck bits from the bottom. 6. Add the Italian seasoning, black pepper, red pepper flakes (if using), and salt. Stir. 7. Add the diced tomatoes and their juices and stir to fully combined. Cover the skillet and cook for 5 minutes. 8. Create 8 wells in the sauce with the back of a large spoon. Gently crack 1 egg into each well. Cover the skillet and cook for 6 minutes, or until the egg whites are set. You may want to slightly undercook the eggs, as they'll continue cooking when reheated. 9.9. With a serving spoon, portion 2 eggs and one-fourth of the sauce into each of 4 large single-compartment glass meal-prep containers. Cover and refrigerate.

Calories: 243, Fat: 14g, Protein: 15g, Carbs: 14g, Fiber: 1.8g, Sugar: 7g, Sodium: 257mg

Mediterranean Air Fried Veggies

Prep Time: 10 minutes, Cook Time: 6 minutes, Serves: 4

1 large zucchini, sliced	1 tsp. mustard
1 cup cherry tomatoes, halved	1 tsp. garlic purée
1 parsnip, sliced	6 tbsps. olive oil
1 green pepper, sliced	Salt and ground black pepper, to taste
1 carrot, sliced	
1 tsp. mixed herbs	

1. Preheat the air fryer to 400ºF (204ºC). 2. Combine all the ingredients in a bowl, making sure to coat the vegetables well. 3. Transfer to the air fryer and air fry for 6 minutes, ensuring the vegetables are tender and browned. 4. Serve immediately.

Calories: 230, Fat: 20g, Protein: 2g, Carbs: 11g, Fiber: 4g, Sugar: 4g, Sodium: 15mg

Tomato-Topped Spaghetti Squash

Prep Time: 11 minutes, Cook Time: 45 minutes, Serves: 2

1 spaghetti squash, cut in half lengthwise	2 tbsps. green onion, chopped
1 tbsp. olive oil	1 tbsp. chopped fresh basil or 3 tsps. dried basil
Sea salt	
Black pepper, freshly ground	3 tbsps. low-fat Parmesan cheese
2 tomatoes, chopped	

1. Preheat oven to 350ºF (180ºC). 2. Line a baking tray with foil. 3. Scoop the seeds of the squash and drizzle the cut sides with the olive oil. 4. Season the cut sides lightly with salt and pepper and lay the squash halves cut-side down on the baking sheet. 5. Bake the squash until tender, about 45 minutes. Cools on the tray for 10 minutes. 6. While the squash is baking, combine the tomatoes, green onion, and basil in a small bowl. 7. Shred the squash strands with a fork into a medium bowl. 8. Top the shredded squash with the tomato mixture and Parmesan cheese. 9. Serve immediately.

Calories: 129, Fat: 5g, Protein: 5g, Carbs: 20g, Fiber: 5g, Sugar: 3g, Sodium: 223mg

Italian Eggplant Parmesan

Prep Time: 14 minutes, Cook Time: 9 hours, Serves: 8 to 10

2 tbsps. olive oil	½ cup chopped toasted almonds
5 large eggplants, peeled and sliced ½-inch thick	2 onions, chopped
2 (8-ounce / 227-g) BPA-free cans low-sodium tomato sauce	6 garlic cloves, minced
	1 tsp. dried Italian seasoning
½ cup grated low-fat Parmesan cheese	

1. Layer the eggplant slices with the onions and garlic in a 6-quart slow cooker. 2. Mix the tomato sauce, olive oil, and Italian seasoning in a medium bowl. Add the tomato sauce mixture into the slow cooker. 3. Cover the slow cooker and cook on low for 8 to 9 hours, or until the eggplant is soft. 4. Mix the Parmesan cheese and almonds in a small bowl. Scatter over the eggplant mixture and serve warm.

Calories: 206, Fat: 8g, Protein: 10g, Carbs: 28g, Fiber: 11g, Sugar: 14g, Sodium: 283mg

Braised Green Cabbage and Onion

Prep Time: 6 minutes, Cook Time: 7 hours, Serves: 8

1 tbsp. olive oil	6 garlic cloves, minced
1 large head green cabbage, cored and chopped	2 tbsps. apple cider vinegar
	2 tbsps. honey
½ cup vegetable broth	½ tsp. salt
3 onions, chopped	

1. Mix all of the ingredients in a 6-quart slow cooker. Cover the slow cooker and cook on low for 6 to 7 hours, or until the cabbage and onions are soft. Serve warm.

Calories: 75, Fat: 2g, Protein: 2g, Carbs: 14g, Fiber: 3g, Sugar: 10g, Sodium: 171mg

Green Beans with Shallot

Prep Time: 10 minutes, Cook Time: 10 minutes, Serves: 4

1½ pounds (680 g) French green beans, stems removed and blanched	½ pound (227 g) shallots, peeled and cut into quarters
	½ tsp. ground white pepper
1 tbsp. salt	2 tbsps. olive oil

1. Preheat the air fryer to 400ºF (204ºC). 2. Coat the vegetables with the rest of the ingredients in a bowl. 3. Transfer to the air fryer basket and air fry for 10 minutes, making sure the green beans achieve a light brown color. 4. Serve hot.

Calories: 145, Fat: 7g, Protein: 2g, Carbs: 19g, Fiber: 4g, Sugar: 5g, Sodium: 596mg

Italian Beets and Tomato

Prep Time: 17 minutes, Cook Time: 7 hours, Serves: 10

2 tbsps. olive oil	4 garlic cloves, minced
10 medium beets, peeled and sliced	1 tsp. dried oregano leaves
4 large tomatoes, seeded and chopped	1 tsp. dried basil leaves
	½ tsp. salt
2 onions, chopped	

1. Mix the beets, tomatoes, onions, and garlic in a 6-quart slow cooker. Add the olive oil and sprinkle with the dried herbs and salt. Toss to mix well. 2. Cover the slow cooker and cook on low for 5 to 7 hours, or until the beets are soft.

Calories: 100, Fat: 4g, Protein: 3g, Carbs: 16g, Fiber: 4g, Sugar: 10g, Sodium: 215mg

Balsamic Brussels Sprouts

Prep Time: 5 minutes, Cook Time: 13 minutes, Serves: 2

2 cups Brussels sprouts, halved	1 tbsp. maple syrup
1 tbsp. olive oil	¼ tsp. sea salt
1 tbsp. balsamic vinegar	

1. Preheat the air fryer to 375ºF (191ºC). 2. Evenly coat the Brussels sprouts with the olive oil, balsamic vinegar, maple syrup, and salt. 3. Transfer to the air fryer basket and air fry for 5 minutes. Give the basket a good shake, turn the heat to 400ºF (204ºC) and continue to air fry for another 8 minutes. 4. Serve hot.

Calories: 120, Fat: 5g, Protein: 3g, Carbs: 17g, Fiber: 4g, Sugar: 9g, Sodium: 160mg

Sesame Taj Tofu

Prep Time: 5 minutes, Cook Time: 25 minutes, Serves: 4

1 block firm tofu, pressed and cut into 1-inch thick cubes	2 tsps. toasted sesame seeds
2 tbsps. soy sauce	1 tsp. rice vinegar
	1 tbsp. cornstarch

1. Preheat the air fryer to 400ºF (204ºC). 2. Add the tofu, soy sauce, sesame seeds, and rice vinegar in a bowl together and mix well to coat the tofu cubes. Then cover the tofu in cornstarch and put it in the air fryer basket. 3. Air fry for 25 minutes, giving the basket a shake at five-minute intervals to ensure the tofu cooks evenly. 4. Serve immediately.

Calories: 160, Fat: 9g, Protein: 11g, Carbs: 10g, Fiber: 1g, Sugar: 1g, Sodium: 321mg

Turmeric Cauliflower and Chickpea Stew

Prep Time: 5 minutes, Cook Time: 45 minutes, Serves: 4

½ head cauliflower, cut into small florets	6 cups water
1 (13-ounce / 369-g) can chickpeas, rinsed and drained	½ tsp. turmeric
1 medium leek, thinly sliced	1 tsp. Himalayan salt
1 yellow onion, thinly sliced	¼ tsp. freshly ground black pepper
	Spice it up:
	½ tsp. garlic powder

1. Combine the cauliflower, chickpeas, onion, leek, salt, turmeric, pepper, garlic powder (if using), and water in a medium stockpot. 2. Bring to a boil, cover, and sauté for about 30 minutes. Uncover and cook for an additional 15 minutes. 3. Serve right away, as is, or over some cooked brown rice.

Calories: 138, Fat: 2g, Protein: 7g, Carbs: 25g, Fiber: 6g, Sugar: 5g, Sodium: 471mg

Honey Roasted Carrots and Parsnips

Prep Time: 11 minutes, Cook Time: 7 hours, Serves: 10

2 tbsps. olive oil	2 red onions, chopped
6 large carrots, peeled and cut into 2-inch pieces	4 garlic cloves, minced
5 large parsnips, peeled and cut into 2-inch pieces	1 tbsp. honey
	½ tsp. salt

1. Mix all of the ingredients in a 6-quart slow cooker and stir gently. Cover the slow cooker and cook on low for 5 to 7 hours, or until the vegetables are soft. Enjoy!

Calories: 138, Fat: 4g, Protein: 2g, Carbs: 26g, Fiber: 6g, Sugar: 10g, Sodium: 199mg

Spicy Cauliflower Roast

Prep Time: 15 minutes, Cook Time: 20 minutes, Serves: 4

For the Cauliflower:	For the Sauce:
5 cups cauliflower florets	½ cup nonfat Greek yogurt or sour cream
3 tbsps. vegetable oil	¼ cup chopped fresh cilantro
½ tsp. ground cumin	1 jalapeño, coarsely chopped
½ tsp. ground coriander	4 cloves garlic, peeled
½ tsp. kosher salt	½ tsp. kosher salt
	2 tbsps. water

1. Preheat the air fryer to 400ºF (204ºC). 2. In a large bowl, combine the cauliflower, oil, cumin, coriander, and salt. Toss to coat. 3. Put the cauliflower in the air fryer basket. Roast for 20 minutes, stirring halfway through the roasting time. 4. Meanwhile, in a blender, combine the yogurt, cilantro, jalapeño, garlic, and salt. Blend, adding the water as needed to keep the blades moving and to thin the sauce. 5. At the end of roasting time, transfer the cauliflower to a large serving bowl. Pour the sauce over and toss gently to coat. Serve immediately.

Calories: 180, Fat: 12g, Protein: 5g, Carbs: 15g, Fiber: 4g, Sugar: 5g, Sodium: 470mg

Asparagus, Mushroom and Tomato Frittata

Prep Time: 8 minutes, Cook Time: 32 minutes, Serves: 4

1 tbsp. extra-virgin olive oil, plus more for greasing the pie dish	8 ounces (227 g) asparagus, woody stems removed and cut into 1-inch pieces
8 large eggs, beaten	½ cup chopped tomatoes
8 ounces (227 g) mushrooms, sliced	½ cup diced yellow onion
	1 tsp. sea salt
	½ tsp. freshly ground black peppe

1. Preheat the oven to 350ºF (180ºC). Grease a 9-inch pie dish lightly and keep aside. 2. In a large sauté pan or skillet, warm the oil over medium-high heat. Place the mushrooms and onion and sauté, stirring occasionally, for about 3 to 4 minutes, until they start to soften. 3. Add the asparagus and continue to sauté, stirring occasionally, for about 2 to 3 minutes. Toss in the tomatoes and season with salt and pepper to taste. Arrange the vegetables evenly in the pie dish. 4. Add the eggs over the vegetable mixture. Bake for about 20 to 25 minutes, until the eggs are set. Remove from the oven and serve hot.

Calories: 213, Fat: 13g, Protein: 16g, Carbs: 8g, Fiber: 2g, Sugar: 3g, Sodium: 729mg

Quick Quinoa Tabbouleh

Prep Time: 9 minutes, Cook Time: 0 minutes, Serves: 4 to 6

¼ cup extra-virgin olive oil	1 large red onion, chopped
2 cups cooked quinoa	Juice of ½ large lemon
3 Persian cucumbers, cut into small cubes	½ tsp. Himalayan salt
1¼ cups fresh parsley, chopped	Spice it up:
	1 tbsp. dried mint flakes

1. Combine the quinoa, parsley, dried mint (if using), onion, and cucumbers in a large bowl. 2. Whisk together oil, lemon juice, and salt in a small bowl, and place it to the large bowl. Toss until everything is well coated. Enjoy!

Calories: 276, Fat: 16g, Protein: 6g, Carbs: 30g, Fiber: 5g, Sugar: 5g, Sodium: 167mg

Roasted Colorful Bell Peppers

Prep Time: 7 minutes, Cook Time: 6 hours, Serves: 8 to 10

1 tbsp. olive oil	1 red onion, chopped
8 to 10 bell peppers of different colors, stemmed, seeded, and halved	1 tsp. dried thyme leaves

1. In a 6-quart slow cooker, put the bell pepper. Do not overfill your slow cooker. Pour in the olive oil, and top with the thyme and red onion. Cover the slow cooker and cook on low for 5 to 6 hours, stirring once if you are home, until the peppers are soft and slightly browned on the edges. 2. Remove the bell pepper skins if you'd like when they are done; and they will come off very easily. Enjoy!

Calories: 59, Fat: 2g, Protein: 2g, Carbs: 9g, Fiber: 3g, Sugar: 5g, Sodium: 6mg

Ratatouille

Prep Time: 20 minutes, Cook Time: 25 minutes, Serves: 4

1 sprig basil	2 red onions, chopped
1 sprig flat-leaf parsley	4 cloves garlic, minced
1 sprig mint	2 red peppers, sliced crosswise
1 tbsp. coriander powder	1 fennel bulb, sliced crosswise
1 tsp. capers	3 large zucchinis, sliced crosswise
½ lemon, juiced	
Salt and ground black pepper, to taste	5 tbsps. olive oil
2 eggplants, sliced crosswise	4 large tomatoes, chopped
	2 tsps. herbs de Provence

1. Blend the basil, parsley, coriander, mint, lemon juice and capers, with a little salt and pepper. Make sure all ingredients are well-incorporated. 2. Preheat the air fryer to 400ºF (204ºC). 3. Coat the eggplant, onions, garlic, peppers, fennel, and zucchini with olive oil. 4. Transfer the vegetables into a baking dish and top with the tomatoes and herb purée. Sprinkle with more salt and pepper, and the herbs de Provence. 5. Air fry for 25 minutes. 6. Serve immediately.

Calories: 252, Fat: 16g, Protein: 4g, Carbs: 26g, Fiber: 9g, Sugar: 12g, Sodium: 154mg

Cauliflower, Chickpea, and Avocado Mash

Prep Time: 10 minutes, Cook Time: 25 minutes, Serves: 4

1 medium head cauliflower, cut into florets	2 tbsps. lemon juice
1 can chickpeas, drained and rinsed	Salt and ground black pepper, to taste
1 tbsp. extra-virgin olive oil	4 flatbreads, toasted
	2 ripe avocados, mashed

1. Preheat the air fryer to 425ºF (218ºC). 2. In a bowl, mix the chickpeas, cauliflower, lemon juice and olive oil. Sprinkle salt and pepper as desired. 3. Put inside the air fryer basket and air fry for 25 minutes. 4. Spread on top of the flatbread along with the mashed avocado. Sprinkle with more pepper and salt and serve.

Calories: 300, Fat: 15g, Protein: 10g, Carbs: 35g, Fiber: 12g, Sugar: 5g, Sodium: 350mg

Roasted Eggplant Slices

Prep Time: 5 minutes, Cook Time: 15 minutes, Serves: 1

1 large eggplant, sliced	¼ tsp. salt
2 tbsps. olive oil	½ tsp. garlic powder

1. Preheat the air fryer to 390ºF (199ºC). 2. Apply the olive oil to the slices with a brush, coating both sides. Season each side with sprinklings of salt and garlic powder. 3. Put the slices in the air fryer and roast for 15 minutes. 4. Serve immediately.

Calories: 160, Fat: 14g, Protein: 1g, Carbs: 10g, Fiber: 5g, Sugar: 4g, Sodium: 299mg

CHAPTER 10 BEEF, LAMB AND PORK RECIPES

Beef Tenderloin Steaks with Brandied Mushrooms ··62	Braised Lamb Ragout ············ 65
Spicy Beef with Worcestershire Sauce ············ 62	Indian Lamb Curry ············ 65
Blue Cheese Crusted Beef Tenderloin ············ 62	Fast Lamb Satay ············ 65
Beef & Veggie Quesadillas ············ 62	Icelandic Lamb with Turnip ············ 65
Sichuan Beef with Vegetable and Almond Butter ··62	Maple-Glazed Spareribs ············ 65
Steak with Green Beans ············ 63	Paprika Pork with Brussels Sprouts ············ 66
Beef Picadillo ············ 63	Jamaican Pork Roast ············ 66
Beer Braised Brisket ············ 63	Paprika Pork Loin Roast ············ 66
Parmesan Beef Burger with Carrot ············ 63	Pork Chops with Peas ············ 66
Lollipop Lamb Chops ············ 63	Mexican Chili Pork ············ 66
Greek Lamb Loaf ············ 64	Indian Roasted Pork ············ 66
Beef Goulash ············ 64	Pine Nut Pork ············ 67
Black Bean Minced Lamb ············ 64	Egg Meatloaf ············ 67
Sloppy Joes in Lettuce ············ 64	Pork with Bell Peppers ············ 67
Feta Lamb Burgers ············ 64	Pulled Pork ············ 67
Classic Lamb and Eggplant Tikka Masala ······ 64	Hawaiian Pulled Pork Roast with Cabbage ······ 67
Air Fried Lamb Ribs ············ 65	Pork Butt with Pear ············ 67

Beef Tenderloin Steaks with Brandied Mushrooms

Prep Time: 10 minutes, Cook Time: 20 minutes, Serves: 4

4 grass-fed beef tenderloin steaks, about ¾ inch thick	1 tsp. balsamic vinegar
3 ½ cups Portobello mushrooms, sliced	½ tsp. salt
1 tbsp. coconut butter	½ tsp. coarsely ground pepper
½ cup brandy, divided	½ tsp. instant coffee granules
	Nonstick cooking spray

1. Heat oven to 200°F (93°C). 2. Salt and pepper both sides of the steaks and let sit 15 minutes. 3. In a small bowl, mix together coffee, vinegar, all but 1 tbsp. brandy, salt and pepper. 4. Spray a large skillet with cooking spray and place over med-high heat. 5. Spray the mushrooms with cooking spray and add to the hot pan. Cook for 5 minutes or until most of the liquid is absorbed. Transfer the mushrooms to a bowl. 6. Add the steaks to the skillet and cook about 3 minutes per side. Reduce heat to med-low and cook for 2 more minutes or to desired doneness. Place on dinner plates, cover with foil and place in oven. 7. Add the brandy mixture to the skillet and bring to a boil. Boil for 1 minute, or until reduced to about ¼ cup liquid. Stir in mushrooms and cook for 1-2 minutes, or most of the liquid has evaporated. 8. Remove from heat and stir in remaining 1 tbsp. brandy and the butter. 9. Spoon evenly over steaks and serve immediately.

Calories: 350, Total Carbs: 1g, Protein: 44g, Fat: 12g, Sugar: 0g, Fiber: 0g

Spicy Beef with Worcestershire Sauce

Prep Time: 10 minutes, Cook Time: 25 minutes, Serves: 5

1 pound (454 g) grass-fed extra-lean ground beef	sauce, no salt added
1 cup chopped onions, fresh or frozen	2 tbsps. red wine vinegar
1 cup chopped green peppers, fresh or frozen	1 tsp. paprika
2 garlic cloves, minced or squeezed through a garlic press	2 tsps. Worcestershire sauce
	½ tsp. chili powder
	½ tsp. black pepper
1 (15-oz. 425 g) can red tomato	dash hot pepper sauce or cayenne pepper

1. Heat a nonstick skillet over medium-high heat. 2. Add ground beef and cook for 3 minutes, turn down heat to medium. 3. Add onions, peppers, and garlic. Continue cooking 5 or more minutes. 4. Put in all other ingredients. Reduce heat and simmer for 10 - 15 minutes.

Calories: 224, Protein: 27g, Carbs: 13g, Fat: 7g, Fiber: 2g, Sodium: 114mg

Blue Cheese Crusted Beef Tenderloin

Prep Time: 10 minutes, Cook Time: 15 minutes, Serves: 4

4 grass-fed beef tenderloin steaks	4½ tsps. bread crumbs
2 tbsps. blue cheese, crumbled	1 tbsp. whole wheat flour
4½ tsps. fresh parsley, diced	1 tbsp. Madeira wine
4½ tsps. chives, diced	¼ tsp. pepper
1½ tsps. almond butter	Nonstick cooking spray
½ cup low sodium beef broth	

1. Heat oven to 350°F (177°C). Spray a large baking sheet with cooking spray. 2. In a small bowl, combine blue cheese, bread crumbs, parsley, chives, and pepper. Press onto one side of the steaks. 3. Spray a large skillet with cooking spray and place over med-high heat. 4. Add steaks and sear 2 minutes per side. Transfer to prepared baking sheet and bake for 6-8 minutes, or steaks reach desired doneness. 5. Melt almond butter in a small saucepan over medium heat. Whisk in flour until smooth. Slowly whisk in broth and wine. Bring to a boil, cook, stirring, 2 minutes or until thickened. 6. Plate the steaks and top with gravy. Serve.

Calories: 263, Total Carbs: 4g, Protein: 36g, Fat: 10g, Sugar: 0g, Fiber: 0g

Beef & Veggie Quesadillas

Prep Time: 15 minutes, Cook Time: 10 minutes, Serves: 4

¾ lb. grass-fed lean ground beef	¼ cup cilantro, diced
2 tomatoes, seeded and diced	4 8-inch whole wheat tortillas, warmed
1 onion, diced	2 cloves garlic, diced
1 zucchini, grated	2 tsps. chili powder
1 carrot, grated	¼ tsp. salt
¾ cup mushrooms, diced	¼ tsp. hot pepper sauce
½ cup low-fat mozzarella cheese, grated	Nonstick cooking spray

1. Heat oven to 400°F (200°C). Spray a large baking sheet with cooking spray. 2. Cook beef and onions in a large nonstick skillet over medium heat, until beef is no longer pink, drain fat. Transfer to a bowl and keep warm. 3. Add the mushrooms, zucchini, carrot, garlic, chili powder, salt and pepper sauce to the skillet and cook until vegetables are tender. 4. Stir in the tomatoes, cilantro and beef. 5. Lay the tortillas on the prepared pan. Cover half of each with beef mixture, and top with cheese. Fold other half over filling. Bake for 5 minutes. Flip over and bake for 5-6 minute more or until cheese has melted. Cut into wedges and serve.

Calories: 319, Total Carbs: 31g, Net Carbs: 26g, Protein: 33g, Fat: 7g, Sugar: 5g, Fiber: 5g

Sichuan Beef with Vegetable and Almond Butter

Prep Time: 10 minutes, Cook Time: 12 minutes, Serves: 2

¾ cup (60ml) tomato juice	1 tbsp. unseasoned dry brandy
3 cups frozen stir-fry vegetable blend	1 tsp. sesame oil
	2 tsps. cornstarch
8 oz. (230 g) grass-fed boneless beef sirloin steak, cut into thin strips	¼ tsp. Chinese five-spice powder
	1 tsp. red pepper flakes
	2 tsps. extra-virgin olive oil
1 tbsp. reduced-sodium almond butter	3 cloves garlic, crushed
	2 tsps. grated fresh ginger

1. Mix together the tomato juice, almond butter, brandy, sesame oil, cornstarch, five-spice, and pepper flakes in a small bowl until smooth. Set aside. 2. Heat 1 tsp. of the olive oil in a large skillet or wok over high heat. Whisk in the beef and stir-fry until no longer pink, 3 to 4 minutes. Using a slotted spoon to remove the beef to a plate, cover to keep warm. 3. Pour the reserving 1 tsp. olive oil to the pan. Spread with the garlic and ginger and stir-

fry for 1 minute. Stir in the vegetables and continue cooking for 2 to 3 minutes, until thawed. Whisk the sauce and pour into the pan, bring to a boil, and cook for 2 to 3 minutes to thicken. Return the beef to the pan, toss to combine, and cook for a further 1 to 2 minutes to heat through.

Calories: 321, Total Fat: 12 g, Saturated Fat: 3 g, Total Carbs: 22g, Protein: 28g, Sodium: 376mg, Fiber: 4g, Sugar: 13g

Steak with Green Beans

Prep Time: 5 minutes, Cook Time: 20 minutes, Serves: 4

1 pound (454 g) microwave-in-bag green beans	flank steak, trimmed of fat
8 cups mixed baby greens or baby spinach	½ tsp. freshly ground black pepper, divided
2 tbsps. fresh dill, finely chopped	1 tbsp. Dijon mustard
	1 tbsp. olive oil
12 ounces (340 g) grass-fed	1 medium onion, sliced
	1 cup (240 ml) no-salt chicken broth

1.Heat the olive oil over medium-high heat in a large skillet. Season the steaks with black pepper, and add the steak to the skillet. Cook until desired doneness: 5 to 7 minutes per side for medium (140°F), or 8 to 10 minutes for medium-well (150°F). Transfer the steak to a cutting board. Cover loosely with foil.2.Cook the onion for 2 minutes in the same skillet, and stir constantly. Stir in the broth, and simmer for 5 minutes, and then whisk in the dill, mustard, and pepper. Transfer to a small bowl. 3.Prepare the green beans according to the package directions. 4.Slice the steak and serve with green beans and baby greens in four equal portions. Serve the sauce on the side.

Calories: 226, Total Fat: 10g, Saturated Fat: 3g, Total Carbs: 13g, Protein: 22g, Sodium: 201mg, Fiber: 6g, Sugar: 0g

Beef Picadillo

Prep Time: 10 minutes, Cook Time: 3-4 hour, Serves: 10

1½ lbs. grass-fed lean ground beef	3 cloves garlic, diced fine
1 onion, diced fine	¼ cup green olives, pitted
1 red bell pepper, diced	2 bay leaves
1 small tomato, diced	1½ tsps. cumin
¼ cup cilantro, diced fine	¼ tsp. garlic powder
1 cup tomato sauce	Salt & pepper, to taste

1.In a large skillet, over medium heat, brown ground beef. Season with salt and pepper. Drain fat. Add onion, bell pepper, and garlic and cook for 3-4 minutes.2.Transfer to crock pot and add remaining ingredients. Cover and cook on high for 3 hours.3.Discard bay leaves. Taste and adjust seasonings as desired. Serve.

Calories: 255, Total Carbs: 6g, Net Carbs: 5g, Protein: 35g, Fat: 9g, Sugar: 3g, Fiber: 1g

Beer Braised Brisket

Prep Time: 10 minutes: Cook Time: 8 hours, Serves: 10

5 lbs. grass-fed beef brisket	3 cloves garlic, diced fine
1 bottle of lite beer	1 tbsp. + 1 tsp. oregano
1 onion, sliced thin	1 tbsp. salt
15 oz. can tomatoes, diced	1 tbsp. black pepper

1.Place the onion on the bottom of the crock pot. Add brisket, fat side up. Add the tomatoes, undrained and beer. Sprinkle the garlic and seasonings on the top.2.Cover and cook on low heat 8 hours, or until beef is fork tender.

Calories: 445, Total Carbs: 4g, Net Carbs: 3g, Protein: 69g, Fat: 14g, Sugar: 2g, Fiber: 1g

Parmesan Beef Burger with Carrot

Prep Time: 10 minutes, Cook Time: 10 minutes, Serves: 4

½ cup cooked pinto beans (or other beans)	2 celery stalks, diced
	3 cloves garlic, minced
½ cup minced onion	½ cup finely chopped red bell pepper
½ cup shredded low-fat parmesan cheese	1 tsp. ground cinnamon
	Salt and freshly ground black pepper
¾ pound 94% lean ground beef	1 tbsp. extra-virgin olive oil
	Lettuce leaves or whole-wheat buns
½ cup cabbage	Fresh basil
1 medium carrot, grated	

1.Lightly mash the beans with the back of a large spoon in a large bowl. Stir in the onion, cabbage, bell pepper, carrot, celery, garlic, beef, cinnamon, parmesan, and a pinch each of salt and pepper and toss to combine well. Form into 4 patties.2.Heat the olive oil in a large skillet over medium-high heat. Add the patties and sear them until dark brown on one side, about 5 minutes. Turn over and cook for another 5 minutes or until reach desired doneness.3.Serve the burgers on lettuce leaves or toasted buns. Garnish with basil.

Calories: 226, Total Fat: 9 g, Saturated Fat: 2 g, Total Carbs: 12g, Protein: 24g, Sodium: 140mg, Fiber: 4g, Sugar: 3g

Lollipop Lamb Chops

Prep Time: 15 minutes, Cook Time: 7 minutes, Serves: 4

½ small clove garlic	½ cup olive oil
¼ cup packed fresh parsley	8 lamb chops (1 rack)
¾ cup packed fresh mint	2 tbsps. vegetable oil
½ tsp. lemon juice	Salt and freshly ground black pepper, to taste
¼ cup grated low-fat Parmesan cheese	
⅓ cup shelled pistachios	1 tbsp. dried rosemary, chopped
¼ tsp. salt	1 tbsp. dried thyme

1.Make the pesto by combining the garlic, parsley and mint in a food processor and process until finely chopped. Add the lemon juice, Parmesan cheese, pistachios and salt. Process until all the ingredients have turned into a paste. With the processor running, slowly pour the olive oil in. Scrape the sides of the processor with a spatula and process for another 30 seconds.2.Preheat the air fryer to 400ºF (204ºC).3.Rub both sides of the lamb chops with vegetable oil and season with salt, pepper, rosemary and thyme, pressing the herbs into the meat gently with the fingers. Transfer the lamb chops to the air fryer basket.4.Air fry the lamb chops for 5 minutes. Flip the chops over and air fry for an additional 2 minutes.5.Serve the lamb chops with mint pesto drizzled on top.

Calories: 584, Fat: 47g, Protein: 27g, Carbs: 8g, Fiber: 2g, Sugar: 1g, Sodium: 395mg

Greek Lamb Loaf

Prep Time: 5 minutes, Cook Time: 15 minutes, Serves: 2

1 pound (454 g) ground lamb meat	1 tsp. rosemary
4 garlic cloves	¾ tsp. salt
½ small onion, chopped	¼ tsp. black pepper
1 tsp. ground marjoram	¾ cup water

1. In a blender, combine the lamb meat, garlic, onions, marjoram, rosemary, salt and pepper. Pulse until well mixed. Shape the lamb mixture into a compact loaf and cover tightly with aluminium foil. Use a fork to make some holes. 2. Pour the water into the Instant Pot and put a trivet in the pot. Place the lamb loaf on the trivet and lock the lid. 3. Select the Manual mode and set the cooking time for 15 minutes on High Pressure. When the timer goes off, use a quick pressure release. 4. Carefully open the lid. Serve warm.

Calories: 563, Fat: 47g, Protein: 28g, Carbs: 6g, Fiber: 1g, Sugar: 1g, Sodium: 792mg

Beef Goulash

Prep Time: 15 minutes, Cook Time: 1 hour, Serves: 6

2 lbs. grass-fed chuck steak, trim fat and cut into bite-sized pieces	1 cup low sodium beef broth
3 onions, quartered	3 cloves garlic, diced fine
1 green pepper, chopped	2 tbsps. tomato paste
1 red pepper, chopped	1 tbsp. olive oil
1 orange pepper, chopped	1 tbsp. paprika
3 cups water	2 tsps. hot smoked paprika
1 can tomatoes, chopped	2 bay leaves
	Salt & pepper, to taste

1. Heat oil in a large soup pot over med-high. Add steak and cook until browned, stirring frequently. Add onions and cook for 5 minutes, or until soft. Add garlic and cook another minute, stirring frequently. 2. Add remaining ingredients. Stir well and bring to a boil. Reduce heat to med-low and simmer for 45-50 minutes, stirring occasionally. Goulash is done when steak is tender. Stir well before serving.

Calories: 413, Total Carbs: 14g, Protein: 53g, Fat: 15g, Sugar: 8g, Fiber: 3g

Black Bean Minced Lamb

Prep Time: 10 minutes, Cook Time: 25 minutes, Serves: 4 to 6

1 pound (454 g) ground lamb	1 can chopped and undrained green chillies
2 tbsps. vegetable oil	1½ cups chicken broth
½ cup chopped onion	1½ tbsps. tomato paste
½ tsp. salt	1½ tbsps. chili powder
2 cans drained black beans	2 tsps. cumin
1 can undrained diced tomatoes	½ tsp. cayenne

1. Set the Instant Pot to the Sauté mode and heat the oil. Add the lamb, onion and salt to the pot and sauté for 5 minutes, stirring constantly. Add the remaining ingredients to the pot and stir well. 2. Select the Manual setting and set the cooking time for 20 minutes on High Pressure. Once the timer goes off, use a natural pressure release for 10 minutes, then release any remaining pressure. Carefully open the lid. 3. Serve immediately.

Calories: 460, Fat: 28g, Protein: 29g, Carbs: 27g, Fiber: 10g, Sugar: 5g, Sodium: 830mg

Sloppy Joes in Lettuce

Prep Time: 15 minutes, Cook Time: 8 hours, Serves: 4

1 pound (454 g) grass-fed extra-lean ground beef	2 onions, chopped
1 (14-ounce, 397 g) can crushed tomatoes	2 green bell peppers, seeded and chopped
½ cup (120 ml) apple cider vinegar	Juice and zest of 1 orange
2 tbsps. honey	¼ tsp. sea salt
	¼ tsp. cayenne pepper
	4 large iceberg lettuce leaves

1. Put the ground beef in your slow cooker. 2. Mix the honey, tomatoes, onions, bell peppers, vinegar, orange juice and orange zest, salt, and cayenne. 3. Cover and cook on low for 8 hours. 4. Spoon the mixture into the lettuce leaves. Serve.

Calories: 261, Total Fat: 5g, Saturated Fat: 2g, Carbs: 26g, Protein: 28g, Fiber: 6g, Sodium: 683mg

Feta Lamb Burgers

Prep Time: 15 minutes, Cook Time: 10 minutes, Serves: 4

⅓ cup sun-dried tomatoes	1 tbsp. tomato paste
Cooking oil spray	½ tsp. cumin
1 pound (454 g) ground lamb	½ tsp. salt
⅓ cup low-fat feta cheese, crumbled	¼ tsp. pepper

1. In a medium bowl, cover sun-dried tomatoes with boiling water and soak until softened, for 10 to 15 minutes. Drain and dice. 2. Preheat the grill to medium. Lightly coat the grill with spray. 3. Combine all of the ingredients and form 4 evenly shaped patties. 4. Grill about 5 minutes per side, until the internal temperature reads 145°F (63°C).

Calories: 368, Fat: 28g, Protein: 20g, Carbs: 5g, Fiber: 1.3g, Sugar: 2.1g, Sodium: 617mg

Classic Lamb and Eggplant Tikka Masala

Prep Time: 7 minutes, Cook Time: 23 minutes, Serves: 4

1 tbsp. extra-virgin olive oil	½ yellow onion, finely diced
1 pound (454 g) boneless lamb, cut into 1-inch cubes	2 cloves garlic, minced
1 (15-ounce / 425-g) can diced tomato	2 tbsps. tomato paste
1 (14-ounce / 397-g) can unsweetened light coconut milk	1½ tsps. garam masala
1 eggplant, diced	1½ tsps. ground cumin
	1 tsp. turmeric
	¼ tsp. ground coriander
	¼ tsp. sea salt, divided

1. In a medium, deep skillet over medium heat, heat the olive oil. Place the onion and garlic and cook for 2 minutes, or until fragrant. Put the eggplant and ⅛ tsp. of sea salt and sauté for about 5 minutes. Pour in the tomato paste and sauté for 1 minute more. If the eggplant starts to stick, add 2 tbsps. of water. Keep aside. 2. Add the lamb, garam masala, cumin, turmeric, coriander, and remaining ⅛ tsp. of salt in the same skillet. Cook for about 8 minutes. Place the tomatoes and scrape the bottom of the pan to deglaze. Pour in the coconut milk and take the eggplant back to the skillet. Mix to combine well, cover, and cook for about 7 minutes. 3. Serve in 4 bowls.

Calories: 289, Fat: 13g, Protein: 26g, Carbs: 17g, Fiber: 5g, Sugar: 10g, Sodium: 500mg

Air Fried Lamb Ribs

Prep Time: 5 minutes, Cook Time: 18 minutes, Serves: 4

2 tbsps. mustard	per, to taste
1 pound (454 g) lamb ribs	¼ cup mint leaves, chopped
1 tsp. rosemary, chopped	1 cup nonfat Greek yogurt
Salt and ground black pep-	

1. Preheat the air fryer to 350ºF (177ºC). 2. Use a brush to apply the mustard to the lamb ribs, and season with rosemary, salt, and pepper. 3. Air fry the ribs in the air fryer for 18 minutes. 4. Meanwhile, combine the mint leaves and yogurt in a bowl. 5. Remove the lamb ribs from the air fryer when cooked and serve with the mint yogurt.

Calories: 328, Fat: 23g, Protein: 22g, Carbs: 5g, Fiber: 1g, Sugar: 3g, Sodium: 245mg

Braised Lamb Ragout

Prep Time: 10 minutes, Cook Time: 1 hour 8 minutes, Serves: 4 to 6

1½ pounds (680 g) lamb, bone-in	6 cloves garlic, minced
1 tsp. vegetable oil	2 tbsps. tomato paste
4 tomatoes, chopped	1 tsp. dried oregano
2 carrots, sliced	Water, as needed
½ pound (227 g) mushrooms, sliced	Salt and ground black pepper, to taste
1 small yellow onion, chopped	Handful chopped parsley

1. Press the Sauté button on the Instant Pot and heat the olive oil. Add the lamb and sear 4 minutes per side, or until browned. 2. Stir in the tomatoes, carrots, mushrooms, onion, garlic, tomato paste, oregano and water. Season with salt and pepper. 3. Set the lid in place. Select the Manual mode and set the cooking time for 60 minutes on High Pressure. Once cooking is complete, perform a quick pressure release. Carefully open the lid. 4. Transfer the lamb to a plate. Discard the bones and shred the meat. Return the shredded lamb to the pot, add the parsley and stir. 5. Serve warm.

Calories: 347, Fat: 18g, Protein: 33g, Carbs: 17g, Fiber: 4g, Sugar: 8g, Sodium: 355mg

Indian Lamb Curry

Prep Time: 15 minutes, Cook Time: 1 hour 3 minutes, Serves: 4

2 tbsps. olive oil	½ tbsp. ground turmeric
1 pound (454 g) lamb meat, cubed	½ tsp. garam masala
2 tomatoes, chopped	1 cup chicken stock
1 onion, chopped	½ cup unsweetened coconut milk
1-inch piece ginger, grated	
2 garlic cloves, minced	¼ cup brown rice, rinsed
½ tbsp. ground cumin	1 tbsp. fish sauce
½ tbsp. chili flakes	¼ cup chopped cilantro

1. Set the Instant Pot on the Sauté mode. Heat the olive oil and sear the lamb shoulder on both sides for 8 minutes, or until browned. Transfer the lamb to a plate and set aside. 2. Add the tomatoes, onion, ginger and garlic to the pot and sauté for 5 minutes. Stir in the cumin, chili flakes, turmeric and garam masala. Cook for 10 minutes, or until they form a paste. Whisk in the chicken stock, coconut milk, rice and fish sauce. Return the lamb back to the pot. 3. Lock the lid. Select Meat/Stew mode and set the cooking time for 35 minutes on High Pressure. Once cooking is complete, do a natural pressure release for 10 minutes, then release any remaining pressure. Open the lid and select the Sauté mode. Cook the curry for 5 minutes, or until thickened. 4. Top with the chopped cilantro and serve warm in bowls.

Calories: 435, Fat: 26g, Protein: 27g, Carbs: 25g, Fiber: 3g, Sugar: 6g, Sodium: 588mg

Fast Lamb Satay

Prep Time: 5 minutes, Cook Time: 8 minutes, Serves: 2

¼ tsp. cumin	2 boneless lamb steaks
1 tsp. ginger	Cooking spray
½ tsp. nutmeg	
Salt and ground black pepper, to taste	

1. Combine the cumin, ginger, nutmeg, salt and pepper in a bowl. 2. Cube the lamb steaks and massage the spice mixture into each one. 3. Leave to marinate for 10 minutes, then transfer onto metal skewers. 4. Preheat the air fryer to 400ºF (204ºC). 5. Spritz the skewers with the cooking spray, then air fry them in the air fryer for 8 minutes. 6. Take care when removing them from the air fryer and serve.

Calories: 226, Fat: 12g, Protein: 24g, Carbs: 2g, Fiber: 0g, Sugar: 0g, Sodium: 85mg

Icelandic Lamb with Turnip

Prep Time: 5 minutes, Cook Time: 45 minutes, Serves: 4

12 ounces (340 g) lamb fillet, chopped	¼ cup scallions, chopped
4 ounces (113 g) turnip, chopped	½ tsp. salt
3 ounces (85 g) celery ribs, chopped	½ tsp. ground black pepper
1 tsp. unsweetened tomato purée	4 cups water

1. Put all ingredients in the Instant Pot and stir well. 2. Close the lid. Select Manual mode and set cooking time for 45 minutes on High Pressure. 3. When timer beeps, use a quick pressure release. Open the lid. 4. Serve hot.

Calories: 161, Fat: 7g, Protein: 18g, Carbs: 7g, Fiber: 2g, Sugar: 3g, Sodium: 358mg

Maple-Glazed Spareribs

Prep Time: 40 minutes, Cook Time: 30 minutes, Serves: 6

2 racks (about 3 pounds / 1.4 kg) baby back pork ribs, cut into 2-rib sections	½ tsp. garlic powder
	¼ tsp. ground coriander
1 tsp. instant coffee crystals	¼ cup soy sauce
1 tsp. sea salt	2 tbsps. pure maple syrup
½ tsp. ground cumin	2 tbsps. tomato paste
½ tsp. chili powder	1 tbsp. apple cider vinegar
½ tsp. ground mustard	1 tbsp. olive oil
½ tsp. cayenne pepper	1 medium onion, peeled and large diced
½ tsp. onion powder	

1. Mix together the coffee, salt, cumin, chili powder, mustard, cayenne pepper, onion powder, garlic powder, and coriander in a mixing bowl. Rub the mixture into the rib sections with your hands. Refrigerate for at least 30 minutes, covered. Set aside. 2. Stir together the soy sauce, maple syrup, tomato paste, and apple cider vinegar in a small mixing bowl. 3. Set your Instant Pot to Sauté and heat the olive oil. Add the onions and sauté for 3 to 5 minutes until translucent. 4. Stir in the soy sauce

mixture. Add a few ribs at a time with tongs and gently stir to coat. Arrange the ribs standing upright, meat-side outward. Secure the lid.5.Select the Manual function and cook for 25 minutes on High Pressure.6.Once cooking is complete, use a natural pressure release for 10 minutes and then release any remaining pressure. Carefully open the lid.7.Transfer the ribs to a serving plate and serve warm.

Calories: 480, Fat: 31g, Protein: 28g, Carbs: 23g, Fiber: 1g, Sugar: 11g, Sodium: 733mg

Paprika Pork with Brussels Sprouts

Prep Time: 10 minutes, Cook Time: 30 minutes, Serves: 4

2 tbsps. olive oil	1½ cups beef stock
2 pounds (907 g) pork shoulder, cubed	1 tbsp. sweet paprika
2 cups Brussels sprouts, trimmed and halved	1 tbsp. chopped parsley

1.Press the Sauté button on the Instant Pot and heat the olive oil.2.Add the pork and brown for 5 minutes. Stir in the remaining ingredients.3.Secure the lid. Select the Manual mode and set the cooking time for 25 minutes at High Pressure.4.Once cooking is complete, do a natural pressure release for 10 minutes, then release any remaining pressure. Carefully open the lid.5.Divide the mix between plates and serve warm.

Calories: 462, Fat: 29g, Protein: 32g, Carbs: 16g, Fiber: 5g, Sugar: 4g, Sodium: 547mg

Jamaican Pork Roast

Prep Time: 10 minutes, Cook Time: 55 minutes, Serves: 6

¼ cup Jamaican jerk spice blend	2 pounds (907 g) pork shoulder
¾ tbsp. olive oil	¼ cup beef broth

1.Rub the jerk spice blend and olive oil all over the pork shoulder and set aside to marinate for 10 minutes.2.When ready, press the Sauté button on the Instant Pot and add the pork.3.Sear for 4 minutes. Flip the pork and cook for 4 minutes.4.Pour the beef broth into the Instant Pot.5.Secure the lid. Select the Manual mode and set the cooking time for 45 minutes at High Pressure.6.Once cooking is complete, do a natural pressure release for 10 minutes, then release any remaining pressure. Carefully open the lid.
7.Serve hot.

Calories: 287, Fat: 19g, Protein: 24g, Carbs: 2g, Fiber: 1g, Sugar: 0g, Sodium: 340mg

Paprika Pork Loin Roast

Prep Time: 6 minutes, Cook Time: 50 minutes, Serves: 9

4 tbsps. olive oil	3 lbs. pork loin roast
4 garlic cloves	Salt and pepper, to taste
½ cup chopped paprika	1 cup water

1.Press the Sauté button on the Instant Pot. Coat the pot with olive oil.2.Add and sauté the garlic and paprika for 1 minute or until fragrant.3.Add the pork loin roast and sear on all sides for 3 minutes or until lightly browned.4.Sprinkle salt and pepper for seasoning. Pour in the water.5.Lock the lid. Press the Meat/Stew button and set the cooking time to 45 minutes at High Pressure.6.Once cooking is complete, perform a natural pressure release for 10 minutes, and then release any remaining pressure. Carefully open the lid.7.Allow to cool for a few minutes. Remove the pork from the pot and baste with the juice remains in the pot before serving.

Calories: 331, Fat: 23g, Protein: 27g, Carbs: 2g, Fiber: 0g, Sugar: 0g, Sodium: 71mg

Pork Chops with Peas

Prep Time: 12 minutes, Cook Time: 10 minutes, Serves: 4

1 tbsp. olive oil	1 cup peas
4 pork chops	½ tsp. salt
1 medium onion, chopped	1 tsp. curry powder

1.Coat the Instant Pot with olive oil and set to Sauté setting.2.Add the pork chops and sear for 3 minutes or until lightly browned.3.Add the onion and sauté for 1 to 2 minutes or until soft.4.Add peas, salt and curry powder and sauté for 3 to 5 minutes or until peas are tender.5.Serve them warm on a large plate.

Calories: 287, Fat: 15g, Protein: 24g, Carbs: 12g, Fiber: 3g, Sugar: 4g, Sodium: 341mg

Mexican Chili Pork

Prep Time: 6 minutes, Cook Time: 35 minutes, Serves: 6

3 tbsps. olive oil	1 tbsp. red chili flakes
2 tsps. minced garlic	1 cup water
2 lbs. pork sirloin, sliced	Salt and pepper, to taste
2 tsps. ground cumin	

1.Press the Sauté button on the Instant pot and heat the olive oil until shimmering.2.Add and sauté the garlic for 30 seconds or until fragrant.3.Add the pork sirloin and sauté for 3 minutes or until lightly browned.4.Add the cumin and chili flakes.5.Pour in the water and sprinkle salt and pepper for seasoning.6.Lock the lid. Press the Meat/Stew button and set the cooking time to 30 minutes at High Pressure.7.Once cooking is complete, perform a natural pressure release for 10 minutes, and then release any remaining pressure. Carefully open the lid.8.Remove the pork from the pot and serve warm.

Calories: 291, Fat: 15g, Protein: 27g, Carbs: 6g, Fiber: 1g, Sugar: 0g, Sodium: 112mg

Indian Roasted Pork

Prep Time: 6 minutes, Cook Time: 8 hours, Serves: 3

1 tbsp. olive oil	2 garlic cloves, roughly chopped
1 lb. pork loin	1 onion, sliced
1 tsp. cumin	Salt and pepper, to taste

1.Coat the Instant Pot with olive oil and add the pork loin. Set aside.2.In a food processor, place the remaining ingredients.3.Pulse until smooth then pour the mixture over the pork loin.4.Lock the lid. Press the Slow Cook button and set the cooking time to 8 hours at High Pressure.5.Once cooking is complete, perform a natural pressure release for 10 minutes, and then release any remaining pressure. Carefully open the lid. 6.Allow to cool for a few minutes. Remove them from the pot and serve warm.

Calories: 329, Fat: 16g, Protein: 34g, Carbs: 10g, Fiber: 2g, Sugar: 4g, Sodium: 171mg

Pine Nut Pork

Prep Time: 20 minutes, Cook Time: 25 minutes, Serves: 4

1½ lbs. pork tenderloin	1 medium onion, finely sliced
1 tsp. sea salt	½ cup pine nuts
1 tbsp. extra virgin olive oil	1 cup pesto sauce

1. On a clean work surface, cut the pork tenderloin into 1-inch thick slices and rub with salt. 2. Place the olive oil in Instant Pot, then set to Sauté setting. 3. Add and brown the pork for 3 minutes, then add onion and sauté for a minute or until translucent. 4. Add the pine nuts and pesto sauce. 5. Lock the lid. Set the pot to Manual mode and set the timer to 20 minutes at High Pressure. 6. Once cooking is complete, use a natural pressure release for 10 minutes, then release any remaining pressure. 7. Carefully open the lid. Allow to cool for a few minutes. Transfer them on a large plate and serve immediately.

Calories: 494, Fat: 38g, Protein: 29g, Carbs: 8g, Fiber: 2g, Sugar: 3g, Sodium: 623mg

Egg Meatloaf

Prep Time: 20 minutes, Cook Time: 25 minutes, Serves: 6

1 tbsp. avocado oil	½ tsp. ground black pepper
1½ cup ground pork	2 tbsps. coconut flour
1 tsp. chives	3 eggs, hard-boiled, peeled
1 tsp. salt	1 cup water

1. Brush a loaf pan with avocado oil. 2. In the mixing bowl, mix the ground pork, chives, salt, ground black pepper, and coconut flour. 3. Transfer the mixture in the loaf pan and flatten with a spatula. 4. Fill the meatloaf with hard-boiled eggs. 5. Pour water and insert the trivet in the Instant Pot. 6. Lower the loaf pan over the trivet in the Instant Pot. Close the lid. 7. Select Manual mode and set cooking time for 25 minutes on High Pressure. 8. When timer beeps, use a natural pressure release for 10 minutes, then release any remaining pressure. Open the lid. 9. Serve immediately.

Calories: 204, Fat: 16g, Protein: 12g, Carbs: 2g, Fiber: 1g, Sugar: 0g, Sodium: 470mg

Pork with Bell Peppers

Prep Time: 10 minutes, Cook Time: 35 minutes, Serves: 4

2 tbsps. olive oil	1 green bell pepper, roughly chopped
4 pork chops	2 cups beef stock
1 red onion, chopped	A pinch of salt and black pepper
3 garlic cloves, minced	1 tbsp. parsley, chopped
1 red bell pepper, roughly chopped	

1. Press the Sauté on your Instant Pot. Add and heat the oil. Brown the pork chops for 2 minutes. 2. Fold in the onion and garlic and brown for an additional 3 minutes. 3. Stir in the bell peppers, stock, salt, and pepper. 4. Lock the lid. Select the Manual mode and cook for 30 minutes on High Pressure. 5. Once cooking is complete, use a natural pressure release for 10 minutes and then release any remaining pressure. Carefully open the lid. 6. Divide the mix among the plates and serve topped with the parsley.

Calories: 324, Fat: 17g, Protein: 28g, Carbs: 15g, Fiber: 2g, Sugar: 5g, Sodium: 489mg

Pulled Pork

Prep Time: 6 minutes, Cook Time: 1 hour, Serves: 12

4 lbs. pork shoulder	1 tsp. cumin powder
1 tsp. cinnamon	1½ cups water
2 tsps. garlic powder	Salt and pepper, to taste
5 tbsps. coconut oil	

1. In the Instant Pot, add all the ingredients. Stir to combine well. 2. Lock the lid. Press the Meat/Stew button and set the cooking time to 1 hour at High Pressure. 3. Once cooking is complete, do a natural pressure release for 10 minutes, and then release any remaining pressure. Carefully open the lid. 4. Remove the meat and shred with two forks to serve.

Calories: 215, Fat: 14g, Protein: 19g, Carbs: 1g, Fiber: 0g, Sugar: 0g, Sodium: 63mg

Hawaiian Pulled Pork Roast with Cabbage

Prep Time: 10 minutes, Cook Time: 1 hour 2 minutes, Serves: 6

1½ tbsps. olive oil	1 tbsp. liquid smoke
3 pounds (1.4 kg) pork shoulder roast, cut into 4 equal-sized pieces	2 cups water, divided
3 cloves garlic, minced	1 tbsp. sea salt
	2 cups shredded cabbage

1. Select Sauté mode and add the olive oil to the Instant Pot. Once the oil is hot, add the pork cuts and sear for 5 minutes per side or until browned. Once browned, transfer the pork to a platter and set aside. 2. Add the garlic, liquid smoke, and 1½ cups water to the Instant Pot. Stir to combine. 3. Return the pork to the pot and sprinkle the salt over top. 4. Lock the lid. Select Manual mode and set cooking time for 1 hour on High Pressure. 5. When cooking is complete, allow the pressure to release naturally for 20 minutes, then release any remaining pressure. 6. Open the lid and transfer the pork to a large platter. Using two forks, shred the pork. Set aside. 7. Add the shredded cabbage and remaining water to the liquid in the pot. Stir. 8. Lock the lid. Select Manual mode and set cooking time for 2 minutes on High Pressure. When cooking is complete, quick release the pressure. 9. Transfer the cabbage to the serving platter with the pork. Serve warm.

Pork Butt with Pear

Prep Time: 12 minutes, Cook Time: 50 minutes, Serves: 12

4 lbs. pork butt	4 pears, peeled, stem removed, deseeded, and cut into ½-inch chunks
2 tbsps. sea salt	
3 tbsps. extra virgin olive oil	1½ cups chicken broth

1. On a clean work surface, rub the pork butt with salt. 2. Set the Instant Pot to Sauté setting, then add and heat the olive oil. 3. Place pork in pot and brown for 5 minutes per side. 4. Add pears and chicken broth. Stir to mix well. 5. Lock the lid. Set the pot to Manual setting and set the timer for 45 minutes at High Pressure. 6. When the timer beeps, press Cancel, then use a quick pressure release. 7. Carefully open the lid and allow to cool for a few minutes. Serve warm.

Calories: 294, Fat: 16g, Protein: 25g, Carbs: 13g, Fiber: 3g, Sugar: 8g, Sodium: 637mg

CHAPTER 10 BEEF, LAMB AND PORK RECIPES

CHAPTER 11 SOUP AND STEW RECIPES

Italian Chickpea and Carrot Soup ······ 69	Lentil and Tomato Barley Soup ······ 71
Carrot and Bean Chili ······ 69	Creamy Broccoli and Cauliflower Soup ······ 71
Adzuki Bean and Celery Soup ······ 69	Celery Root and Pear Soup ······ 71
Healthy Veggie Minestrone Soup ······ 69	Pozole ······ 72
Tomato and Bean Stew ······ 69	Creamy Vegetable Soup ······ 72
Carrot, Celery and Barley Soup ······ 69	French Chicken, Mushroom and Wild Rice Stew · 72
Black Bean Wild Rice Chili ······ 70	Rustic Tomato Soup ······ 72
Black Bean and Tomato Soup with Lime Yogurt 70	Gazpacho with Avocado ······ 72
Cauliflower and Beef Soup ······ 70	Beef and Eggplant Tagine ······ 73
Delicious Roasted Beet Soup ······ 70	Pasta Vegetables Stew ······ 73
Nourishing Vegetable Stew ······ 70	Beef Chili Bean ······ 73
Green Lentil and Carrot Stew ······ 70	Lemon Chicken and Zucchini Soup ······ 73
Authentic Ratatouille Soup ······ 71	Quick Lentil Bisque ······ 73
Kale and White Bean Soup with Tofu ······ 71	

Italian Chickpea and Carrot Soup

Prep Time: 20 minutes, Cook Time: 6 hours, Serves: 7

- 2 (15-ounce / 425-g) BPA-free cans no-salt-added chickpeas, drained and rinsed
- 2 (14-ounce / 397-g) BPA-free cans diced tomatoes, undrained
- 4 carrots, peeled and cut into chunks
- 2 medium parsley roots, peeled and sliced
- 2 onions, chopped
- 3 garlic cloves, minced
- 6 cups vegetable broth
- 1 tsp. dried basil leaves
- ¼ tsp. freshly ground black pepper

1. Layer all the ingredients in a 6-quart slow cooker. Cover the slow cooker and cook on low for 5 to 6 hours, or until the vegetables are soft. 2. Stir in the soup and top with pesto, if desired. Serve warm.

Calories: 154, Fat: 2g, Protein: 6g, Carbs: 30g, Fiber: 6g, Sugar: 10g, Sodium: 469mg

Carrot and Bean Chili

Prep Time: 10 minutes, Cook Time: 41 minutes, Serves: 4

- 1 tbsp. olive oil
- 1 small red onion, peeled and diced
- 1 medium green bell pepper, deseeded and diced
- 1 large carrot, peeled and diced
- 4 cloves garlic, peeled and minced
- 1 small jalapeño, deseeded and diced
- 1 (28-ounce / 794-g) can diced tomatoes, undrained
- 1 (15-ounce / 425-g) can cannellini beans, drained and rinsed
- 1 (15-ounce / 425-g) can kidney beans, drained and rinsed
- 1 (15-ounce / 425-g) can black beans, drained and rinsed
- 2 tbsps. chili powder
- 1 tsp. ground cumin
- 1 tsp. salt
- ¼ cup vegetable broth

1. Press the Sauté button on the Instant Pot and heat the oil. Add the onion, bell pepper and carrot to the pot and sauté for 5 minutes, or until the onion is translucent. Add the garlic and sauté for 1 minute. 2. Stir in the remaining ingredients. 3. Set the lid in place. Select the Meat/Stew setting and set the cooking time for 35 minutes on High Pressure. When the timer goes off, perform a natural pressure release for 15 minutes, then release any remaining pressure. Open the lid. 4. Ladle the chili into 4 bowls and serve warm.

Calories: 307, Fat: 4g, Protein: 16g, Carbs: 59g, Fiber: 17g, Sugar: 12g, Sodium: 789mg

Adzuki Bean and Celery Soup

Prep Time: 6 minutes, Cook Time: 35 minutes, Serves: 4 to 6

- ⅛ cup extra-virgin olive oil
- 2 (13-ounce / 369-g) cans adzuki beans, drained and rinsed
- 1 large carrot, finely diced
- 1 long celery stalk, finely diced
- 1 leek, chopped
- 1 small yellow onion, finely chopped
- 6 cups water
- 1½ tsps. Himalayan salt
- Spice it up:
- 2 bay leaves

1. In a medium saucepan, heat the olive oil over medium heat. Place the leeks, onions, carrots, and celery. Cook for 5 minutes. 2. Put the salt and bay leaves (if using), then pour in the beans and water. 3. Cover and cook over medium-low heat for 30 minutes, until some of the water evaporates and the vegetables are cooked through. If you like thinner stew, shorten the cook time a little. 4. Remove and discard the bay leaves. Serve immediately.

Calories: 301, Fat: 7g, Protein: 13g, Carbs: 47g, Fiber: 13g, Sugar: 3g, Sodium: 640mg

Healthy Veggie Minestrone Soup

Prep Time: 6 minutes, Cook Time: 32 minutes, Serves: 4

- 3 tbsps. extra-virgin olive oil
- 1 (13-ounce / 369-g) can chickpeas, rinsed and drained
- 2 medium green zucchinis, cubed
- 1 small head broccoli, broken into small, bite-size florets
- 2½ cups tomato purée
- 4 cups water
- 1 large yellow onion, thinly sliced
- 1 tsp. Himalayan salt
- Spice it up:
- ¾ to 1 tsp. oregano
- ¾ to 1 tsp. basil

1. In a medium stockpot, heat the oil over medium heat. 2. Add the onion and cook for 2 minutes. 3. Place the salt, oregano and basil (if using), followed by the broccoli, zucchinis, and chickpeas. 4. Pour in the water and tomato purée. Stir, cover, and cook on low heat for 30 minutes, until the liquid reduces by half and the vegetables are soft. 5. Serve hot.

Calories: 313, Fat: 13g, Protein: 12g, Carbs: 42g, Fiber: 12g, Sugar: 11g, Sodium: 576mg

Tomato and Bean Stew

Prep Time: 12 minutes, Cook Time: 20 minutes, Serves: 4

- 1 tbsp. olive oil
- 1 large onion, chopped
- 2 large tomatoes, roughly chopped
- 1 lb. green beans
- 2 cups low-sodium chicken stock
- Salt and pepper, to taste
- ¼ cup low-fat Parmesan cheese

1. Press the Sauté bottom on the Instant Pot. 2. Add and heat the olive oil. 3. Add the onions and sauté for 2 minutes until translucent and softened. 4. Add the tomatoes and sauté for 3 to 4 minutes or until soft. 5. Add the beans and stock. Sprinkle with salt and pepper. 6. Lock the lid. Press Manual. Set the timer to 15 minutes at High Pressure. 7. Once the timer goes off, press Cancel. Do a quick pressure release. 8. Open the lid, transfer them in a large bowl and serve with Parmesan cheese on top.

Calories: 173, Fat: 5g, Protein: 8g, Carbs: 27g, Fiber: 7g, Sugar: 8g, Sodium: 415mg

Carrot, Celery and Barley Soup

Prep Time: 11 minutes, Cook Time: 9 hours, Serves: 6

- 1 bunch (about 6) large carrots, cut into 2-inch chunks and tops reserved
- 1½ cups hulled barley
- 1 large celery root, peeled and cubed
- 8 cups vegetable broth
- 2 cups bottled unsweetened carrot juice
- 2 onions, chopped
- 5 garlic cloves, minced
- 1 bay leaf
- 2 tbsps. freshly squeezed lemon juice
- 1 tsp. dried dill weed

CHAPTER 11 SOUP AND STEW RECIPES | 69

1. Mix the barley, carrots, celery root, onions, and garlic in a 6-quart slow cooker. 2. Pour in the vegetable broth, carrot juice, dill weed, and bay leaf. 3. Cover the slow cooker and cook on low for 8 to 9 hours, or until the barley and vegetables are soft. Remove the bay leaf and discard. 4. Dice the carrot tops and add 1 cup to the slow cooker. Pour in the lemon juice. Cover and cook on low for 15 minutes more. Serve warm.

Calories: 220, Fat: 1g, Protein: 6g, Carbs: 43g, Fiber: 9g, Sugar: 9g, Sodium: 240mg

Black Bean Wild Rice Chili

Prep Time: 19 minutes, Cook Time: 7 hours, Serves: 10 to 12

2 (15-ounce / 425-g) BPA-free cans no-salt-added black beans, drained and rinsed	2 red bell peppers, stemmed, seeded, and chopped
1½ cups wild rice, rinsed and drained	5 cups vegetable broth
2 cups sliced cremini mushrooms	3 cups low-sodium tomato juice
	2 onions, chopped
	3 garlic cloves, minced
	1 tbsp. chili powder
	½ tsp. ground cumin

1. Mix all of the ingredients in a 6-quart slow cooker. Cover the slow cooker and cook on low for 6 to 7 hours, or until the wild rice is tender. Enjoy!

Calories: 288, Fat: 5g, Protein: 13g, Carbs: 58g, Fiber: 10g, Sugar: 9g, Sodium: 564mg

Black Bean and Tomato Soup with Lime Yogurt

Prep Time: 8 hours 10 minutes, Cook Time: 1 hour 33 minutes, Serves: 8

2 tbsps. avocado oil	1 tsp. ground cumin
1 medium onion, chopped	3 garlic cloves, minced
1 (10-ounce / 284-g) can diced tomatoes and green chilies	6 cups chicken bone broth, vegetable broth, or water
1 pound (454 g) dried black beans, soaked in water for at least 8 hours, rinsed	Kosher salt, to taste
	1 tbsp. freshly squeezed lime juice
	¼ cup nonfat plain Greek yogurt

1. Heat the avocado oil in a nonstick skillet over medium heat until shimmering. 2. Add the onion and sauté for 3 minutes or until translucent. 3. Transfer the onion to a pot, then add the tomatoes and green chilies and their juices, black beans, cumin, garlic, broth, and salt. Stir to combine well. 4. Bring to a boil over medium-high heat, then reduce the heat to low. Simmer for 1 hour and 30 minutes or until the beans are soft. 5. Meanwhile, combine the lime juice with Greek yogurt in a small bowl. Stir to mix well. 6. Pour the soup in a large serving bowl, then drizzle with lime yogurt before serving.

Calories: 285, Fat: 6g, Protein: 19g, Carbs: 42g, Fiber: 10g, Sugar: 3g, Sodium: 174mg

Cauliflower and Beef Soup

Prep Time: 10 minutes, Cook Time: 14 minutes, Serves: 4

1 cup grass-fed ground beef	1 tsp. minced garlic
½ cup cauliflower, shredded	1 tsp. dried oregano
1 tsp. unsweetened tomato purée	½ tsp. salt
¼ cup unsweetened coconut milk	4 cups water

1. Put all ingredients in the Instant Pot and stir well. 2. Close the lid. Select Manual mode and set cooking time for 14 minutes on High Pressure. 3. When timer beeps, make a quick pressure release and open the lid. 4. Blend with an immersion blender until smooth. 5. Serve warm.

Calories: 148, Fat: 11g, Protein: 9g, Carbs: 4g, Fiber: 1g, Sugar: 1g, Sodium: 327mg

Delicious Roasted Beet Soup

Prep Time: 12 minutes, Cook Time: 35 minutes, Serves: 4

8 medium beets, peeled and cut in quarters	1 tbsp. olive oil
½ small sweet onion, peeled and cut into chunks	2 tbsps. apple cider vinegar
2 garlic cloves, peeled	2 cups unsweetened almond milk
	¼ cup fresh parsley, chopped

1. Preheat the oven to 350°F (180°C). Line a baking sheet with foil. 2. On the baking sheet, arrange the beets, onion, and garlic and drizzle the vegetables with the oil. 3. Bake until the beets are fork tender, about 35 minutes. 4. In a food processor or blender, combine the vegetables, including any juices on the baking sheet, with the vinegar and almond milk, and process until very smooth. 5. Serve warm, topped with parsley.

Calories: 152, Fat: 6g, Protein: 4g, Carbs: 26g, Fiber: 5g, Sugar: 16g, Sodium: 159mg

Nourishing Vegetable Stew

Prep Time: 16 minutes, Cook Time: 30 minutes, Serves: 4

1 tsp. olive oil	vegetable stock
1 small sweet onion, peeled and chopped	2 large tomatoes, chopped
1 tsp. garlic, minced	½ cup canned sodium-free white kidney beans, rinsed and drained
½ tsp. cumin, ground	1 tsp. fresh lemon juice
½ tsp. coriander, ground	1 cup kale, chopped
1 red bell pepper, seeded and chopped	Pinch of red pepper flakes, crushed
2 large carrots, peeled and chopped	Black pepper, freshly ground, to taste
2 cups fat-free, low-sodium	

1. In a large pot over medium heat, heat the oil and sauté the onion and garlic for about 3 minutes, or until softened. 2. Add the cumin, and coriander, and stir to coat, about 1 minute. 3. Add the red pepper and carrots and sauté for 5 minutes. 4. Stir in the vegetable stock, tomatoes, and kidney beans. 5. Bring the stew to a boil and then lower the heat. 6. Simmer until the vegetables are tender, stirring often, about 15 to 17 minutes. 7. Add the lemon juice and kale and heat for 3 minutes or until the kale is wilted. 8. Stir in the red pepper flakes and pepper. Serve.

Calories: 101, Fat: 2g, Protein: 4g, Carbs: 18g, Fiber: 3g, Sugar: 7g, Sodium: 63mg

Green Lentil and Carrot Stew

Prep Time: 5 minutes, Cook Time: 30 minutes, Serves: 4

2 tbsps. extra-virgin olive oil	6 cups water
2 cups green lentils, rinsed	1 tsp. Himalayan salt
1 carrot, chopped	Spice it up:
2 celery stalks, chopped	1 tbsp. cumin
1 yellow onion, chopped	Freshly ground black pepper

CHAPTER 11 SOUP AND STEW RECIPES

1. In a sauté pan or skillet, heat the oil over medium heat. Place the carrots, celery, and onion. Cook until the onion is translucent. 2. Place the lentils, salt, cumin (if using), and water. Stir, cover, reduce the heat to low, and sauté for about 25 to 30 minutes. 3. Season with more salt and black pepper, if desired. Serve right away.

Calories: 418, Fat: 8g, Protein: 24g, Carbs: 65g, Fiber: 12g, Sugar: 4g, Sodium: 324mg

Authentic Ratatouille Soup

Prep Time: 18 minutes, Cook Time: 9 hours, Serves: 6

2 tbsps. olive oil	1½ cups shredded low-fat Swiss cheese
6 large tomatoes, seeded and chopped	6 cups vegetable broth
2 medium eggplants, peeled and chopped	2 onions, chopped
2 red bell peppers, stemmed, seeded, and chopped	4 garlic cloves, minced
	2 tsps. herbes de Provence
	2 tbsps. cornstarch

1. Mix the olive oil, onions, garlic, eggplants, bell peppers, tomatoes, vegetable broth, and herbes de Provence in a 6-quart slow cooker. Cover the slow cooker and cook on low for 7 to 9 hours, or until the vegetables are soft. 2. Toss the cheese with the cornstarch in a small bowl. Place the cheese mixture to the slow cooker. Cover and allow to stand for 10 minutes, then stir in the soup and serve warm.

Calories: 215, Fat: 10g, Protein: 9g, Carbs: 23g, Fiber: 8g, Sugar: 11g, Sodium: 144mg

Kale and White Bean Soup with Tofu

Prep Time: 7 minutes, Cook Time: 23 minutes, Serves: 4

3 tbsps. extra-virgin olive oil	1 large yellow onion, thinly sliced
1 (14-ounce / 397-g) package extra-firm tofu, drained and cubed	4 cups vegetable stock
4 cups kale, coarsely chopped	4 cups water
1 (13-ounce / 369-g) can cannellini beans, rinsed and drained	1 tsp. Himalayan salt
	Spice it up:
	½ tsp. crushed red pepper flakes
	½ tsp. garlic powder

1. In a medium saucepan, heat the olive oil over medium heat. Place the onion and cook until translucent. 2. Place the stock, kale, beans, and water, and bring it to a boil. Put the tofu, salt, and garlic powder (if using). Sauté for 20 minutes, partly covered. 3. Sprinkle with some red pepper flakes before serving (if using).

Calories: 302, Fat: 17g, Protein: 18g, Carbs: 25g, Fiber: 7g, Sugar: 5g, Sodium: 433mg

Lentil and Tomato Barley Soup

Prep Time: 10 minutes, Cook Time: 7 hours, Serves: 6

3 large tomatoes, seeded and chopped	12 cups vegetable broth
4 large carrots, peeled and sliced	2 onions, chopped
2 cups chopped kale	1 leek, chopped
1½ cups pearl barley	4 garlic cloves, minced
1½ cups Puy lentils	1 tsp. dried dill weed

1. Mix the onions, leek, garlic, carrots, tomatoes, barley, lentils, vegetable broth, and dill weed in a 6-quart slow cooker. Cover the slow cooker and cook on low for 6 to 7 hours, or until the barley and lentils are soft. 2. Toss in the kale. Cover and cook on low for about 15 to 20 minutes, or until the kale wilts. Enjoy!

Calories: 347, Fat: 2g, Protein: 16g, Carbs: 66g, Fiber: 14g, Sugar: 10g, Sodium: 250mg

Creamy Broccoli and Cauliflower Soup

Prep Time: 4 minutes, Cook Time: 23 minutes, Serves: 3

1 small head broccoli, broken into florets	1 tbsp. low-fat Pecorino Romano cheese
½ head cauliflower, broken into florets	6 cups water
1 small carrot, chopped	1¾ tsps. Himalayan salt
1 small yellow onion, cut in half	½ tsp. basil (optional)

1. Combine the broccoli, cauliflower, onion, carrot, salt, basil (if using), and 6 cups water in a medium stockpot. 2. Bring to a boil, then reduce the heat to medium and simmer for about 20 minutes, covered, until the veggies are soft. 3. Drain the water with a colander, reserving 2 cups of cooking liquid. 4. Place the vegetables to a high-speed blender with 1 cup of the reserved liquid. Gently blend to desired consistency, working in batches, if needed. If you like bisque to be on the thinner side, pour in more of the reserved liquid. 5. Take the bisque back in the pot and bring to a boil. 6. Stir in the cheese, then cover and allow soup to rest for about 3 minutes. 7. Serve hot with some high-fiber crackers or a piece of whole-grain toast.

Calories: 106, Fat: 2g, Protein: 7g, Carbs: 19g, Fiber: 7g, Sugar: 6g, Sodium: 430mg

Celery Root and Pear Soup

Prep Time: 9 minutes, Cook Time: 1 hour, Serves: 4

1 tbsp. extra-virgin olive oil, plus additional for garnish	¾ cup organic vegetable broth
1 pound (454 g) celery root, peeled and diced	4 tarragon sprigs
1 pear, peeled and cored	2 bay leaves
1 yellow onion, diced	1 garlic clove, minced
3 cups water	¼ tsp. sea salt
	¼ tsp. cayenne pepper
	¼ tsp. ground white pepper

1. In a large pot, heat the olive oil over medium heat. Place the onion and cook for about 5 to 8 minutes, until tender and translucent. Put the celery root and garlic, and sauté for 5 minutes, stirring constantly. Add the pear and sauté for another 3 minutes, stirring constantly. 2. Add vegetable broth, tarragon, bay leaves, cayenne pepper, and white pepper to the pot. Sprinkle with salt. Increase the heat to high and cook, stirring occasionally, until most of the liquid has evaporated. 3. Pour the water to the pot and bring to a boil. Turn the heat to low, cover the pot, and allow to simmer for about 20 to 25 minutes, until the celery root is tender. Remove the bay leaves and tarragon sprigs and discard. 4. With an immersion blender, blend the soup right in the pot until completely smooth. Divide the soup equally among 4 bowls and drizzle with olive oil. Enjoy!

Calories: 79, Fat: 4g, Protein: 1g, Carbs: 11g, Fiber: 4g, Sugar: 5g, Sodium: 325mg

Pozole

Prep Time: 20 minutes, Cook Time: 53 minutes, Serves: 6

2½ pounds (1.1 kg) boneless pork shoulder, cut into pieces
1 tsp. salt, divided
1 tsp. ground black pepper, divided
2 tbsps. vegetable oil
2 medium yellow onions, peeled and chopped
2 medium poblano peppers, deseeded and diced
1 chipotle pepper in adobo, minced
4 cloves garlic, peeled and minced
1 cinnamon stick
1 tbsp. smoked paprika
2 tsps. chili powder
1 tsp. dried oregano
1 tsp. ground cumin
½ tsp. ground coriander
1 (12-ounce / 340-g) can lager-style beer
4 cups chicken broth
2 (15-ounce / 425-g) cans hominy, drained and rinsed
1 tbsp. lime juice
½ cup chopped cilantro

1. Season the pork pieces with ½ tsp. of the salt and ½ tsp. of the pepper. 2. Press the Sauté button on the Instant Pot and heat the oil. Add half the pork to the pot in an even layer, making sure there is space between pieces to prevent steam from forming. Sear the pork for 3 minutes on each side, or until lightly browned. Remove the pork to a plate. Repeat with the remaining pork. 3. Add the onions and poblano peppers to the pot and sauté for 5 minutes, or until just softened. Add the chipotle pepper, garlic, cinnamon, paprika, chili powder, oregano, cumin and coriander to the pot. Sauté for 1 minute, or until fragrant. 4. Return the pork to the pot and turn to coat with the spices. Pour in the beer and chicken broth. 5. Lock the lid. Select the Manual mode and set the cooking time for 35 minutes on High Pressure. When the timer beeps, perform a natural pressure release for 20 minutes, then release any remaining pressure. Carefully open the lid. 6. Season with the remaining ½ tsp. of the salt and ½ tsp. of the pepper. Stir in the hominy, lime juice and cilantro. Serve hot.

Calories: 482, Fat: 26g, Protein: 36g, Carbs: 26g, Fiber: 7g, Sugar: 3g, Sodium: 854mg

Creamy Vegetable Soup

Prep Time: 15 minutes, Cook Time: 40 minutes, Serves: 6

1 tsp. olive oil
¼ cup sweet onion, chopped
2 celery stalks, diced
1 tsp. garlic, minced
4 cups fat-free, low-sodium vegetable stock
2 cups cauliflower florets, chopped
1 cup broccoli florets, chopped
1 cup spinach, shredded
8 ounces (227 g) silken tofu
1 tsp. white wine vinegar
½ tsp. nutmeg, ground
Black pepper, freshly ground

1. In a large pot over medium heat, heat the oil and sauté the onion, celery, and garlic until softened, about 3 minutes. Add the stock and bring to a boil. 2. Add the cauliflower and broccoli and lower the heat so the soup simmers. 3. Cover the pot and cook until the vegetables are tender, about 25 minutes. 4. Add the spinach and simmer an additional 3 minutes. 5. Transfer the soup to a food processor or blender and purée until it is smooth. 6. Add the tofu and vinegar and purée until silky and smooth. 7. Season with the nutmeg and pepper to taste. 8. Serve warm.

Calories: 89, Fat: 3g, Protein: 8g, Carbs: 8g, Fiber: 3g, Sugar: 3g, Sodium: 126mg

French Chicken, Mushroom and Wild Rice Stew

Prep Time: 14 minutes, Cook Time: 9 hours, Serves: 9

10 boneless, skinless chicken thighs, cut into 2-inch pieces
2 (14-ounce / 397-g) BPA-free cans diced tomatoes, undrained
2 cups sliced cremini mushrooms
3 large carrots, sliced
1 cup wild rice, rinsed and drained
2 leeks, chopped
½ cup sliced ripe olives
8 cups vegetable broth
3 garlic cloves, minced
2 tsps. dried herbes de Provence

1. Mix all the ingredients in a 6-quart slow cooker. Cover the slow cooker and cook on low for 7 to 9 hours, or until the chicken is cooked to 165ºF (74ºC) and the wild rice is soft. Serve warm.

Calories: 363, Fat: 12g, Protein: 32g, Carbs: 31g, Fiber: 3g, Sugar: 5g, Sodium: 470mg

Rustic Tomato Soup

Prep Time: 9 minutes, Cook Time: 30 minutes, Serves: 4

1 tsp. olive oil
1 sweet onion, peeled and diced
3 tsps. garlic, minced
2 celery stalks, diced
10 large ripe tomatoes, chopped
3 medium carrots, peeled and diced
4 cups fat-free, low-sodium vegetable stock
2 tbsps. fresh basil, chopped
2 tbsps. fresh parsley, chopped
1 tsp. fresh oregano, chopped
Black pepper, freshly ground

1. In a large pot on medium heat, heat the olive oil and sauté the onion, garlic, and celery until softened, about 5 minutes. 2. Add the tomatoes, carrots, and stock and bring to a boil. 3. Lower the heat and simmer the soup until the carrots are tender, about 25 minutes. 4. Remove the soup from the heat and purée with a blender or a food processor until the soup reaches chunky consistency. 5. Stir in the basil, parsley, and oregano; season with pepper and serve warm.

Calories: 134, Fat: 2g, Protein: 5g, Carbs: 30g, Fiber: 8g, Sugar: 16g, Sodium: 112mg

Gazpacho with Avocado

Prep Time: 10 minutes, Cook Time: 30 minutes, Serves: 4

8 ripe plum tomatoes, chopped
1 large English cucumber, chopped
1 large red bell pepper, seeded and chopped
¼ small red onion, peeled and chopped
4 tbsps. chopped fresh cilantro
3 tsps. fresh lemon juice
1 tsp. garlic, minced
Black pepper, freshly ground, to taste
Hot pepper sauce
1 cup low-sodium prepared vegetable juice or fresh vegetable juice
1 ripe avocado, peeled and diced

1. In a food processor or blender, combine all the ingredients except the juice and the avocado. Process until well combined but chunky. 2. Add the vegetable juice and pulse to combine to the desired consistency. 3. Store the soup in a sealed container in the refrigerator until ready to use. 4. Serve topped with chopped avocado.

Calories: 166, Fat: 8g, Protein: 5g, Carbs: 25g, Fiber: 6g, Sugar: 14g, Sodium: 231mg

Beef and Eggplant Tagine

Prep Time: 15 minutes, Cook Time: 25 minutes, Serves: 6

1 pound (454 g) grass-fed beef fillet, chopped
1 eggplant, chopped
6 ounces (170 g) scallions, chopped
4 cups beef broth
1 tsp. ground allspices
1 tsp. erythritol
1 tsp. coconut oil

1. Put all ingredients in the Instant Pot. Stir to mix well. 2. Close the lid. Select Manual mode and set cooking time for 25 minutes on High Pressure. 3. When timer beeps, use a natural pressure release for 15 minutes, then release any remaining pressure. Open the lid. 4. Serve warm.

Calories: 183, Fat: 7g, Protein: 18g, Carbs: 15g, Fiber: 5g, Sugar: 5g, Sodium: 686mg

Pasta Vegetables Stew

Prep Time: 9 minutes, Cook Time: 7½ hours, Serves: 6

1½ cups whole-wheat orzo pasta
6 large tomatoes, seeded and chopped
2 cups sliced cremini mushrooms
2 cups sliced button mushrooms
2 cups chopped yellow summer squash
2 red bell peppers, stemmed, seeded, and chopped
8 cups vegetable broth
2 onions, chopped
5 garlic cloves, minced
2 tsps. dried Italian seasoning

1. Mix the onions, garlic, mushrooms, summer squash, bell peppers, tomatoes, vegetable broth, and Italian seasoning in a 6-quart slow cooker. Cover the slow cooker and cook on low for 6 to 7 hours, or until the vegetables are soft. 2. Place the pasta and stir. Cover and cook on low for 20 to 30 minutes more, or until the pasta is tender. Enjoy!

Calories: 248, Fat: 1g, Protein: 11g, Carbs: 48g, Fiber: 9g, Sugar: 10g, Sodium: 462mg

Beef Chili Bean

Prep Time: 16 minutes, Cook Time: 10 hours, Serves: 7

2½ pounds (1.1 kg) grass-fed sirloin tip, cut into 2-inch cubes
2 cups dried beans, rinsed and drained
4 large tomatoes, seeded and chopped
1 (6-ounce / 170-g) BPA-free can tomato paste
2 jalapeño peppers, minced
2 onions, chopped
6 garlic cloves, minced
11 cups vegetable broth
2 tbsps. chili powder
1 tsp. ground cumin

1. Mix all of the ingredients in a 6-quart slow cooker. Cover the slow cooker and cook on low for 8 to 10 hours, or until the beans are soft. Serve warm.

Calories: 459, Fat: 10g, Protein: 45g, Carbs: 47g, Fiber: 14g, Sugar: 10g, Sodium: 290mg

Lemon Chicken and Zucchini Soup

Prep Time: 8 minutes, Cook Time: 68 minutes, Serves: 4

1 tbsp. extra-virgin olive oil
1 cup shredded cooked chicken
1 zucchini, diced
½ cup quinoa
2 celery stalks, chopped
4 cups chicken stock
1 cup water
2 scallions, sliced
2 garlic cloves, minced
1 tbsp. chopped fresh dill
1 tbsp. chopped fresh parsley
1 tbsp. red pepper flakes
1 tbsp. freshly squeezed lemon juice
½ tsp. lemon zest
½ tsp. sea salt
¼ tsp. freshly ground black pepper

1. In a large pot over high heat, bring the quinoa and water to a boil, stirring constantly. Turn the heat to low and allow to simmer for about 15 to 20 minutes, stirring occasionally. Once the liquid is absorbed and the quinoa is soft, take the pot from the heat. 2. When the quinoa is cooking, heat the olive oil over medium heat in a large pot. Add the scallions and cook for about 3 to 4 minutes, until soft and tender. 3. Place the celery and garlic to the pot and cook for another 2 minutes, stirring constantly. Add the zucchini, salt, and pepper, and sauté for another 10 minutes, stirring constantly. 4. Pour the chicken stock and lemon zest to the pot. Raise the heat to high and bring to a boil. Turn the heat to low, cover the pot, and let simmer for about 30 minutes. 5. Stir in the cooked quinoa, chicken, parsley, dill and and simmer for an additional 2 minutes. Divide the soup equally among 4 bowls and garnish with the lemon juice and red pepper flakes. Enjoy!

Calories: 190, Fat: 7g, Protein: 15g, Carbs: 18g, Fiber: 2g, Sugar: 2g, Sodium: 420mg

Quick Lentil Bisque

Prep Time: 2 minutes, Cook Time: 20 minutes, Serves: 2 to 4

1 cup red lentils, washed and drained
1 yellow onion, chopped
2 garlic cloves, minced
4 cups water
¾ tsp. Himalayan salt
¼ tsp. freshly ground black pepper
1½ tsps. cumin (optional)

1. Combine the lentils, onion, garlic, salt, cumin (if using), and water in a medium stockpot. 2. Bring to a boil, cover, reduce the heat to low and simmer for 20 minutes. 3. Serve right away with freshly ground black pepper, or blend it for a smoother texture.

Calories: 370, Fat: 2g, Protein: 24g, Carbs: 67g, Fiber: 11g, Sugar: 2g, Sodium: 358mg

CHAPTER 12: APPETIZER AND SIDES RECIPES

Creamy Spinach with Mushrooms 75	Green Beans with Shallots 77
Simple Poached Eggs 75	Braised Kale 77
Pesto Spaghetti Squash 75	Smoky Carrots and Collard Greens 78
Grilled Carrots with Dill 75	Roasted Coconut Brussels Sprouts 78
Ginger-Garlic Spicy Kale 75	Green Broccolini Sauté 78
Instant Pot Pinto Beans 75	Braised Cabbage 78
Italian Roasted Vegetables 76	Lemony Peas 78
Herbed Cauliflower with Orange Juice 76	Artichokes with Mayonnaise Dip 78
Sumptuous Beet Salad with Vinaigrette 76	Baked Parmesan Broccoli Fritters 79
Curried Cauliflower 76	Brussels Sprouts with Sesame Seeds 79
Classic Tex-Mex Kale 76	Zucchini Noodles with Lemon Artichoke Pesto 79
Caramelized Onions and Garlic 76	Spicy Green Beans 79
Cranberry Green Beans with Walnut 77	Quinoa with Brussels Sprouts and Avocado 79
Thai Curry Roasted Veggies 77	Garlicky Broccoli 79
Black-Eyed Peas with Greens 77	Roasted Red Pepper and Dry Sherry 80
Beet and Grapefruit Salad 77	Cannellini Mandarin Salsa 80

Creamy Spinach with Mushrooms

Prep Time: 10 minutes, Cook Time: 10 minutes, Serves: 4

1 tbsp. olive oil	2 cups sliced portabella mushrooms
1 cup sliced fennel	1 cup unsweetened coconut milk
2 cloves garlic, crushed and minced	½ cup vegetable broth
	½ tsp. salt
¼ cup white wine	1 tsp. coarse ground black pepper
10 cups fresh spinach	1 tsp. nutmeg
	½ tsp. thyme

1. Press the Sauté button on the Instant Pot and heat the oil. Add the fennel and garlic. Sauté the mixture for 3 minutes. 2. Add the white wine and sauté an additional 2 minutes, or until the wine reduces. Add the remaining ingredients and stir. 3. Lock the lid. Select the Manual mode and set the cooking time for 5 minutes on High Pressure. Once the timer goes off, perform a natural pressure release for 10 minutes, then release any remaining pressure. Carefully open the lid. 4. Stir before serving.

Calories: 124, Fat: 9g, Protein: 5g, Carbs: 7g, Fiber: 3g, Sugar: 1g, Sodium: 368mg

Simple Poached Eggs

Prep Time: 2 minutes, Cook Time: 5 minutes, Serves: 1

6 cups water	1 tsp. vinegar
A pinch of salt	2 large eggs

1. Add the salt and the vinegar to a medium saucepan with water and bring it to a boil over high heat. 2. Crack each egg in its own small bowl. 3. When reaching a boil, turn down the heat until it comes to a slow and steady simmer. 4. Swirl the water in a circle with a spoon to create a vortex and slide the egg(s) into water. 5. Cook for 4 minutes and then remove the eggs with a slotted spoon. 6. If you prefer your yolks on the runnier side, cook for 3 minutes. If you prefer them hard, cook longer, for 5 to 6 minutes.

Calories: 152, Fat: 9g, Protein: 12g, Carbs: 0.8g, Fiber: 0g, Sugar: 0.2g, Sodium: 298mg

Pesto Spaghetti Squash

Prep Time: 5 minutes, Cook Time: 12 minutes, Serves: 6

1½ cups plus 3 tbsps. water, divided
1 (3-pound / 1.4-kg) spaghetti squash, pierced with a knife about 10 times
¼ cup pesto

1. Pour 1½ cups of the water and insert the trivet in the Instant Pot. Put the pan on the trivet. Place the squash on the trivet. 2. Lock the lid. Select the Manual mode and set the cooking time for 12 minutes on High Pressure. Once the timer goes off, perform a natural pressure release for 10 minutes, then release any remaining pressure. Carefully open the lid. 3. Using tongs, carefully transfer the squash to a cutting board to cool for about 10 minutes. 4. Halve the spaghetti squash lengthwise. Using a spoon, scoop out and discard the seeds. Using a fork, scrape the flesh of the squash and shred into long "noodles". Place the noodles in a medium serving bowl. 5. In a small bowl, mix the pesto with the remaining 3 tbsps. of the water. Drizzle over the squash, toss to combine, and serve warm.

Calories: 94, Fat: 6g, Protein: 2g, Carbs: 10g, Fiber: 2g, Sugar: 2g, Sodium: 95mg

Grilled Carrots with Dill

Prep Time: 6 minutes, Cook Time: 10 minutes, Serves: 4

1 pound (454 g) carrots, washed and cut into batons	1 tbsp. fresh dill, chopped
	1 tbsp. fresh lemon juice
1 tsp. olive oil	

1. Preheat the barbecue to medium-high heat or preheat the broiler. 2. On the barbecue, grill the carrots until softened and lightly charred, turning frequently, about 10 minutes. Or in the oven, broil the carrots, turning once, until tender, about 8 minutes. 3. In a large bowl, combine the carrots with the remaining ingredients and toss. 4. Serve warm.

Calories: 59, Fat: 2g, Protein: 1g, Carbs: 11g, Fiber: 4g, Sugar: 6g, Sodium: 80mg

Ginger-Garlic Spicy Kale

Prep Time: 5 minutes, Cook Time: 6 minutes, Serves: 4

1 tbsp. olive oil	8 cups kale, stems removed and chopped
5 cloves garlic	
1 tbsp. fresh grated ginger	1½ cups vegetable broth
1 tbsp. crushed red pepper flakes	1 tbsp. garlic chili paste

1. Press the Sauté button on the Instant Pot and heat the oil. Add in the garlic, ginger and crushed red pepper flakes. Sauté the mixture for 2 minutes or until highly fragrant. 2. Add in the vegetable broth and garlic chili paste. Whisk until well blended. Add in the kale and stir. 3. Lock the lid. Select the Manual mode and set the cooking time for 4 minutes on High Pressure. Once the timer goes off, perform a natural pressure release for 5 minutes, then release any remaining pressure. Carefully open the lid. 4. Stir before serving.

Calories: 80, Fat: 4g, Protein: 3g, Carbs: 10g, Fiber: 2g, Sugar: 1g, Sodium: 364mg

Instant Pot Pinto Beans

Prep Time: 10 minutes, Cook Time: 20 minutes, Serves: 4

3 cups water	½ fine sea salt, or more to taste
1 cup dried pinto beans, soaked for 8 hours and drained	
2 cloves garlic, minced	Pinch of cayenne pepper (optional)
½ yellow onion, chopped	Chopped fresh cilantro, for garnish
1 tsp. chili powder	
1 tsp. ground cumin	Lime wedges, for garnish
¼ tsp. freshly ground black pepper	

1. In the Instant Pot, combine the water, beans, garlic, and onion. 2. Lock the lid. Select the Manual mode and set the cooking time for 20 minutes at High Pressure. 3. Once cooking is complete, do a natural pressure release for 10 minutes, then release any remaining pressure. Carefully open the lid. 4. Drain the beans and reserve the liquid. 5. Return the cooked beans to the pot and stir in ½ cup of the reserved liquid. Add the chili powder, cumin, black pepper, salt, and cayenne pepper (if desired) and stir well. Using a potato masher, mash the beans until smooth, leaving some texture if you like. If you prefer a more smooth texture, you can purée the beans with an immersion blender. 6. Taste and add more salt, if desired. Garnish with the cilantro and lime wedges and serve warm.

Calories: 143, Fat: 0.5g, Protein: 8g, Carbs: 28g, Fiber: 7g, Sugar: 1g, Sodium: 300mg

Italian Roasted Vegetables

Prep Time: 8 minutes, Cook Time: 30 minutes, Serves: 6

2 tbsps. extra-virgin olive oil	1 red bell pepper, cut into chunks
8 ounces (227 g) Brussels sprouts, halved	½ red onion, cut into chunks
2 cups cauliflower florets	3 tbsps. balsamic vinegar
1 medium zucchini, cut into 1-inch chunks	2 tsp. store-bought Italian seasoning
	1 tsp. kosher salt

1. Preheat the oven to 400ºF (205ºC). Gently line a large rimmed baking sheet with parchment paper. 2. Arrange the Brussels sprouts, zucchini, bell pepper, red onion, and cauliflower on the lined baking sheet. 3. Whisk together the balsamic vinegar, olive oil, Italian seasoning, and salt in a small bowl. Pour the liquid over the vegetables and toss to combine well, then arrange the vegetables back out in an even layer. 4. Roast for about 25 to 30 minutes, until the vegetables are fork-tender and beginning to brown. Serve warm.

Calories: 84, Fat: 5g, Protein: 3g, Carbs: 9g, Fiber: 3g, Sugar: 3g, Sodium: 413mg

Herbed Cauliflower with Orange Juice

Prep Time: 12 minutes, Cook Time: 4 hours, Serves: 10

2 heads cauliflower, rinsed and cut into florets	1 tsp. dried thyme leaves
½ cup orange juice	1 tsp. grated orange zest
2 onions, chopped	½ tsp. dried basil leaves
	½ tsp. salt

1. Mix the cauliflower and onions in a 6-quart slow cooker. Top with the orange juice and orange zest, and sprinkle with the thyme, basil, and salt. 2. Cover the slow cooker and cook on low for 4 hours, or until the cauliflower is soft when pierced with a fork. Serve warm.

Calories: 75, Fat: 0g, Protein: 5g, Carbs: 16g, Fiber: 5g, Sugar: 8g, Sodium: 212mg

Sumptuous Beet Salad with Vinaigrette

Prep Time: 10 minutes, Cook Time: 20 minutes, Serves: 4

For the Salad:	¾ cup low-fat Feta cheese
1 pound (454 g) beets, each about 2½ inches in diameter	1 cup water
2 navel oranges, peeled and cut into segments	For the Vinaigrette:
	¼ cup extra-virgin olive oil
1 large avocado, pitted, peeled and sliced	2 tbsps. fresh lemon juice
	½ tsp. dried oregano
1 (5- to 6-ounce / 142- to 170-g) bag baby spinach	¼ tsp. fine sea salt
	¼ tsp. freshly ground black pepper
4 sprigs fresh mint, leaves removed and torn if large	1 clove garlic, minced

1. Pour the water into the Instant Pot and place the wire metal steam rack in the pot. Arrange the beets in a single layer on the steam rack. 2. Set the lid in place. Select the Manual mode and set the cooking time for 20 minutes on High Pressure. 3. While the beets are cooking, prepare an ice bath. 4. To make the vinaigrette: In a widemouthed 1-pint jar, combine the oil, lemon juice, oregano, salt, pepper, and garlic. Using an immersion blender, blend until an emulsified vinaigrette forms. Set aside. 5. When the timer goes off, do a quick pressure release. Carefully open the lid. Using tongs, transfer the beets to the ice bath and let cool for 10 minutes. 6. Using a paring knife, remove the skins from the beets; they should peel off very easily. Trim and discard the ends of the beets, then slice them into wedges. 7. In a large bowl, toss the spinach with half of the vinaigrette. Arrange the spinach on a large serving plate or on individual salad plates, then top with the beets, oranges, avocado, and mint. 8. Using a pair of spoons, scoop bite-sized pieces of the feta out of its container and dollop it onto the salad. Spoon the rest of the vinaigrette over the salad and serve immediately.

Calories: 366, Fat: 26g, Protein: 9g, Carbs: 29g, Fiber: 9g, Sugar: 15g, Sodium: 636mg

Curried Cauliflower

Prep Time: 5 minutes, Cook Time: 13 minutes, Serves: 4

2 tbsps. olive oil	½ tsp. curry powder
1 medium head cauliflower, cut into florets	⅛ tsp. salt
	⅛ tsp. black pepper

1. Press the Sauté button on your Instant Pot. Add the oil and let heat for 1 minute. 2. Add the remaining ingredients and stir well. Lock the lid and sauté for 12 minutes, or until the florets are crisp-tender. 3. Transfer to a plate and serve hot.

Calories: 92, Fat: 7g, Protein: 2g, Carbs: 7g, Fiber: 3g, Sugar: 2g, Sodium: 99mg

Classic Tex-Mex Kale

Prep Time: 11 minutes, Cook Time: 5 hours, Serves: 10

4 bunches kale, washed, stemmed, and cut into large pieces	2 onions, chopped
	8 garlic cloves, minced
	1 tbsp. chili powder
4 large tomatoes, seeded and chopped	½ tsp. salt
2 jalapeño peppers, minced	⅛ tsp. freshly ground black pepper

1. Mix the kale, onions, garlic, jalapeño peppers, and tomatoes in a 6-quart slow cooker. 2. Scatter with the chili powder, salt, and pepper, and stir to mix well. 3. Cover the slow cooker and cook on low for 4 to 5 hours, or until the kale is wilted and soft. Serve warm.

Calories: 52, Fat: 1g, Protein: 3g, Carbs: 11g, Fiber: 3g, Sugar: 5g, Sodium: 223mg

Caramelized Onions and Garlic

Prep Time: 8 minutes, Cook Time: 10 hours, Serves: 12

¼ cup olive oil	2 tbsps. balsamic vinegar
10 large yellow onions, peeled and sliced	1 tsp. dried thyme leaves
20 garlic cloves, peeled	¼ tsp. salt

1. Mix all the ingredients in a 6-quart slow cooker. Cover the slow cooker and cook on low for 8 to 10 hours, stirring once or twice if you have the time. 2. Refrigerate the onions up to 1 week, or evenly divide them into 1-cup portions and freeze up to 3 months.

Calories: 109, Fat: 4g, Protein: 2g, Carbs: 16g, Fiber: 3g, Sugar: 9g, Sodium: 56mg

Cranberry Green Beans with Walnut

Prep Time: 15 minutes, Cook Time: 7 hours, Serves: 10

2 pounds (907 g) fresh green beans
1 cup dried cranberries
1 cup coarsely chopped toasted walnuts
1 onion, chopped
⅓ cup orange juice
½ tsp. salt
⅛ tsp. freshly ground black pepper

1. Mix the green beans, onion, cranberries, orange juice, salt, and pepper in a 6-quart slow cooker. Cover the slow cooker and cook on low for 5 to 7 hours, or until the green beans are soft. 2. Place the walnuts and serve warm.

Calories: 100, Fat: 3g, Protein: 2g, Carbs: 18g, Fiber: 3g, Sugar: 11g, Sodium: 151mg

Thai Curry Roasted Veggies

Prep Time: 10 minutes, Cook Time: 8 hours, Serves: 8 to 10

4 large carrots, peeled and cut into chunks
2 parsnips, peeled and sliced
2 jalapeño peppers, minced
½ cup vegetable broth
2 onions, peeled and sliced
6 garlic cloves, peeled and sliced
⅓ cup canned unsweetened coconut milk
3 tbsps. lime juice
2 tbsps. grated fresh ginger root
2 tsps. curry powder

1. Mix the carrots, onions, garlic, parsnips, and jalapeño peppers in a 6-quart slow cooker. 2. Mix the vegetable broth, coconut milk, lime juice, ginger root, and curry powder in a small bowl, until well blended. Pour this mixture into the slow cooker. 3. Cover the slow cooker and cook on low for 6 to 8 hours, or until the vegetables are soft when pierced with a fork. Enjoy!

Calories: 69, Fat: 3g, Protein: 1g, Carbs: 13g, Fiber: 3g, Sugar: 6g, Sodium: 95mg

Black-Eyed Peas with Greens

Prep Time: 10 minutes, Cook Time: 15 minutes, Serves: 2

1 tbsp. olive oil
½ yellow onion, diced
2 garlic cloves, minced
½ pound (227 g) dried black-eyed peas
2 cups chopped Swiss chard or kale
1 cup chicken stock
1½ tsps. red pepper flakes
½ tsp. dried thyme or 2 fresh thyme sprigs
½ tbsp. kosher salt
¼ tsp. freshly ground black pepper
1 tbsp. apple cider vinegar
1 to 2 tsps. hot sauce (optional)

1. Press the Sauté button on the Instant Pot and heat the oil until shimmering. 2. Add the onion and cook for 2 minutes until tender, stirring frequently. 3. Stir in the garlic and cook for about 1 minute until fragrant. 4. Add the peas, Swiss chard, chicken stock, red pepper flakes, thyme, salt, and pepper. Using a wooden spoon, scrape the bottom of the pot, then mix well. 5. Lock the lid. Select the Manual mode and set the cooking time for 10 minutes at High Pressure. 6. Once cooking is complete, do a natural pressure release for 10 minutes, then release any remaining pressure. Carefully open the lid. 7. Whisk in the vinegar and hot sauce, if desired. Taste and adjust the seasoning, if needed. Serve warm.

Calories: 304, Fat: 6g, Protein: 16g, Carbs: 47g, Fiber: 12g, Sugar: 4g, Sodium: 831mg

Beet and Grapefruit Salad

Prep Time: 5 minutes, Cook Time: 20 minutes, Serves: 8

6 medium fresh beets
1½ cups water
¼ cup extra-virgin olive oil
3 tbsps. lemon juice
2 tbsps. cider vinegar
2 tbsps. honey
¼ tsp. salt
¼ tsp. black pepper
2 large grapefruits, peeled and sectioned
2 small red onions, halved and sliced

1. Scrub the beets, trimming the tops to 1 inch. 2. Pour the water and insert the trivet in the Instant Pot. Place the beets on the trivet. 3. Set the lid in place. Select the Manual mode and set the cooking time for 20 minutes on High Pressure. When the timer goes off, do a quick pressure release. Carefully open the lid. 4. Whisk together the remaining ingredients, except for the grapefruits and onion. Pour over beets. Stir in the grapefruits and onion and serve.

Calories: 130, Fat: 6g, Protein: 2g, Carbs: 19g, Fiber: 3g, Sugar: 14g, Sodium: 120mg

Green Beans with Shallots

Prep Time: 5 minutes, Cook Time: 6 minutes, Serves: 4

¾ tsp. salt, divided
1 cup water
1 pound (454 g) green beans, trimmed
2 tbsps. olive oil
1 medium shallot, peeled and minced
½ tsp. black pepper

1. Add ½ tsp. of salt and the water to the Instant Pot and insert a steamer basket. Place green beans on top of the basket. Lock the lid. 2. Press the Steam button on the Instant Pot and set the cooking time for 0 minutes on High Pressure. 3. When the timer goes off, do a quick pressure release and then carefully open the lid. Remove the green beans and drain the cooking liquid. 4. Select the Sauté mode and add the oil to the pot. 5. Add the green beans and shallot and sauté for 6 minutes, or until the green beans are crisp-tender. 6. Sprinkle with the remaining ¼ tsp. of salt and pepper. 7. Transfer to a serving plate and serve.

Calories: 87, Fat: 6g, Protein: 1g, Carbs: 8g, Fiber: 3g, Sugar: 3g, Sodium: 376mg

Braised Kale

Prep Time: 5 minutes, Cook Time: 5 minutes, Serves: 4

1 large bunch kale
2 tbsps. extra-virgin olive oil
6 cloves garlic, thinly sliced crosswise
½ cup vegetable broth
¼ tsp. sea salt
Freshly ground black pepper, to taste

1. Remove and discard the middle stems from the kale and roughly chop the leafy parts. Rinse and drain the kale. 2. Press the Sauté button on the Instant Pot and heat the oil. Add the garlic and sauté for about 2 minutes until tender and golden. Transfer the garlic and oil to a small bowl and set aside. 3. Add the broth to the inner pot. Place the kale on top and sprinkle with salt and pepper. 4. Set the lid in place. Select the Manual mode and set the cooking time for 3 minutes on Low Pressure. When the timer goes off, do a quick pressure release. Carefully open the lid. 5. Return the garlic and oil to the pot, and toss to combine. 6. Serve immediately.

Calories: 85, Fat: 7g, Protein: 2g, Carbs: 1g, Fiber: 0g, Sugar: 0g, Sodium: 220mg

Smoky Carrots and Collard Greens

Prep Time: 10 minutes, Cook Time: 12 minutes, Serves: 4 to 6

1 tbsp. extra-virgin olive oil
1 yellow onion, diced
8 ounces (227 g) carrots, peeled and diced
2 bunches collard greens, stems discarded and leaves sliced into 1-inch ribbons
½ tsp. smoked paprika
½ tsp. fine sea salt, plus more as needed
¼ tsp. freshly ground black pepper
½ cup water
1 tbsp. tomato paste

1.Select the Sauté setting on the Instant Pot, add the oil, and heat for 1 minute. Add the onion and carrots and sauté for about 4 minutes, or until the onion begins to soften. Stir in the collards and sauté for about 2 minutes, or until wilted. Stir in the smoked paprika, salt, pepper, and water. Dollop the tomato paste on top, but do not stir it in.2.Set the lid in place. Select the Manual mode and set the cooking time for 5 minutes on High Pressure. When the timer goes off, do a quick pressure release. Carefully open the lid.3.Stir to incorporate the tomato paste. Taste and adjust the seasoning with salt, if needed.4.Spoon the collards into a serving bowl or onto serving plates. Serve warm.

Calories: 66, Fat: 3g, Protein: 2g, Carbs: 9g, Fiber: 4g, Sugar: 3g, Sodium: 334mg

Roasted Coconut Brussels Sprouts

Prep Time: 12 minutes, Cook Time: 30 minutes, Serves: 4

2 pounds (907 g) Brussels sprouts, trimmed and cut in half
2 tsps. coconut oil, melted
¼ cup unsweetened toasted shredded coconut

1.Preheat the oven to 400ºF (205ºC). Line a baking sheet with foil.2.In a large bowl, toss the Brussels sprouts with the melted coconut oil until the vegetables are well coated.3.Spread the Brussels sprouts on the prepared baking sheet in one layer and roast until they are tender and browned, about 20 to 30 minutes. 4.Serve topped with toasted coconut.

Calories: 117, Fat: 3g, Protein: 8g, Carbs: 21g, Fiber: 9g, Sugar: 5g, Sodium: 57mg

Green Broccolini Sauté

Prep Time: 8 minutes, Cook Time: 10 minutes, Serves: 4

3 tsps. olive oil
4 cups broccolini, chopped (about 3 bunches)
3 green onions, chopped
4 roasted garlic cloves, sliced or chopped
½ tsp. black pepper, freshly ground
¼ tsp. red pepper flakes, crushed
3 cups baby spinach
¼ cup fresh parsley, chopped
Zest and juice of 1 lemon

1.In a large skillet over medium heat, heat the oil and sauté the broccolini, green onions, and roasted garlic until the broccolini is bright green but still crisp, about 5 minutes.2.Add the black pepper and red pepper flakes and stir to combine.3.Add the spinach, parsley, and lemon zest and sauté until the spinach is wilted, about 3 minutes.4.Add the lemon juice to the skillet and stir.5.Serve immediately.

Calories: 81, Fat: 4g, Protein: 4g, Carbs: 8g, Fiber: 2g, Sugar: 3g, Sodium: 47mg

Braised Cabbage

Prep Time: 5 minutes, Cook Time: 7 to 8 minutes, Serves: 4

1 tbsp. olive oil
¼ cup minced shallots
¼ cup white wine
4 cups savoy cabbage
1 cup vegetable broth

1.Press the Sauté button on the Instant Pot and heat the oil. Add in the shallots and sauté for 3 minutes. Add the white wine and cook for 1 to 2 minutes, or until the wine reduces. Add the savoy cabbage and the vegetable broth to the pot.2.Lock the lid. Select the Manual mode and set the cooking time for 3 minutes on High Pressure. Once the timer goes off, perform a natural pressure release for 5 minutes, then release any remaining pressure. Carefully open the lid.3.Serve immediately.

Calories: 56, Fat: 3g, Protein: 1g, Carbs: 7g, Fiber: 2g, Sugar: 3g, Sodium: 260mg

Lemony Peas

Prep Time: 5 minutes, Cook Time: 2 minutes, Serves: 4

4 cups fresh peas, not in pods
1 cup vegetable broth
1 tbsp. coconut oil, melted
¼ cup chopped fresh mint
¼ cup chopped fresh parsley
1 tsp. lemon zest

1.Combine the peas and vegetable broth in the Instant Pot.2.Set the lid in place. Select the Manual mode and set the cooking time for 2 minutes on High Pressure. When the timer goes off, do a quick pressure release. Carefully open the lid.3.Drain off the excess liquid from the peas and place them in a bowl.4.Drizzle the peas with the melted coconut oil and toss to coat.5.Add the mint, parsley and lemon zest to the bowl and stir.6.Serve immediately.

Calories: 105, Fat: 3g, Protein: 4g, Carbs: 16g, Fiber: 5g, Sugar: 5g, Sodium: 211mg

Artichokes with Mayonnaise Dip

Prep Time: 10 minutes, Cook Time: 15 minutes, Serves: 4

2 large artichokes, rinsed
1 medium lemon, halved
¾ tsp. salt, divided
3 cloves garlic, crushed
1 cup water
For the Mayonnaise Dip:
3 tbsps. low-fat mayonnaise
⅛ tsp. black pepper
¼ tsp. chili powder

1.Cut off top ½ inch of each artichoke.
2.Slice one half of the lemon into wedges and set the other half aside.3.Add the lemon wedges, ½ tsp. of salt, garlic, and water to your Instant Pot.4.Put the trivet in the bottom of the pot and place the artichokes on top. Lock the lid. You may need to trim the artichoke stems to secure the lid.5.Press the Manual button on your Instant Pot and set the cooking time for 15 minutes at High Pressure.6.Once cooking is complete, do a quick pressure release. Carefully open the lid and remove the artichokes.7.Meanwhile, make the mayonnaise dip by stirring together the juice from the remaining ½ lemon, the remaining ¼ tsp. of salt, mayonnaise pepper, and chili powder in a small bowl.8.Cut the artichokes in half and serve alongside the mayonnaise dip.

Calories: 98, Fat: 3g, Protein: 2g, Carbs: 18g, Fiber: 7g, Sugar: 2g, Sodium: 586mg

Baked Parmesan Broccoli Fritters

Prep Time: 9 minutes, Cook Time: 25 minutes, Makes: 10 fritters

2 tbsps. extra-virgin olive oil	¼ cup grated low-fat Parmesan cheese
1 head broccoli, florets only	1 tsp. lemon zest
1 large egg, beaten	½ tsp. garlic powder
½ cup cassava or almond flour	1 tsp. sea salt
¼ cup finely diced yellow onion	

1. Preheat the oven to 400ºF (205ºC). Gently line a baking sheet with parchment paper. 2. In a food processor, add the broccoli florets and pulse until finely chopped. Then pour into a large bowl. 3. Place the onion, flour, egg, lemon zest, garlic powder, salt, and Parmesan, and mix well to form a dough. Form 8 patties and arrange on the prepared baking sheet. 4. Spray patties with olive oil and bake for about 25 to 30 minutes, flipping halfway through, until lightly browned on both sides. Enjoy!

Calories: 84, Fat: 4g, Protein: 4g, Carbs: 9g, Fiber: 2g, Sugar: 0g, Sodium: 303mg

Brussels Sprouts with Sesame Seeds

Prep Time: 5 minutes, Cook Time: 4 minutes, Serves: 4

25 Brussels sprouts, halved lengthwise	1 tbsp. balsamic vinegar
1 cup water	1 tsp. kosher salt
1 tbsp. extra-virgin olive oil	½ tsp. freshly ground black pepper
2 garlic cloves, finely chopped	1 tbsp. roasted sesame seeds

1. Place the Brussels sprouts in the steamer basket. Pour the water and insert the trivet in the Instant Pot. Place the basket on the trivet. 2. Set the lid in place. Select the Manual mode and set the cooking time for 1 minute on High Pressure. When the timer goes off, do a quick pressure release. Carefully open the lid. 3. Using tongs, carefully transfer the Brussels sprouts to a serving plate. Discard the water and wipe the inner pot dry. 4. Press the Sauté button on the Instant Pot and heat the oil. Add the garlic and sauté for 1 minute. Add the Brussels sprouts, vinegar, salt, and pepper, and sauté for 2 minutes. Sprinkle with the roasted sesame seeds and serve hot.

Calories: 66, Fat: 3g, Protein: 3g, Carbs: 10g, Fiber: 4g, Sugar: 2g, Sodium: 625mg

Zucchini Noodles with Lemon Artichoke Pesto

Prep Time: 26 minutes, Cook Time: 0 minutes, Serves: 4

1 cup artichoke hearts, chopped	¼ cup olive oil
½ cup packed fresh basil leaves	2 large zucchini, julienned
½ cup pecan halves, chopped	2 cups cherry tomatoes, halved
2 tsps. garlic, minced	Pinch of red pepper flakes, crushed
Zest and juice of 1 lemon	
Pinch of black pepper, freshly ground	

1. In a food processor or blender, add half the artichoke hearts with the basil, pecans, garlic, lemon zest, lemon juice, and black pepper. Pulse until very finely chopped. 2. Add the olive oil and pulse until blended. 3. In a large bowl, toss the zucchini "noodles" with the remaining artichoke hearts, cherry tomatoes, and red pepper flakes until well mixed. 4. Add the pesto by tbsps. until it reaches the desired flavor and texture. 5. Store any leftover pesto in a sealed container in the fridge for up to 2 weeks. 6. Serve immediately.

Calories: 259, Fat: 23g, Protein: 5g, Carbs: 14g, Fiber: 5g, Sugar: 5g, Sodium: 106mg

Spicy Green Beans

Prep Time: 5 minutes, Cook Time: 3 minutes, Serves: 4 to 6

1½ pounds (680 g) green beans, ends trimmed	2 tsps. garlic powder
¼ cup low-sodium soy sauce	1 tsp. onion powder
¼ cup vegetable or garlic broth	2 tbsps. chopped almonds (optional)
3 cloves garlic, minced	¼ tsp. crushed red pepper flakes (optional)
2 tbsps. sriracha	¼ tsp. cayenne pepper (optional)
2 tbsps. sesame oil	
1 tbsp. paprika	
1 tbsp. rice vinegar	

1. Stir together all the ingredients in the Instant Pot. 2. Lock the lid. Select the Manual mode and set the cooking time for 3 minutes at High Pressure. 3. Once cooking is complete, do a quick pressure release. Carefully open the lid. 4. Serve warm.

Calories: 90, Fat: 5g, Protein: 2g, Carbs: 10g, Fiber: 4g, Sugar: 3g, Sodium: 617mg

Quinoa with Brussels Sprouts and Avocado

Prep Time: 14 minutes, Cook Time: 6 hours, Serves: 6 to 8

2 cups quinoa, rinsed	4 cups vegetable broth
3 cups Brussels sprouts	1 onion, finely chopped
2 avocados, peeled and sliced	3 garlic cloves, minced
1 cup broken walnuts	2 tbsps. lemon juice
½ cup pomegranate seeds	1 tsp. dried marjoram leaves

1. Mix the quinoa, onion, garlic, vegetable broth, Brussels sprouts, marjoram, and lemon juice in a 6-quart slow cooker. Cover the slow cooker and cook on low for 5 to 6 hours, or until the quinoa is tender. 2. Place the avocados, pomegranate seeds, and walnuts on top, and serve.

Calories: 358, Fat: 17g, Protein: 10g, Carbs: 42g, Fiber: 8g, Sugar: 6g, Sodium: 83mg

Garlicky Broccoli

Prep Time: 5 minutes, Cook Time: 9 minutes, Serves: 4

3 tbsps. olive oil	½ tsp. salt
2 medium heads broccoli, cut into florets	½ tsp. black pepper
	4 cloves garlic, minced

1. Press the Sauté button on your Instant Pot. Add the oil and let heat for 1 minute. 2. Add the broccoli and sprinkle with the salt and pepper. Secure the lid and sauté for 4 minutes. 3. Stir in the garlic and lock the lid. Sauté for another 4 minutes. 4. Transfer to a serving bowl and serve hot.

Calories: 128, Fat: 10g, Protein: 3g, Carbs: 9g, Fiber: 4g, Sugar: 2g, Sodium: 304mg

Roasted Red Pepper and Dry Sherry

Prep Time: 25 minutes, Cook Time: 55 minutes, Serves: 2¾ cups

- 1 medium red onion, minced
- ½ cup (120 ml) low-sodium vegetable broth
- ½ cup (120 ml) no-salt-added tomato sauce
- 3 large red bell peppers
- 2 tbsps. extra-virgin olive oil, plus more for brushing peppers
- 3 cloves garlic, minced
- 2 tsps. dried thyme
- 1 tsp. dried cumin
- ½ tsp. dried rosemary
- 2 tbsps. tomato paste
- 2 tsps. dry sherry
- ½ tsp. salt
- 2 tbsps. chopped fresh sage

1. Preheat the broiler. 2. Cut the bell peppers in half lengthwise, seeded, and press open to flatten. Place the peppers skin side up under the broiler and cook until lightly charred, about 10 minutes. Remove the pepper halves, stacking one on top of the other inside of a small paper bag to create steam or place in a bowl and cover. Let rest for 10 minutes, then remove as much charred skin as possible. Cut into strips. 3. heat the 2 tbsps. olive oil in a large skillet over medium-high heat until it begins to shimmer. Stir in the pepper strips, onion, garlic, dried thyme, rosemary, and thyme and cook, stirring, until the peppers, onion, and garlic are tender and the herbs are fragrant, about 5 minutes. 4. Lower the heat to medium, pour in the vegetable broth and simmer until the mixture is reduced to a sauce, about 15 minutes. 5. Pour in the tomato sauce, tomato paste, and 1½ cups water, lower the heat, and cook, uncovered, for 25 minutes. 6. Transfer the sauce to a blender and process until smooth. Return the sauce to the skillet and bring to a very low simmer. Sprinkle with the sherry, salt, and sage. Serve warm.

Calories: 92, Total Fat: 5g, Saturated Fat: <1g, Total Carbs: 11g, Protein: 1g, Sodium: 238mg, Fiber: 3g, Sugar: 5g

Cannellini Mandarin Salsa

Prep Time: 10 minutes, Cook Time: 10 minutes, Serves: 4 cups

- 3 mandarins, finely diced
- ½ cup chopped fresh dill
- 1 Plum tomato, coarsely chopped
- 1 (15-oz./430 g) can cannellini beans, rinsed and drained
- ¼ cup finely minced red onion
- 2 cloves garlic, crushed
- ½ to 1 jalapeño pepper, seeded and diced
- 1 tsp. freshly ground black pepper
- Juice of 1 lime
- Dash of salt

1. Mix together the mandarins, cannellini beans, onion, garlic, tomato, jalapeño to taste, the dill, and lime juice in a medium bowl and toss to combine well. Cover and store in refrigerate for at least 10 minutes and up to one day to meld the flavors. 2. Store in an airtight container in the refrigerator for 5 to 7 days. 3. Taste the salsa before serving and sprinkle with pepper and salt to season.

Calories: 17, Total Fat: 0g, Saturated Fat: 0g, Total Carbs: 3g, Protein: 1g, Sodium: 3mg, Fiber: 1g, Sugar: 1g

CHAPTER 13

SMOOTHIE RECIPES

Vanilla Avocado Peach Smoothie ········· 82
Fruit Smoothie with Yogurt ················· 82
Green Smoothie with Pear ··················· 82
Quick Berry Banana Smoothie ············· 82
Quick Healthy Strawberry Yogurt Smoothie ···· 82
Fresh Green Strawberry Smoothie ········ 82
Apple and Banana Smoothie ················ 82
Spinach and Berries Smoothie ·············· 82
Healthy Green Smoothie Bowl ·············· 83
Quick Healthy Peaches and Greens Smoothie ·· 83
Healthy Green Avocado Smoothie ········· 83
Strawberry Cucumber Delight Smoothie ····· 83
Savory Melon Mélange Smoothie ·········· 83
Creamy Chocolate-Cherry Smoothie ······· 83
Healthy Peach Green Smoothie ············· 84
Banana Blueberry Smoothie ················· 84
Mint Chocolate Spinach Smoothie ········· 84
Fruit and Beet Smoothie ······················ 84
Carrot and Banana Smoothie Bowl ········ 84
Spinach and Banana Smoothie ·············· 84
Avocado Smoothie ····························· 84
Kale and Avocado Smoothie Bowl ········· 84
Strawberry and Banana Bowl ··············· 85
Summer Cucumber Ginger Smoothie ····· 85
Easy Strawberry Kiwi Smoothie ············ 85
Carrot and Banana Smoothie ················ 85
Green Smoothie with Berry and Banana ···· 85
Healthy Green Smoothie ····················· 85
Strawberry and Peach Smoothie ··········· 85
Savory Banana Almond Smoothie ········· 85
Healthy Green Smoothie for Diabetics ···· 86
Green Apple and Oat Bran Smoothie ····· 86

Vanilla Avocado Peach Smoothie

Prep Time: 15 minutes, Cook Time: 5 minutes, Serves: 2

1 cup (240 ml) nonfat plain or vanilla Greek yogurt
1 avocado, peeled and pitted
1½ tsps. stevia, granulated
1 tsp. pure vanilla extract
1 to 2 cups ice cubes
1½ cups peaches, frozen
1½ cups (360 ml) nonfat milk
1 tbsp. flaxseed, ground

1. Combine all ingredients in a blender. Purée until smooth. 2. Serve immediately.

Calories: 323, Total Fat: 15g, Saturated Fat: 2g, Total Carbs: 32g, Protein: 21g, Fiber: 8g, Sugar: 21g, Sodium: 142mg

Fruit Smoothie with Yogurt

Prep Time: 10 minutes, Cook Time: 5 minutes, Serves: 2

1 cup (240 ml) unsweetened almond milk
3 cups kale or spinach
1 small green apple
1 cup frozen peaches
¼ cup (60 ml) nonfat coconut yogurt
1 banana, peeled
1 orange, peeled

1. Put all ingredients in a blender in the order listed and blend thoroughly until smooth. 2. Serve.

Calories: 306, Fat: 2.27g, Carbs: 73g, Protein: 4.2g, Cholesterol: 0mg, Sodium: 104mg, Fiber: 8.1g

Green Smoothie with Pear

Prep Time: 10 minutes, Cook Time: 5 minutes, Serves: 2

1 cup chopped kale
¾ cup water
1 cup spinach
1 green apple, coarsely chopped
½ cup chopped unpeeled cucumber
1 tbsp. ground flaxseed
1 pear, coarsely chopped

1. In a blender, put the spinach, kale, and water. Start mix on low speed until the mixture begins to decompose, then turn to medium speed and stir until it is completely decomposed and smooth. 2. Place the cucumber, apple, pear, and flaxseed, and blend for 1 minute on medium to high until desired consistency is reached. Remove from the blender and enjoy.

Calories: 114, Fat: 2g, Protein: 3g, Carbs: 25g, Fiber: 5g, Sugar: 14g, Sodium: 32mg

Quick Berry Banana Smoothie

Prep Time: 15 minutes, Cook Time: 5 minutes, Serves: 2

1 tsp. almond extract
1 cup nonfat coconut yogurt
1 banana, cut into 4 pieces
1 cup fresh or frozen blueberries
1 cup unsweetened coconut milk

1. Prepare a blender and put the banana, blueberries, yogurt, milk and almond extract in it. 2. Start mixing at a high speed, about 1-2 minutes until the desired consistency is reached. Enjoy!

Calories: 216, Fat: 5.3g, Protein: 9.7g, Carbs: 34.9g, Fiber: 5g, Sugar: 16g, Sodium: 124mg

Quick Healthy Strawberry Yogurt Smoothie

Prep Time: 5 minutes, Cook Time: 1 minute, Serves: 1

1 cup frozen strawberries
½ frozen banana
½ cup unsweetened coconut milk
½ orange, peeled
1 cup nonfat coconut yogurt

1. In a large bowl, place the banana, orange, strawberries, milk, yogurt to a blender and process until the mixture smooth purée. 2. Remove from the blender to a bowl and enjoy immediately.

Calories: 305, Total Fat: 1g, Saturated Fat: 0g, Protein: 29g, Total Carbs: 52g, Fiber: 6g, Sugar: 37g, Sodium: 170mg

Fresh Green Strawberry Smoothie

Prep Time: 8 minutes, Cook Time: 0 minutes, Serves: 2

1½ cups unsweetened almond milk
2 cups packed baby spinach greens
1 cup frozen unsweetened strawberries
1 banana
1 cup ice

1. In a blender, combine the almond milk, spinach, strawberries, and banana. Purée until smooth. 2. Add the ice and blend until it reaches milkshake consistency. Pour into 2 glasses to serve.

Calories: 107, Fat: 2g, Protein: 2g, Carbs: 22g, Fiber: 5g, Sugar: 12g, Sodium: 159mg

Apple and Banana Smoothie

Prep Time: 10 minutes, Cook Time: 5 minutes, Serves: 2

1 cup (240 ml) nonfat milk
½ cup (120 ml) 100% apple juice
½ tsp. pure vanilla extract
½ tsp. stevia, granulated
1 to 2 cups ice cubes
2 tbsps. walnuts, chopped
1 small carrot, peeled and chopped
½ tsp. cinnamon, ground
2 tbsps. unsweetened coconut flakes
2 bananas, frozen

1. Place the apple juice, walnuts, milk, and coconut flakes in the blender. Set 5 minutes. 2. Add the frozen bananas, vanilla extract, cinnamon, stevia, carrot, and ice cubes to the pitcher. Purée until smooth. 3. Serve immediately.

Calories: 276, Total Fat: 8g, Saturated Fat: 4g, Total Carbs: 46g, Protein: 6g, Fiber: 6g, Sugar: 30g, Sodium: 72mg

Spinach and Berries Smoothie

Prep Time: 5 minutes, Cook Time: 0 minutes, Serves: 1

1 cup packed spinach leaves
¾ cup frozen blueberries
4 large fresh or frozen strawberries
½ large, ripe banana
¾ cup water (or more, as needed)
1 tbsp. ground flaxseed

1. In a blender, combine the spinach, blueberries, strawberries, banana, flaxseed, and water and blend until completely smooth and creamy. 2. Serve cold.

Calories: 184, Fat: 4g, Protein: 4g, Carbs: 38g, Fiber: 8g, Sugar: 21g, Sodium: 26mg

Healthy Green Smoothie Bowl

Prep Time: 10 minutes, Cook Time: 3 minutes, Serves: 2

1 green apple, thinly sliced, divided	1 cup unsweetened coconut milk
1 banana, cut into chunks	¼ cup unsweetened coconut flakes
1 pear, chopped	½ lemon, thinly sliced
1 cup chopped kale leaves	
1 cup baby spinach	

1. In a small dry skillet, toast the coconut flakes over medium heat for 2 to 3 minutes, or until lightly browned. Set side. 2. In a blender, well blend three-quarters of the apple slices, all the banana, pear, kale, spinach, and milk. Pour into a storage container. Store the smoothie, remaining apple slices, the lemon slices, and toasted coconut separately. 3. For each serving, pour half the smoothie into a bowl. Top with half the remaining apple slices, half the lemon slices, and coconut flakes.

Calories: 262, Total Fat: 6.5g, Carbs: 47g, Fiber: 7.5g, Protein: 8g, Sodium: 94mg

Quick Healthy Peaches and Greens Smoothie

Prep Time: 5 minutes, Cook Time: 1 minute, Serves: 1

½ cup nonfat or low-fat milk	1 cup frozen peaches (or fresh, pitted)
2 cups fresh spinach (or ⅓ cup frozen)	1 cup ice
½ cup plain nonfat or low-fat Greek yogurt	Optional: no-calorie sweetener of choice
½ tsp. vanilla extract	

1. In a large bowl, place the spinach, vanilla extract, peaches, milk, yogurt and ice to a blender and process until the mixture smooth purée. 2. Remove from the blender to a bowl and enjoy immediately.

Calories: 191, Total Fat: 0g, Saturated Fat: 0g, Protein: 18g, Total Carbs: 30g, Fiber: 3g, Sugar: 23g, Sodium: 157mg

Healthy Green Avocado Smoothie

Prep Time: 15 minutes, Cook Time: 10 minutes, Serves: 2

¾–1 cup water	1 tangerine, peeled and separated into segments
1 cup chopped kale	1 green apple, chopped
3–4 ice cubes	2 small kiwifruits, peeled and halved
1 small avocado, pitted, peeled, and chopped	

1. In a blender, put the kale and water. Stir on low speed until the kale starts to decompose, then increase to medium speed and stir for one minute until it is completely decomposed and smooth. Add the apple, kiwifruits, avocado, tangerine, ice cubes in the blender. 2. Mix on medium-high speed for about 1 minute until the desired consistency is reached. Remove from the blender and enjoy.

Calories: 271, Fat: 15g, Protein: 4g, Carbs: 39g, Fiber: 13g, Sugar: 10g, Sodium: 29mg

Strawberry Cucumber Delight Smoothie

Prep Time: 10 minutes, Cook Time: 5 minutes, Serves: 2

4 mint leaves	3–4 ice cubes
¾ cup water	1½ cups frozen strawberries
Juice of ½ large orange	
2 cups chopped unpeeled cucumber	

1. In a blender, add the strawberries, cucumber, orange, leaves, ice cubes, and water to mix. At first, stir at low speed. 2. When the contents begin to decompose, increase to medium speed and stir for about 1 minute until the desired consistency is reached. Remove the mixture from the blender and enjoy.

Calories: 61, Fat: 0.7g, Protein: 4g, Carbs: 14g, Fiber: 4g, Sugar: 9g, Sodium: 4mg

Savory Melon Mélange Smoothie

Prep Time: 15 minutes, Cook Time: 10 minutes, Serves: 2

2 cups spinach	½ cup frozen strawberries
½–¾ cup water	¾ cup chopped cantaloupe
¾ cup chopped honeydew melon	2 tbsps. flax seeds
	4 ice cubes

1. In a blender, add spinach and water. First, stir at low speed. When the spinach starts to decompose, increase to a medium speed, about 1 minute, until the mixture is completely decomposed and smooth. 2. Add the fruit, flax seeds, and ice cubes to the blender and mix on high speed for one minute until the mixture reaches the desired consistency. Enjoy!

Calories: 77, Fat: 2g, Protein: 3g, Carbs: 15g, Fiber: 3g, Sugar: 7g, Sodium: 29 mg

Creamy Chocolate-Cherry Smoothie

Prep Time: 5 minutes, Cook Time: 5 minutes, Serves: 1

For the Smoothie:	½ medium banana, sliced and frozen
½ cup (120 ml) unsweetened vanilla almond or cashew milk	3 to 4 ice cubes
1 tsp. vanilla extract	For Serving:
1 cup fresh baby spinach	¼ cup berries, such as blueberries, raspberries, or strawberries
1 tbsp. almond butter	
1 tbsp. unsweetened cocoa powder	½ small banana, sliced
½ cup (120 ml) nonfat plain Greek yogurt	1 tsp. sliced almonds
¾ cup frozen cherries	½ tbsp. cacao nibs

1. Combine the spinach, milk, vanilla, almond butter, yogurt, cocoa, cherries, banana, and ice in a high-powered blender. Blend until thick and creamy. 2. Pour the mixture into a bowl and top with the sliced banana, berries, almonds, and cacao nibs. Serve.

Calories: 412, Total Fat: 14g, Saturated Fat: 2g, Total Carbs: 61g, Protein: 20g, Sodium: 182mg, Fiber: 13g, Sugar: 35g

Healthy Peach Green Smoothie

Prep Time: 15 minutes, Cook Time: 5 minutes, Serves: 2

2 cups spinach	1 tbsp. coconut oil
½ cup frozen strawberries	1 small frozen banana, chopped
1½ cups frozen peach	
1 cup water	

1. In a blender, put the spinach and water. Start mix on low speed until the spinach begins to decompose, then turn on medium speed and stir until it is completely decomposed and smooth. 2. Add the fruit and coconut oil and start combine on medium-high speed for 1 minute until the desired consistency is reached. Remove from the blender and enjoy.

Calories: 178, Fat: 7g, Protein: 3g, Carbs: 30g, Fiber: 5g, Sugar: 8g, Sodium: 27mg

Banana Blueberry Smoothie

Prep Time: 5 minutes, Cook Time: 5 minutes, Serves: 1

1 cup blueberries, frozen	½ cup (120 ml) low-fat cow's or rice milk, unsweetened
½ cup silken tofu	
1 banana	

1. Put berries, banana, milk, and tofu in a blender. 2. Blend until smooth and serve immediately.

Calories: 133, Fat: 4.6g, Carbs: 18.8g, Protein: 1.8g, Cholesterol: 0mg, Sodium: 89mg, Fiber: 2g

Mint Chocolate Spinach Smoothie

Prep Time: 4 minutes, Cook Time: 0 minutes, Serves: 1

1 cup spinach leaves	1 cup crushed ice
½ very ripe banana	1 tbsp. cocoa powder
4 or 5 fresh mint leaves	3 tbsps. unsweetened almond milk

1. In a blender, mix the banana, ice, cocoa powder, almond milk, spinach and mint, and blend until completely smooth and creamy. 2. Serve right away.

Calories: 148, Fat: 2g, Protein: 3g, Carbs: 35g, Fiber: 6g, Sugar: 19g, Sodium: 59mg

Fruit and Beet Smoothie

Prep Time: 5 minutes, Cook Time: 5 minutes, Serves: 1

¾ cup (180 ml) unsweetened almond milk	½ cup sliced cooked beets
1 tbsp. hemp seeds	½ cup frozen strawberries
1 tsp. honey	½ navel orange, peeled, quartered, and frozen
½ tsp. vanilla extract	3 to 4 ice cubes
½ cup (120 ml) nonfat plain Greek yogurt	

1. Mix the almond milk and hemp seeds in a high-powered blender and blend on low for 20 to 30 seconds. 2. Add the yogurt, honey, vanilla, orange, strawberries, beets, and ice. Blend until creamy.

Calories: 251, Total Fat: 6g, Saturated Fat: <1g, Total Carbs: 32g, Protein: 17g, Sodium: 239mg, Fiber: 7g, Sugar: 18g

Carrot and Banana Smoothie Bowl

Prep Time: 7 minutes, Cook Time: 0 minutes, Serves: 1

For the Smoothie Bowl:	For the Topping:
1 frozen banana	2 Medjool dates, pitted and torn
½ cup carrot juice	¼ cup walnuts
½ cup ice	2 tbsps. unsweetened shredded coconut
2 Medjool dates, pitted	Ground cinnamon
¼ tsp. pure vanilla extract	
¼ tsp. ground cinnamon	

1. In a blender, add all the smoothie bowl ingredients in the order listed. Blend until smooth, scraping down the sides of the blender if needed. 2. Place the smoothie into a bowl and garnish with the topping. Serve right away.

Calories: 484, Fat: 17g, Protein: 7g, Carbs: 64g, Fiber: 9g, Sugar: 37g, Sodium: 111mg

Spinach and Banana Smoothie

Prep Time: 4 minutes, Cook Time: 0 minutes, Serves: 2

12 ounces (340 g) unsweetened vanilla almond milk	1 measure plant-based, vanilla protein powder
1 cup baby spinach	1 tbsp. peanut butter
1 banana, frozen	

1. Combine the milk, banana, protein powder, peanut butter, and spinach in a high-speed blender. 2. Blend until creamy. Enjoy.

Calories: 256, Fat: 8g, Protein: 16g, Carbs: 34g, Fiber: 5g, Sugar: 16g, Sodium: 123mg

Avocado Smoothie

Prep Time: 5 minutes, Cook Time: 5 minutes, Serves: 2

1 large avocado	2 tbsps. honey
1½ cups (360 ml) low-fat milk	

1. Put all ingredients in your blender and mix until smooth and creamy. Serve immediately.

Calories: 316, Fat: 18.36g, Carbs: 34.66g, Protein: 8.1g, Sodium: 94mg, Fiber: 6.8g

Kale and Avocado Smoothie Bowl

Prep Time: 9 minutes, Cook Time: 0 minutes, Serves: 1

For the Smoothie Bowl:	1 tbsp. agave
1 cup kale, chopped	For the Topping:
1 cup unsweetened almond milk	1 kiwi, peeled and sliced
½ frozen banana	½ banana
½ avocado	½ cup fresh raspberries
½ cup ice	1 tsp. chia seeds

1. In a blender, add all the smoothie bowl ingredients in the order listed. Blend until smooth, scraping down the sides of the blender if needed. 2. Place the smoothie into a bowl and garnish with the topping. Serve right away.

Calories: 399, Fat: 20g, Protein: 7g, Carbs: 58g, Fiber: 18g, Sugar: 22g, Sodium: 188mg

Strawberry and Banana Bowl

Prep Time: 10 minutes, Cook Time: 0 minutes, Serves: 1

For the Smoothie Bowl:
1 cup frozen strawberries
½ frozen banana
½ beet, peeled and chopped
½ cup unsweetened almond milk

For the Topping:
3 fresh strawberries, sliced
¼ cup fresh blueberries
1 tbsp. goji berries
1 tbsp. unsweetened coconut flakes

1. In a blender, add all the smoothie bowl ingredients in the order listed. Blend until smooth, scraping down the sides of the blender if needed. 2. Place the smoothie into a bowl and garnish with the topping. Serve right away.

Calories: 216, Fat: 4g, Protein: 4g, Carbs: 45g, Fiber: 10g, Sugar: 24g, Sodium: 138mg

Summer Cucumber Ginger Smoothie

Prep Time: 3 minutes, Cook Time: 0 minutes, Serves: 2

1 large English cucumber, washed and cut into chunks
1 tsp. fresh ginger, grated
1 cup water, plus more if necessary

Juice of ½ large lemon
¼ cup mint leaves
1 cup ice cubes

1. Combine the cucumber, ginger, water, lemon juice, and mint in a blender. Blend until smooth. 2. Add the ice and blend until smooth, adding more water if too thick. 3. Pour to bowls and serve.

Calories: 35, Fat: 1g, Protein: 1g, Carbs: 7g, Fiber: 2g, Sugar: 2g, Sodium: 10mg

Easy Strawberry Kiwi Smoothie

Prep Time: 5 minutes, Cook Time: 0, Serves: 2

1 cup fresh strawberries
2 kiwifruits, peeled and cut into quarters

1 cup nonfat coconut yogurt
1 cup unsweetened coconut milk

1. Add strawberries, kiwi, yogurt and milk to the blender. Blend on high until smooth. 2. Serve with fresh diced strawberries, kiwis, and a straw as desired.

Calories: 164, Protein: 9.22g, Fat: 4.52g, Carbs: 22.75g, Fiber: 7g, Sugar: 14g, Sodium: 167 mg

Carrot and Banana Smoothie

Prep Time: 5 minutes, Cook Time: 0 minutes, Serves: 2

1 frozen ripe banana
2 medium carrots, chopped
¾ cup unsweetened coconut milk, plus more if needed

1 (½ inch) piece ginger
1 tbsp. pure maple syrup
¼ tsp. ground turmeric
Ice (optional)

1. Combine the banana, carrots, ginger, turmeric, coconut milk, and maple syrup in a high-speed blender. Blend until smooth. If you'd like a thicker consistency, place some ice cubes and blend again. For a thinner consistency, pour in additional coconut milk. Enjoy!

Calories: 297, Fat: 20g, Protein: 3g, Carbs: 31g, Fiber: 5g, Sugar: 19g, Sodium: 58mg

Green Smoothie with Berry and Banana

Prep Time: 15 minutes, Cook Time: 5 minutes, Serves: 2

2 cups spinach
1 tbsp. almond butter
¾ cup frozen blackberries
1 cup water

1 small frozen banana, chopped
¾ cup frozen blueberries

1. In a blender, put the spinach and water. Start mix on low speed until the spinach begins to decompose, then turn on medium speed and stir until it is completely decomposed and smooth. 2. Put the blackberries, blueberries, banana, and almond butter, and start combine on medium-high speed for 1 minute until the desired consistency is reached. Remove from the blender and enjoy.

Calories: 159, Fat: 5g, Protein: 4g, Carbs: 29g, Fiber: 7g, Sugar: 13g, Sodium: 30mg

Healthy Green Smoothie

Prep Time: 5 minutes, Cook Time: 0 minutes, Serves: 1

2 cups baby spinach
½ cucumber, chopped
½ apple, chopped

¼ avocado, chopped
½ lemon, squeezed
1 cup water

1. Combine the spinach, avocado, cucumber, lemon, apple, and water in a high-speed blender. Blend until smooth. 2. Enjoy immediately or refrigerate for up to several hours.

Calories: 180, Fat: 8g, Protein: 5g, Carbs: 28g, Fiber: 9g, Sugar: 12g, Sodium: 53mg

Strawberry and Peach Smoothie

Prep Time: 6 minutes, Cook Time: 0 minutes, Serves: 1

10 large strawberries, hulled
1 cup unsweetened almond milk
½ peach, frozen

2 tbsps. oat bran
1 tbsp. raw honey

1. Combine the strawberries, peach, almond milk, oat bran, and honey in a high-speed blender. 2. Blend until smooth. 3. Enjoy right away or refrigerate for up to several hours.

Calories: 271, Fat: 4g, Protein: 5g, Carbs: 62g, Fiber: 8g, Sugar: 38g, Sodium: 154mg

Savory Banana Almond Smoothie

Prep Time: 10 minutes, Cook Time: 5 minutes, Serves: 1

1 tbsp. unsalted almond butter
3–4 ice cubes
⅛ tsp. vanilla extract
1 cup unsweetened almond milk

⅛ tsp. ground cinnamon
1 tbsp. wheat germ
1 large banana

1. In a blender, put the almond milk, almond butter, banana, wheat germ, vanilla extract, ice cubes, and ground cinnamon. 2. Start mix on low speed until the mixture begins to decompose, then turn on medium speed and stir for 1 minute until it is completely decomposed and smooth. Remove from the blender and enjoy.

Calories: 338, Fat: 13g, Protein: 10g, Carbs: 52g, Fiber: 8g, Sugar: 25g, Sodium: 183mg

Healthy Green Smoothie for Diabetics

Prep Time: 15 minutes, Cook Time: 5 minutes, Serves: 2

¾ cup water
2 cups spinach
1 tbsp. ground flaxseeds
1 large frozen banana, chopped
1 tbsp. almond butter or peanut butter, optional
2 large kale leaves, chopped (about 1½ cups)
½ cup frozen peach
½ cup frozen berries

1. In a blender, put the spinach, kale, and water. Start mixing on low speed until the mixture begins to decompose, then turn to medium speed and stir until it is completely decomposed and smooth. 2. Place the fruit, flaxseeds, and nut butter (if using), and blend on medium to high until desired consistency is reached. Remove from the blender and enjoy.

Calories: 157, Fat: 2g, Protein: 5g, Carbs: 35g, Fiber: 7g, Sugar: 16g, Sodium: 48mg

Green Apple and Oat Bran Smoothie

Prep Time: 5 minutes, Cook Time: 5 minutes, Serves: 1

¾ cup (180 ml) unsweetened vanilla almond or cashew milk
2 tbsps. oat bran
¼ tsp. apple pie spice or ground cinnamon
½ tsp. vanilla extract
1 cup baby spinach or ⅓ cup frozen
½ cup (120 ml) nonfat plain Greek yogurt
1 tbsp. avocado
½ medium banana, sliced and frozen
½ cup green apple, unpeeled, chopped and frozen
¼ cup cooked or canned white beans, rinsed and drained
½ cup ice

1. Mix the milk, oat bran, vanilla, spinach, apple pie spice, yogurt, banana, apple, beans, avocado, and ice in a high-powered blender. Blend until smooth.

Calories: 319, Total Fat: 5g, Saturated Fat: <1g, Total Carbs: 50g, Protein: 21g, Sodium: 226mg, Fiber: 10g, Sugar: 19g

CHAPTER 14　SNACK AND DESSERT RECIPES

Chickpea Tortillas ········· 88	Brown Rice Pudding ········· 90
Roasted Cherry Tomato with Parmesan ········· 88	Chia and Raspberry Pudding ········· 90
Roasted Za'atar Edamame ········· 88	Date and Almond Balls with Seeds ········· 90
Spicy Roasted Maple Nuts ········· 88	Peanut Butter Pie ········· 90
Buffalo Bites ········· 88	Orange and Peach Ambrosia ········· 90
Roasted Chickpeas with Herbs ········· 88	Mini Peppers Stuffed with Black Bean ········· 91
Roasted Harissa Cucumber ········· 88	Pita Pizza with Feta and Cucumber ········· 91
Peach Bruschetta with Tarragon ········· 89	Roasted Asparagus with Apple Cider ········· 91
Spicy Nuts ········· 89	Coconut Yogurt and Pistachio Stuffed Peaches ········· 91
Red Bean with Pine Nuts ········· 89	Peach, Banana and Almond Pancakes ········· 91
Almond Cheesecake Bites ········· 89	Crispy Apple Chips ········· 91
Almond Flour Crackers ········· 89	Strawberry Sorbet ········· 91
Easy Banana Mug Cake ········· 89	Apple Cinnamon Chimichanga ········· 92
Old-Fashioned Cherry French Toast ········· 89	Crispy Apple and Pecan Bake ········· 92
Toffee Apple Mini Pies ········· 90	

Chickpea Tortillas

Prep Time: 5 minutes, Cook Time: 10 minutes, Serves: 4

1 cup chickpea flour	¼ tsp. salt
1 cup water	Nonstick cooking spray

1. In a large bowl, whisk all together until no lumps remain. 2. Spray a skillet with cooking spray and place over medium-high heat. 3. Pour batter in, ¼ cup at a time, and tilt pan to spread thinly. 4. Cook until golden brown on each side, about 2 minutes per side. 5. Use for taco shells, enchiladas, quesadillas or whatever you desire.

Calories: 90, Fat: 2g, Protein: 5.1g, Carbs: 13.1g, Fiber: 3g, Sugar: 3g, Sodium: 161mg

Roasted Cherry Tomato with Parmesan

Prep Time: 15 minutes, Cook Time: 30 minutes, Serves: 4

2 pints (about 20 oz./570 g) cherry tomatoes	1 tsp. rosemary
8 oz. (230 g) fresh, unsalted parmesan, cut into bite-size slices	5 garlic cloves, smashed
	2 tbsps. extra-virgin olive oil
Loaf of crusty whole-wheat bread for serving	½ tsp. kosher salt
	¼ cup dill, chopped

1. Preheat the oven to 350°F(180ºC). Line a baking sheet with foil. 2. Put the tomatoes, rosemary, garlic, olive oil, and salt into a large bowl and toss to combine well. spread on the prepared baking sheet evenly. Roast for 30 minutes, or until the tomatoes are bursting and juicy. 3. Place the mozzarella on a platter or in a bowl. Pour all the tomato mixture, including the juices, over the parmesan. Garnish with the dill. 4. Serve with crusty bread.

Calories: 250, Total Fat: 17g, Saturated Fat: 7g, Total Carbs: 9g, Protein: 17g, Sodium: 157mg, Fiber: 2g, Sugar: 4g

Roasted Za'atar Edamame

Prep Time: 5 minutes, Cook Time: 60 minutes, Serves: 8

3 tbsps. za'atar	4 cups cooked edamame, or 2 (15-oz./425 g) cans, drained and rinsed
2 tbsps. extra-virgin olive oil	
½ tsp. kosher salt	
¼ tsp. freshly ground black pepper	

1. Preheat the oven to 400°F(205ºC). Line a baking sheet with foil. 2. Mix together the za'atar, olive oil, salt, and black pepper in a large bowl. Stir in the chickpeas and toss to combine well. 3. Spread the edamame evenly on the prepared baking sheet. Bake for 45 to 60 minutes, or until golden brown and crispy. Let sit to cool and store in an airtight container at room temperature for up to 1 week.

Calories: 150, Total Fat: 6g, Saturated Fat: 1g, Total Carbs: 17g, Protein: 6g, Sodium: 230mg, Fiber 6g, Sugar: 3g

Spicy Roasted Maple Nuts

Prep Time: 5 minutes, Cook Time: 10 minutes, Serves: 2

1 tsp. extra-virgin olive oil	½ tsp. pure maple syrup
1 tsp. ground sumac	¼ tsp. kosher salt
2 cups raw walnuts or pecans (or a mix of nuts)	¼ tsp. ground ginger
	2 to 4 rosemary sprigs

1. Preheat the oven to 350°F(177ºC). Line a baking sheet with parchment paper or foil. 2. In a large bowl, combine the nuts, olive oil, sumac, maple syrup, salt, and ginger, mix together. Spread in a single layer on the prepared baking sheet. Add the rosemary. Roast for 8 to 10 minutes, or until golden and fragrant. 3. Remove the rosemary leaves from the stems and place in a serving bowl. 4. Add the nuts and toss to combine before serving.

Calories: 175, Total Fat: 18g, Saturated Fat: 2g, Sodium: 35mg, Total Carbs: 4g, Fiber: 2g, Sugar: 1g, Protein: 3g

Buffalo Bites

Prep Time: 5 minutes, Cook Time: 10 minutes, Serves: 4

1 egg	½ cup hot sauce
½ head of cauliflower, separated into florets	½ tsp. salt
	½ tsp. garlic powder
1 cup panko bread crumbs	Black pepper
1 cup low-fat ranch dressing	Nonstick cooking spray

1. Heat oven to 400°F (200°C). Spray a baking sheet with cooking spray. 2. Place the egg in a medium bowl and mix in the salt, pepper and garlic. Place the panko crumbs into a small bowl. 3. Dip the florets first in the egg then into the panko crumbs. Place in a single layer on prepared pan. 4. Bake for 8-10 minutes, stirring halfway through, until cauliflower is golden brown and crisp on the outside. 5. In a small bowl stir the dressing and hot sauce together. Use for dipping.

Calories: 132, Total Carbs: 15g, Net Carbs: 14g, Protein: 6g, Fat: 5g, Sugar: 4g, Fiber: 1g

Roasted Chickpeas with Herbs

Prep Time: 5 minutes, Cook Time: 30 minutes, Serves: 8

2 tbsps. olive oil	Two (15-ounce, 425 g) cans low-salt chickpeas, drained and rinsed
1 tsp. cumin	
	1 tsp. dried thyme

1. Preheat oven to 400°F. Mix chickpeas, cumin, olive oil and thyme in a medium bowl. Toss to combine. 2. Spread chickpeas in a single layer on a jelly roll pan. Roast for 30 minutes, stir. 3. Chickpeas are done when crisp outside and creamy inside. Serve immediately.

Calories: 165, Fat: 5.5g, Carbs: 23g, Protein: 7g, Cholesterol: 0mg, Sodium: 6mg, Fiber: 6g

Roasted Harissa Cucumber

Prep Time: 10 minutes, Cook Time: 15 minutes, Serves: 4

1 pound (450 g) cucumber, peeled and sliced into 1-inch-thick rounds	2 tbsps. harissa
	1 tsp. nutmeg
	1 tsp. ground rosemary
½ cup fresh coriander, chopped	½ tsp. kosher salt
2 tbsps. extra-virgin olive oil	

1. Preheat the oven to 450°F (235ºC). Line a baking sheet with foil. 2. Mix together the cucumber, olive oil, harissa, nutmeg, rosemary, and salt in a large bowl. Spread evenly on the baking sheet. Roast for 15 minutes. Remove from the oven, add the coriander, and toss to combine well.

Calories: 120, Total Fat: 8g, Saturated Fat: 1g, Total Carbs: 13g, Protein: 1g, Sodium: 255mg, Fiber: 4g, Sugar: 7g

Peach Bruschetta with Tarragon

Prep Time: 15 minutes, Cook Time: 20 minutes, Serves: 4

8 oz. (230 g) assorted peaches, halved
⅓ cup fresh tarragon, chopped
¼ cup low-fat feta cheese
4 slices whole-wheat bread, toasted
1 tsp. lime juice
1 tbsp. extra-virgin olive oil
¼ tsp. kosher salt
⅛ tsp. freshly ground black pepper

1. Mix together the peaches, tarragon, lime juice olive oil, salt, and black pepper in a medium bowl and toss to combine well. 2. Sprinkle 1 tbsp. of feta cheese onto each slice of toast. Spoon one-quarter of the peach mixture onto each bruschetta.

Calories: 100, Total Fat: 6g, Saturated Fat: 1g, Total Carbs: 10g, Protein: 4g, Sodium: 135mg, Fiber: 2g, Sugar: 2g

Spicy Nuts

Prep Time: 5 minutes, Cook Time: 4 hours, Serves: 6

2 tbsps. honey
1 tbsp. olive oil
1 tsp. ground cinnamon
½ tsp. ground ginger
¼ tsp. ground nutmeg
Nonstick cooking spray
½ tsp. sea salt
⅛ tsp. cayenne pepper
Zest of 1 orange
1 cup unsalted raw pecans (or other raw nuts of your choice)

1. Spray the jar of your slow cooker with nonstick cooking spray. 2. Whisk together the honey, olive oil, cinnamon, orange zest, ginger, nutmeg, sea salt, and cayenne in a small bowl. 3. Add the nuts to the slow cooker. Pour the spice mixture over the top. 4. Cover and cook on low for 4 hours. 5. Turn off the slow cooker. Uncover and cool down the nuts for 2 hours, stirring occasionally to keep the nuts coated.

Calories: 125, Total Fat: 11g, Saturated Fat: 1g, Carbs: 8g, Protein: 1g, Fiber: 2g, Sodium: 195mg

Red Bean with Pine Nuts

Prep Time: 10 minutes, Cook Time: 20 minutes, Serves: 4

1 (14.5-oz./410g) can no-salt-added diced onion
1 (14.5-oz./410g) can low-sodium red beans, drained and rinsed
½ cup roasted unsalted pine nuts
1 6-inch multigrain pita, torn into small pieces
2 red bell peppers, or 1 (12-oz./570 g) jar roasted sweet red peppers in water, drained
3 garlic cloves, mince
1 tsp. chili powder
1 tbsp. fresh dill, chopped
1 tsp. sweet or smoked paprika
1 tsp. kosher salt
¼ tsp. ground black pepper
¼ cup (60 ml) extra-virgin olive oil
2 tbsps. brandy
2 tbsps. ginger

1. Add the garlic in a blender and puree until finely minced. Scrape down the sides of the bowl and pour in pine nuts, pita, and chili powder, and puree until minced. Scrape down the sides of the bowl and add the bell peppers, onion, beans, dill, paprika, salt, and black pepper. Process until smooth. 2. With the blender running, add the olive oil, ginger and brandy, and process until smooth.

Calories: 180, Total Fat: 10g, Saturated Fat: 1g, Total Carbs: 20g, Protein: 6g, Sodium: 285mg, Fiber: 4g, Sugar: 3g

Almond Cheesecake Bites

Prep Time: 5 minutes, Chill time: 30 minutes, Serves: 6

½ cup reduced-fat cream cheese, soft
½ cup almonds, ground fine
¼ cup almond butter
2 drops liquid stevia

1. In a large bowl, beat cream cheese, almond butter and stevia on high speed until mixture is smooth and creamy. Cover and chill 30 minutes. 2. Use your hands to shape the mixture into 12 balls. 3. Place the ground almonds in a shallow plate. Roll the balls in the nuts completely covering all sides. Serve immediately.

Calories: 68, Total Carbs: 3g, Net Carbs: 2 Protein 5g, Fat: 5g, Sugar: 0g, Fiber: 1g

Almond Flour Crackers

Prep Time: 5 minutes, Cook Time: 15 minutes, Serves: 8

½ cup coconut oil, melted
1½ cups almond flour
¼ cup Stevia

1. Heat oven to 350ºF (177ºC). Line a cookie sheet with parchment paper. 2. In a mixing bowl, combine all ingredients and mix well. 3. Spread dough onto prepared cookie sheet, ¼-inch thick. Use a paring knife to score into 24 crackers. 4. Bake for 10-15 minutes or until golden brown. 5. Separate and store in air-tight container.

Calories: 281, Total Carbs: 16g, Net Carbs: 14g, Protein: 4g, Fat: 23g, Sugar: 13g, Fiber: 2g

Easy Banana Mug Cake

Prep Time: 10 minutes, Cook Time: 1 minutes, Serves: 1

½ ripe banana, mashed
3 tbsps. egg white
1 tsp. oat flour
½ tbsp. vanilla protein powder
1 tsp. rolled oats
1 tsp. cocoa powder
½ tsp. baking powder
2 tbsps. stevia
1 tsp. olive oil
2 tsps. chopped walnuts

1. Whisk together the banana and egg whites in a bowl. 2. Add the flour, vanilla protein powder, rolled oats, cocoa powder, baking powder, and stevia to the bowl. Stir to mix well. 3. Grease a microwave-safe mug with olive oil. 4. Pour the mixture in the bowl, then scatter with chopped walnuts. 5. Microwave them for 1 minutes or until puffed. 6. Serve immediately.

Calories: 211, Fat: 12.0g, Protein: 11.3g, Carbs: 46.7g, Fiber: 2.8g, Sugar: 6.6g, Sodium: 97mg

Old-Fashioned Cherry French Toast

Prep Time: 10 minutes, Cook Time: 40 minutes, Serves: 2

1 cup nonfat milk
1 egg
1 pint fresh or frozen cherries
1 cup water, divided
1 tbsp. cornstarch
1 tbsp. maple syrup
1 tsp. almond extract
½ cup nonfat yogurt
3 slices whole grain bread
Nutmeg

1. Combine the cherries with ½ cup water in a non-stick saucepan. Heat over medium-high heat and bring to a gentle boil. Mix the remaining ½ cup water with the cornstarch in a bowl,

CHAPTER 14 SNACK AND DESSERT RECIPES

then stir it into the cherries. Let it simmer until thickened and remove from heat. Stir in the maple syrup and almond extract and set aside.2.Preheat oven to 375ºF(190ºC).3.Whisk the milk and egg together until thoroughly mixed and then whisk in the yogurt.4.Lightly coat a glass baking dish with canola oil spray and then spread the cherry mixture evenly in the dish. Pour the milk mixture into a shallow pan (or a pie pan), cut the bread slices in half and soak them in the milk mixture. Arrange them on top of the cherry mixture in the baking dish and sprinkle lightly with nutmeg.5.Bake for 30–40 minutes or until the toast slices are golden brown on top.6.Transfer the slices with a spatula onto a plate and serve with the cherry mixture on the top.

Calories: 322, Protein: 17.29g, Fat: 8.22g, Carbs: 44.4g, Fiber: 3g, Sugar: 14g, Sodium: 375mg

Toffee Apple Mini Pies

Prep Time: 20 minutes, Cook Time: 25 minutes, Serves: 12

2 (9-inch) pie crusts, soft	1½ tsps. fresh lemon juice
2 cups Gala apples, diced fine	2 tbsps. toffee bits
1 egg, beaten	1 tbsp. Splenda
1 tbsp. almond butter, cut in 12 cubes	½ tsp. cinnamon
	Nonstick cooking spray

1.Heat oven to 375ºF (190ºC). Spray a cookie sheet with cooking spray.2.In a medium bowl, stir together apples, toffee, Splenda, lemon juice, and cinnamon.3.Roll pie crusts, one at a time, out on a lightly floured surface. Use a 3-inch round cookie cutter to cut 12 circles from each crust. Place 12 on prepared pan.4.Brush the dough with half egg. Spoon 1 tbsp. of the apple mixture on each round, leaving ½- inch edge. Top with pat of almond butter. Place second dough round on top and seal edges closed with a fork. Brush with remaining egg.5.Bake for 25 minutes, or until golden brown. Serve warm.

Calories: 154, Total Carbs: 17g, Net Carbs: 16g, Protein: 1g, Fat: 9g, Sugar: 6g, Fiber: 1g

Brown Rice Pudding

Prep Time: 5 minutes, Cook Time: 35 minutes, Serves: 6

2 cups short-grain brown rice	more for serving
6 cups fat-free milk	¼ tsp. orange extract
1 tsp. ground nutmeg, plus more for serving	Juice of 2 oranges (about ¾ cup)
1 tsp. ground cinnamon, plus	½ cup erythritol or other brown sugar replacement

1.In an electric pressure cooker, stir the rice, milk, nutmeg, cinnamon, orange extract, orange juice, and erythritol together.2.Close and lock the lid, and set the pressure valve to sealing.3.Select the Manual/Pressure Cook setting, and cook for 35 minutes.4.Once cooking is complete, quick-release the pressure. Carefully remove the lid.5.Stir well and spoon into serving dishes. Enjoy with an additional sprinkle of nutmeg and cinnamon.

Calories: 321, Fat: 2.1g, Protein: 12.9g, Carbs: 60.9g, Fiber: 2.1g, Sugar: 15.1g, Sodium: 131mg

Chia and Raspberry Pudding

Prep Time: 1 hours, Cook Time: 0 minutes, Serves: 4

1 cup unsweetened vanilla almond milk	1½ tsps. lemon juice
2 cups plus ½ cup raspberries, divided	½ tsp. lemon zest
¼ cup chia seeds	1 tbsp. honey

1.Stir together the almond milk, 2 cups of raspberries, chia seeds, lemon juice, lemon zest, and honey in a small bowl.2.Transfer the bowl to the fridge to thicken for at least 1 hour, or until a pudding-like texture is achieved.3.When the pudding is ready, give it a good stir. Scatter with the remaining ½ cup raspberries and serve immediately.

Calories: 122, Fat: 5.2g, Protein: 3.1g, Carbs: 17.9g, Fiber: 9g, Sugar: 6.8g, Sodium: 51mg

Date and Almond Balls with Seeds

Prep Time: 15 minutes, Cook Time: 0 minutes, Serves: 36 Balls

1 pound (454 g) pitted dates	1 tsp. ground cardamom
½ pound (227 g) blanched almonds	1 tsp. vanilla extract
¼ cup water	½ tsp. ground cinnamon
¼ cup coconut butter, at room temperature	2 tbsps. ground flaxseed
	1 cup toasted sesame seeds

1.In a food processor, add the pitted dates, almonds, water, butter, cardamon, vanilla, and cinnamon, and pulse until the mixture has broken down into a smooth paste.2.Scoop out the paste and form into 36 equal-sized balls with your hands.3.Spread out the flaxseed and sesame seeds on a baking sheet. Roll the balls in the seed mixture until they are evenly coated on all sides.4.Serve immediately or store in an airtight container in the fridge for 2 days.

Calories: 113, Fat: 7.1g, Protein: 2.9g, Carbs: 12g, Fiber: 2g, Sugar: 7.8g, Sodium: 10mg

Peanut Butter Pie

Prep Time: 10 minutes, Chill time: 4 hours, Serves: 8

1½ cups skim milk	1 (1½ oz.) pkg. sugar-free peanut butter cups, chopped
1½ cups frozen fat-free whipped topping, thawed and divided	1 (9-inch) reduced-fat graham cracker pie crust
1 small pkg. sugar-free instant vanilla pudding mix	⅓ cup reduced-fat peanut butter
	½ tsp. vanilla

1.In a large bowl, whisk together milk and pudding mix until it thickens. Whisk in peanut butter, vanilla, and 1 cup whip cream. Fold in peanut butter cups.2.Pour into pie crust and spread remaining whip cream over top. Cover and chill at least 4 hours before serving.

Calories: 191, Total Carbs: 27g, Protein: 4g, Fat: 6g, Sugar: 6g, Fiber: 0g

Orange and Peach Ambrosia

Prep Time: 10 minutes, Cook Time: 0 minutes, Serves: 8

3 oranges, peeled, sectioned, and quartered	1 cup shredded, unsweetened coconut
2 (4-ounce / 113-g) cups diced peaches in water, drained	1 (8-ounce / 227-g) container fat-free crème fraîche

1.In a large mixing bowl, combine the oranges, peaches, coconut, and crème fraîche. Gently toss until well mixed. Cover and refrigerate overnight.

Calories: 113, Fat: 5.1g, Protein: 2.1g, Carbs: 12.1g, Fiber: 2.9g, Sugar: 8.1g, Sodium: 8mg

Mini Peppers Stuffed with Black Bean

Prep Time: 15 minutes, Cook Time: 20 minutes, Serves: 8 (4 pepper halves)

1 (16-oz./454 g) bag sweet mini peppers (about 16 mini peppers)
1 (15-oz./425 g) can black beans, rinsed and drained
½ cup part-skim pecorino cheese
2 tsps. extra-virgin olive oil
1 tsp. dried thyme
1 tsp. mint
¼ tsp. freshly ground black pepper
¼ tsp. salt

1. Cut the stems off the peppers and halve the peppers lengthwise and use a soup spoon and scrape the seeds off. Set aside. 2. Mix the black beans, pecorino, olive oil, thyme, onion powder, black pepper, and salt in a blender and puree 4 or 5 times. The mixture should still have some texture to it. 3. Stuff each pepper half with about 2 tbsps. of the mixture. 4. Serve immediately or store in an airtight container and refrigerate for up to 3 days.

Calories: 93, Total Fat: 3 g, Saturated Fat: <1 g, Total Carbs: 13g, Protein: 5g, Sodium: 113mg, Fiber: 3g, Sugar: 4g

Pita Pizza with Feta and Cucumber

Prep Time: 15 minutes, Cook Time: 10 minutes, Serves: 4

4 (6-inch) whole-wheat pitas
1 tbsp. extra-virgin olive oil
½ cup hummus (store-bought or Roasted Red Pepper Hummus)
½ bell pepper, sliced
½ cucumber, sliced
¼ cup dates, halved and pitted
¼ cup crumbled low-fat feta cheese
¼ tsp. red pepper flakes
¼ cup fresh coriander, chopped

1. Preheat the broiler to low. Line a baking sheet with foil. 2. Spread the pitas on the prepared baking sheet and spritz both sides with the olive oil. Broil 1 to 2 minutes per side until just golden brown. 3. 3. Top each pita with 2 tbsps. hummus. Spread bell pepper, cucumber, dates, feta cheese, and red pepper flakes over the pitas. Broil again until the cheese softens and starts to get golden brown, 4 to 6 minutes, being careful not to burn the pitas. 4. Remove from broiler and top with the coriander.

Calories: 185, Total Fat: 11g, Saturated Fat: 2g, Total Carbs: 17g, Protein: 5g, Sodium: 285mg, Fiber: 3g, Sugar: 3g

Roasted Asparagus with Apple Cider

Prep Time: 5 minutes, Cook Time: 25 minutes, Serves: 4

1 cup asparagus
2 tbsps. apple cider
1 tbsp. extra-virgin olive oil
5 garlic cloves, peeled
1 tsp. cinnamon
1 tsp. chives

1. Preheat the oven to 400°F(205°C). Line the baking sheet with foil. 2. Mix together the asparagus, apple cider, olive oil, and garlic in a medium bowl and toss to combine well. Spread evenly on the prepared baking sheet. Sprinkle with cinnamon. Roast for 25 minutes, tossing halfway through. 3. Place in a serving bowl and sprinkle with chives, and serve.

Calories: 100, Total Fat: 9g, Saturated Fat: 1g, Total Carbs: 4g, Protein: 0g, Sodium: 260mg, Fiber: 0g, Sugar: 0g

Coconut Yogurt and Pistachio Stuffed Peaches

Prep Time: 5 minutes, Cook Time: 10 minutes, Serves: 4

2 peaches, halved and pitted
1 tsp. pure vanilla extract
½ cup nonfat coconut yogurt
2 tbsps. unsalted pistachios, shelled and broken into pieces
¼ cup unsweetened dried coconut flakes

1. Preheat the broiler to high. 2. Place the peach halves on a baking sheet, cut side down, and broil for 7 minutes or until soft and lightly browned. 3. Meanwhile, combine the vanilla and yogurt in a bowl. 4. Divide the mixture among the the pits of peach halves, then scatter the pistachios and coconut flakes on top before serving.

Calories: 103, Fat: 4.9g, Protein: 5.1g, Carbs: 10.8g, Fiber: 2.1g, sugars: 7.8g, Sodium: 10mg

Peach, Banana and Almond Pancakes

Prep Time: 15 minutes, Cook Time: 15 minutes, Serves: 7

2 cups peaches, chopped
4 ripe bananas, peeled
2 medium egg whites
1 medium egg
¼ tsp. almond extract
¾ cup almond meal

1. Preheat the oven to 400ºF (205ºC). 2. Put all the ingredients in a food processor, and pulse until mix well and it has a thick consistency. 3. Pour the mixture in a baking dish lined with parchment paper. 4. Bake in the preheated oven for 10 minutes or until a toothpick inserted in the center of the pancakes comes out clean. 5. Remove the pancakes from the oven and slice to serve.

Calories: 166, Fat: 6.9g, Protein: 6.1g, Carbs: 21.8g, Fiber: 4.2g, sugars: 11.8g, Sodium: 22mg

Crispy Apple Chips

Prep Time: 10 minutes, Cook Time: 2 hours, Serves: 4

2 medium apples, sliced
1 tsp. ground cinnamon

1. Preheat the oven to 200ºF (93ºC). Line a baking sheet with parchment paper. 2. Arrange the apple slices on the prepared baking sheet, then sprinkle with cinnamon. 3. Bake in the preheated oven for 2 hours or until crispy. Flip the apple chips halfway through the cooking time. 4. Allow to cool for 10 minutes and serve warm.

Calories: 50, Fat: 0g, Protein: 0g, Carbs: 13g, Fiber: 2g, Sugar: 9g, Sodium: 0mg

Strawberry Sorbet

Prep Time: 5 minutes, Chill time: 4 hours, Serves: 4

10 oz. strawberries, frozen
2 cups water
1 tbsp. stevia

1. Place strawberries, water, and stevia in a blender and process until smooth and creamy. 2. Pour mixture into ice cream maker and process according to instructions. 3. Transfer to a plastic container with an airtight lid and freeze for 4 hours before serving.

Calories: 38g, Total Carbs: 9g, Net Carbs: 7g, Protein: 0g, Fat: 0g, Sugar: 7g, Fiber: 2g

Apple Cinnamon Chimichanga

Prep Time: 15 minutes, Cook Time: 15 minutes, Serves: 4

2 apples, cored and chopped
3 tbsps. splenda, divided
¼ cup water
½ tsp. ground cinnamon
4 (8-inch) whole-wheat flour tortillas
Nonstick cooking spray
Special Equipment:
4 toothpicks, soaked in water for at least 30 minutes

1. Preheat the oven to 400ºF (205ºC). Line a baking sheet with parchment paper and set aside. 2. Make the apple filling: Add the apples, 2 tbsps. of splenda, water, and cinnamon to a medium saucepan over medium heat. Stir to combine and allow the mixture to boil for 5 minutes, or until the apples are fork-tender, but not mushy. 3. Remove the apple filling from the heat and let it cool to room temperature. 4. Make the chimichangas: Place the tortillas on a lightly floured surface. 5. Spoon 2 tsps. of prepared apple filling onto each tortilla and fold the tortilla over to enclose the filling. Roll each tortilla up and run the toothpicks through to secure. Spritz the tortillas lightly with nonstick cooking spray. 6. Arrange the tortillas on the prepared baking sheet, seam-side down. Scatter the remaining splenda all over the tortillas. 7. Bake in the preheated oven for 10 minutes, flipping the tortillas halfway through, or until they are crispy and golden brown on each side. 8. Remove from the oven to four plates and serve while warm.

Calories: 201, Fat: 6.2g, Protein: 3.9g, Carbs: 32.8g, Fiber: 5g, Sugar: 7.9g, Sodium: 241mg

Crispy Apple and Pecan Bake

Prep Time: 10 minutes, Cook Time: 15 minutes, Serves: 4

2 apples, peeled, cored, and chopped
½ tsp. cinnamon
½ tsp. ground ginger
2 tbsps. pure maple syrup
¼ cup pecans, chopped

1. Preheat the oven to 350ºF (180ºC). 2. Combine all the ingredients, except for the pecans, in a bowl. Stir to mix well. 3. Pour the mixture in a baking dish, and spread the pecans over the mixture. 4. Bake in the preheated oven for 15 minutes or until the apples are soft. 5. Remove them from the oven and serve warm.

Calories: 124, Fat: 5.1g, Protein: 1.1g, Carbs: 20.8g, Fiber: 3.2g, Carbs: 18.6g, Sodium: 1mg

CHAPTER 15 — SAUCE AND DRESSING RECIPES

Herb Vinaigrette ·········· 94	Creamy Poppy Seed Dressing ·········· 95
Tahini Yogurt Dressing ·········· 94	Cannellini Bean Dip ·········· 96
Creamy Avocado Alfredo Sauce ·········· 94	Healthy Black Bean Hummus ·········· 96
Basic Salsa ·········· 94	Spicy Red Mexican Salsa ·········· 96
Authentic Greek Tzatziki Sauce ·········· 94	Apple Cider Vinaigrette ·········· 96
Olive & Mint Vinaigrette ·········· 94	Lemon Paleo Caesar Dressing ·········· 96
Italian Salad Dressing ·········· 94	Fresh Tomato Basil Sauce ·········· 96
BBQ Sauce ·········· 94	Chinese Hot Mustard ·········· 96
Tahini Lemon Dressing ·········· 95	Greek Yogurt Dressing with Basil ·········· 97
Cucumber and Roasted Pine Nut Spread ·········· 95	Super Simple Tomato Sauce ·········· 97
Horseradish Mustard Sauce ·········· 95	Garlic Dipping Sauce ·········· 97
Lemony Spicy Pumpkin Dip ·········· 95	Cinnamon-Vanilla Applesauce ·········· 97
Citrus Vinaigrette ·········· 95	Spicy Red Mexican Salsa ·········· 97
Meaty Spagetti Sauce ·········· 95	

Herb Vinaigrette

Prep Time: 5 minutes, Cook Time: 5 minutes, Serves: 12

2 tbsps. shallot, diced fine
1 tbsp. fresh basil, diced
1 tbsp. fresh oregano, diced
1 tbsp. fresh tarragon, diced
¼ cup extra virgin olive oil
¼ cup low sodium chicken broth
¼ cup red-wine vinegar
¼ tsp. salt
¼ tsp. freshly ground pepper

1. Place all ingredients in a jar with an air tight lid. Secure lid and shake vigorously to combine. 2. Refrigerate until ready to use. Will keep up to 2 days. Serving size is 1 tablespoon.

Calories: 39, Total Carbs: 0g, Protein 0g, Fat: 4g, Sugar: 0g, Fiber: 0g

Tahini Yogurt Dressing

Prep Time: 5 minutes, Cook Time: 0, Serves: makes 1 cup

½ cup nonfat coconut yogurt
⅓ cup tahini
¼ cup freshly squeezed orange juice
½ tsp. kosher salt

1. In a medium mixing bowl, whisk together the tahini, orange juice and salt until the tahini becomes smooth. Add more juice if needed to help smooth it out. 2. Place in the refrigerator until ready to serve. 3. Store any leftovers in an airtight container and refrigerate up to 5 days.

Calories: 70, Total Fat: 2g, Saturated Fat: 1g, Sodium: 80mg, Total Carbs: 4g, Fiber: 1g, Sugar: 1g, Protein: 4g

Creamy Avocado Alfredo Sauce

Prep Time: 10 minutes, Cook Time: 2 minutes, Serves: 4

1 ripe avocado, peeled and pitted
1 tbsp. olive oil
1 tbsp. dried basil
1 clove garlic
1 tbsp. lemon juice
⅛ tsp. salt

1. Add the avocado, basil, garlic clove, lemon juice, olive oil, and salt to a food processor. Blend until a smooth, creamy sauce forms. 2. Pour the sauce over hot pasta or vegetable noodles.

Calories: 104, Total Fat: 10g, Saturated Fat: 1g, Sodium: 43mg, Total Carbs: 4g, Fiber: 3g, Sugar: 0g, Protein: 1g

Basic Salsa

Prep Time: 15 minutes, Chill time: 1 hour: Serves: 8

8 tomatoes
2-3 jalapeno peppers, depending on how spicy you like it
2 limes, juiced
4 cloves garlic
1 tbsp. salt
Nonstick cooking spray

1. Heat oven to broil. Spray a baking sheet with cooking spray. 2. Place tomatoes, peppers, and garlic on prepared pan and broil 8-10 minutes, turning occasionally, until skin on the vegetables begins to char and peel way. 3. Let cool. Remove skins. 4. Place vegetables in a food processor and pulse. Add salt and lime juise and pulse until salsa reaches desired consistency. 5. Store in a jar with an airtight lid in the refrigerator up to 7 days. Serving size is ¼ cup.

Calories: 31, Total Carbs: 7g, Net Carbs: 5g, Protein: 1g, Fat: 0g, Sugar: 4g, Fiber: 2g

Authentic Greek Tzatziki Sauce

Prep Time: 10 minutes, Cook Time: 0, Serves: makes 1½ cups

1 cup nonfat plain Greek yogurt
2 Persian cucumbers or ½ hot-house or English cucumber
1 tbsp. extra-virgin olive oil
2 tbsps. fresh dill, chopped
2 tbsps. fresh mint, chopped
1 garlic clove, minced
2 tbsps. lemon juice
½ tsp. kosher salt

1. Using a box grater to grate the cucumbers. 2. In a medium bowl, mix the grated cucumbers, yogurt, dill, mint, lemon juice, olive oil, garlic, and salt well.

Calories: 45, Total Fat: 0g, Saturated Fat: 0g, Sodium: 105mg, Total Carbs: 3g, Fiber: 0g, Sugar: 2g, Protein: 3g

Olive & Mint Vinaigrette

Prep Time: 5 minutes, Cook Time: 0, Serves: makes ½ cup

¼ cup white wine vinegar
¼ cup olives, pitted and minced
2 tbsps. fresh mint, minced
¼ tsp. honey
¼ tsp. kosher salt
¼ tsp. freshly ground black pepper
¼ cup extra-virgin olive oil

1. Put the vinegar, honey, salt, and black pepper in a bowl and whisk together. 2. Slowly pour in the olive oil, whisking all the while, and continue whisking until smooth. 3. Add the olives and mint, and mix well. 4. Transfer all the ingredients into an airtight container and refrigerate for up to 5 days.

Calories: 135, Total Fat: 15g, Saturated Fat: 2g, Sodium: 135mg, Total Carbs: 1g, Fiber: 0g, Sugar: 0g, Protein: 0g

Italian Salad Dressing

Prep Time: 5 minutes, Cook Time: 0 minutes, Serves: 8

2 tbsps. lemon juice
¾ cup olive oil
¼ cup red wine vinegar
2 cloves of garlic, diced
2 tsps. Italian seasoning
1 tsp. oregano
½ tsp. honey
½ tsp. salt
¼ tsp. black pepper
¼ tsp. red pepper flakes

1. Combine all ingredients in a measuring cup or jar. Whisk well. 2. Store in jar or bottle with an air tight lid for up to 1 week. Serving size is 1 tablespoon.

Calories: 167, Total Carbs: 1g, Protein: 0g, Fat: 18g, Sugar: 0g, Fiber: 0g

BBQ Sauce

Prep Time: 5 minutes, Cook Time: 20 minutes, Serves: 20

2½ (6 oz.) cans tomato paste
1½ cup water
½ cup apple cider vinegar
⅓ cup swerve confectioners
2 tbsps. Worcestershire sauce
1 tbsp. liquid hickory smoke
2 tsps. smoked paprika
1 tsp. garlic powder
½ tsp. onion powder
½ tsp. salt
¼ tsp. chili powder
¼ tsp. cayenne pepper

1. Whisk all ingredients, but water, together in a saucepan. Add water, starting with 1 cup, whisking it in, until mixture resembles a thin barbecue sauce. 2. Bring to a low boil over med-high heat. Reduce heat to med-low and simmer, stirring frequently, 20 minutes, or sauce has thickened slightly. 3. Taste and adjust

seasoning until you like it. Cool completely. Store in a jar with an airtight lid in the refrigerator. Serving size is 2 tbsps. of sauce.

Calories: 24, Total Carbs: 9g, Net Carbs: 8g, Protein: 1g, Fat: 0g, Sugar: 7g, Fiber: 1g

Tahini Lemon Dressing

Prep Time: 5 minutes, Cook Time: 0, Serves: makes ½ cup

- ¼ cup tahini
- 3 tbsps. lemon juice
- 3 tbsps. warm water
- ¼ tsp. kosher salt
- ¼ tsp. maple syrup
- ¼ tsp. ground cumin
- ⅛ tsp. cayenne pepper

1. Put the tahini, lemon juice, water, salt, maple syrup, cumin, and cayenne pepper in a medium bowl and whisk together until smooth. 2. Place in the refrigerator until ready to serve. 3. Store any leftovers in an airtight container and refrigerate up to 5 days.

Calories: 90, Total Fat: 7g, Saturated Fat: 1g, Sodium: 80mg, Total Carbs: 5g, Fiber: 1g, Sugar: 1g, Protein: 3g

Cucumber and Roasted Pine Nut Spread

Prep Time: 5 minutes, Cook Time: 20 minutes, Serves: 4 cups

- 1 cup red cucumber, rinsed
- ½ cup pine nuts, chopped
- 1 celery stalk, diced
- 2 cloves garlic, crushed
- 1 tsp. dried cumin
- ½ tsp. ground allspice
- 2 tbsps. tomato paste
- 2 tsps. fresh tomato juice
- ¼ tsp. salt
- ¼ tsp. freshly ground black pepper

1. Mix together the cucumber and 2 cups water in a small saucepan and bring to a boil over high heat. Reduce the heat to low, cover, and cook until the cucumber are softened but not mushy and the water is absorbed, about 15 minutes. Drain well. Transfer to a blender. 2. In the meantime, toast the pine nuts in a dry medium skillet over low heat, stirring consistently, until they begin to brown and are fragrant, 2 to 3 minutes. Scrape them into the blender over the cucumber. 3. Pour the celery, garlic, cumin, allspice, tomato paste, tomato juice, salt, and pepper to the blender. Puree the mixture until smooth and well combined, stopping occasionally to scrape the bowl. If the mixture is too thick, add water 1 tbsp. at a time until it reaches a smooth spreadable consistency similar to hummus. 4. Serve immediately or store in an airtight container in the refrigerator for up to 5 days.

Calories: 70, Total Fat: 2 g, Saturated Fat: <1 g, Total Carbs: 8g, Protein: 4g, Sodium: 38mg, Fiber: 1g, Sugar: 1g

Horseradish Mustard Sauce

Prep Time: 5 minutes, Cook Time: 0 minutes, Serves: 8

- ¼ cup fat free sour cream
- ¼ cup lite mayonnaise
- 1½ tsps. lemon juice
- 1 tsp. Splenda
- ½ tsp. ground mustard
- ½ tsp. Dijon mustard
- ½ tsp. horseradish

1. In a small bowl, combine all ingredients until thoroughly combined. 2. Store in an air tight jar in the refrigerator until ready to use. Serving size is 1 tablespoon.

Calories: 36, Total Carbs: 2g, Protein: 0g, Fat: 2g, Sugar: 1g, Fiber: 0g

Lemony Spicy Pumpkin Dip

Prep Time: 5 minutes, Cook Time: 15 minutes, Serves: 4

- 1 tbsp. olive oil
- ½ yellow onion, finely chopped
- 1 tsp. smoked sweet paprika
- ½ tsp. ground cumin
- ½ tsp. ground ginger
- ½ tsp. curry powder
- 2 garlic cloves, minced
- One (15-ounce, 425 g) can pumpkin puree or cooked winter squash
- Unsalted pita chips
- 1 tbsp. water (optional)
- 1 tbsp. lemon juice

1. Heat oil over medium heat in a sauté pan. Add onion and garlic, and sauté for about 6 minutes. Add the pumpkin and cook for 5 minutes. 2. Add paprika, curry, cumin and ginger, and cook for about 2 minutes, until spices have infused. Add a little water if needed to prevent scorching. 3. Remove from heat. Put in some lemon juice, mix and serve with pita chips.

Calories: 90, Fat: 3.7g, Carbs: 13.9g, Protein: 2.0g, Cholesterol: 0mg, Sodium: 8.7mg, Fiber: 4.3g

Citrus Vinaigrette

Prep Time: 10 minutes, Cook Time: 0 minutes, Serves: 6

- 1 orange, zested and juiced
- 1 lemon, zested and juiced
- ¼ cup extra virgin olive oil
- 1 tsp. Dijon mustard
- 1 tsp. honey
- 1 clove garlic, crushed
- Salt & pepper, to taste

1. Place the zest and juices, mustard, honey, garlic, salt and pepper in a food processor. Pulse to combine. 2. With the machine running, slowly pour in the olive oil and process until combined. 3. Use right away, or store in a jar with an airtight lid in the refrigerator.

Calories: 94, Total Carbs: 6g, Net Carbs: 5g, Protein: 0g, Fat: 8g, Sugar: 4g, Fiber: 1g

Meaty Spagetti Sauce

Prep Time: 15 minutes, Cook Time: 30 minutes, Serves: 6

- 1 pound (454 g) extra-lean ground beef, 95% lean
- 1 15-oz. (425 g) can tomato sauce, no salt added
- 1 14½-oz. (410 g) can diced tomatoes, no salt added
- 2 garlic cloves, minced or squeezed through garlic press
- ½ cup chopped onions, fresh or frozen
- 1 tsp. Italian seasoning
- 1 tsp. dried basil

1. Add ground beef in a large nonstick skillet over medium-high heat. Cook for 3 minutes, turn down heat to medium. Put in onions and garlic. Continue cooking for about 5 more minutes, or until thoroughly browned. 2. Add diced tomatoes and tomato sauce and simmer for 10 - 15 minutes. Sprinkle seasonings in last few minutes of cooking.

Calories: 184, Protein: 24g, Carbs: 8g, Fat: 6g, Cholesterol: 67mg, Fiber: 2g, Sodium: 105mg

Creamy Poppy Seed Dressing

Prep Time: 5 minutes, Cook Time: 0 minutes, Serves: 6

- ⅓ cup light mayonnaise
- ¼ cup skim milk
- 3 tbsps. Splenda
- 4 tsps. cider vinegar
- 2 tsps. poppy seeds

1. In a small bowl, whisk all ingredients together until thoroughly combined. Store in an airtight jar in the refrigerator.

Calories: 90, Total Carbs: 10g, Protein: 1g, Fat: 5g, Sugar: 7g, Fiber: 0g

Cannellini Bean Dip

Prep Time: 20 minutes, Cook Time: 0, Serves: 8

15 whole-wheat crackers or pita wedges	½ cup (120 ml) low-fat sour cream
15 celery sticks	1 tbsp. dried dill
One (15-ounce, 425 g) can low-salt cannellini beans, rinsed and drained	15 baby carrots
	1 cup (240 ml) nonfat plain yogurt
	1 tsp. cumin
	1½ tbsp. lemon juice

1. Mix beans, yogurt, sour cream, dill, lemon juice, and cumin in a food processor, and pulse for one minute, until beans are broken down and all ingredients combined. Scrape down the sides if necessary. 2. Serve with celery sticks, carrots and crackers.

Calories: 87, Fat: 3.1g, Carbs: 11.7g, Protein: 5.7g, Cholesterol: 6.9mg, Sodium: 131.1mg, Fiber: 1.9g

Healthy Black Bean Hummus

Prep Time: 5 minutes, Cook Time: 5 minutes, Serves: 8

1 (15-ounce (425g)) can no-salt-added black beans, drained and rinsed	¾ tsp. ground cumin
1 tbsp. extra-virgin olive oil	2 tbsps. tahini
⅓ cup fresh cilantro leaves	¼ tsp. paprika
2 tbsps. fresh lime juice	1 garlic clove, peeled
	6 Kalamata olives, pitted
	¼ tsp. salt

1. Add the black beans, cilantro leaves, olives, garlic, lime juice, tahini, oil, cumin, paprika, and salt in a blender or food processor, stirring often, until smooth purée. 2. Remove from the blender to a storage container.

Calories: 94, Total Fat: 5g, Carbs: 9g, Protein: 4g, Fiber: 3g, Sodium: 126mg

Spicy Red Mexican Salsa

Prep Time: 15 minutes, Cook Time: 20 minutes, Serves: 12 (2-tablespoon) servings

2 large Roma tomatoes, cut into large pieces	¾ cup fresh cilantro
½ cup water	20 dried red chiles/chiles de arbol
½ white onion, cut into large pieces	1 large clove garlic
	¼ tsp. sea salt

1. Prepare a large frying pan and heat it on high heat. Without oil, put peppers, garlic, onions and tomatoes in the pan. When the tomato skin and chili start to turn black, immediately remove the chili from the frying pan and put it in a small pot with water. 2. Cover the lid and simmer for 8 to 10 minutes to soften the peppers. When the peppers are soft, put the cooked ingredients and coriander in a blender. 3. Stir on low speed and cover the top with a kitchen towel so that the steam can escape, but the salsa will not explode from the top of the blender. Season with salt at the end and enjoy.

Calories: 10, Fat: 0.1g, Protein: 0.2g, Carbs: 2g, Fiber: 0.3g, Sugar: 0g, Sodium: 132mg

Apple Cider Vinaigrette

Prep Time: 5 minutes, Cook Time: 0 minutes, Serves: 8

½ cup sunflower oil	1 tbsp. lemon juice
¼ cup apple cider vinegar	½ tsp. salt
¼ cup apple juice, unsweetened	Freshly ground black pepper, to taste
2 tbsps. honey	

1. Place all ingredients in a mason jar. Screw on lid and shake until everything is thoroughly combined. Store in refrigerator until ready to use. Shake well before using.

Calories: 138, Total Carbs: 4g, Protein: 0g, Fat: 13g, Sugar: 4g, Fiber: 0g

Lemon Paleo Caesar Dressing

Prep Time: 10 minutes, Cook Time: 0, Serves: ½ cup

2 tbsps. extra-virgin olive oil	½ tsp. lemon zest
2 garlic cloves, minced	1 tbsp. white wine vinegar
¼ cup Paleo mayonnaise	½ tsp. anchovy paste
2 tbsps. freshly squeezed lemon juice	¼ tsp. salt
	Freshly ground black pepper

1. Combine all of the ingredients except the black pepper in a small bowl, whisk them until well mixed and emulsified. 2. Use pepper to season. Cover and place in the refrigerator for up to 1 week.

Calories: 167, Total Fat: 18.9 g, Saturated Fat: 2.4g, Carbs: 1.3g, Protein: 0.2g, Fiber: 0.3g, Sodium: 170mg

Fresh Tomato Basil Sauce

Prep Time: 5 minutes, Cook Time: 10 minutes, Serves: 6

2 tbsps. olive oil	1 tbsp. dried basil
4 (15-ounce, 425g) cans no-salt, crushed, or chopped tomatoes	Salt
3 garlic cloves, finely chopped	Freshly ground black pepper

1. Heat the oil in a large saucepan and sauté the garlic for about a minute until lightly browned, being careful not to burn. Add the tomatoes and basil, season with salt and pepper, and cook uncovered over medium heat for about 10 minutes. 2. Serve over pasta, grains, beans, or vegetables.

Calories: 103, Total Fat: 5g, Saturated Fat: 1g, Sodium: 32mg, Total Carbs: 15g, Fiber: 3g, Sugar: 0g, Protein: 3g

Chinese Hot Mustard

Prep Time: 15 minutes, Cook Time: 15 minutes, Serves: 4

1 tbsp. mustard powder	½ tsp. rice vinegar
1½ tsp. hot water	⅛ tsp. salt
½ tsp. vegetable oil	⅛ tsp. white pepper

1. In a small bowl, mix together the dry ingredients. Add water and stir until mixture resembles liquid paste and dry ingredients are absorbed. 2. Stir in oil and vinegar until thoroughly combined. Cover and let rest 10 minutes. 3. Stir again. Taste and adjust any seasonings if desired. Cover and refrigerate until ready to use.

Calories: 19, Total Carbs: 1g, Protein: 1g, Fat: 1g, Sugar: 0g, Fiber: 0g

Greek Yogurt Dressing with Basil

Prep Time: 5 minutes, Cook Time: 10 minutes, Serves: 2 cups

¼ cup chopped fresh basil
¼ cup chopped sage
1 cup (240 ml) nonfat (0%) plain Greek yogurt
½ cup chopped fresh coriander
1 small onion, minced
2 cloves garlic, minced
2 tbsps. extra-virgin olive oil
2 tbsps. juice from 1 orange
½ tsp. maple syrup
⅛ tsp. salt
⅛ tsp. freshly ground black pepper

1. Mix together the basil, sage, and coriander in a food processor and puree a few times until they have been ground up slightly. Scrape down the sides. 2. Pour in the onion, garlic, Greek yogurt, olive oil, orange juice, ¼ cup water, maple syrup, salt, and pepper and puree until smooth and the ingredients have been fully incorporated. 3. Use immediately or store in an airtight container in the refrigerator for up to 1 week.

Calories: 26, Total Fat: 2g, Saturated Fat: <1g, Total Carbs: 1g, Protein: 2g, Sodium: 27mg, Fiber: <1g, Sugar: 1g

Super Simple Tomato Sauce

Prep Time: 10 minutes, Cook Time: 20 minutes, Serves: 2 cups

¼ cup extra-virgin olive oil
3 garlic cloves, minced
2 pints grape tomatoes, halved
2 tbsps. chopped fresh basil
¼ tsp. salt
¼ tsp. freshly ground black pepper
¼ tsp. red pepper flakes (optional)

1. In a large skillet, heat the oil over medium heat. Add the garlic and cook, stirring constantly, for 30 seconds to 1 minute. 2. Then stir in the tomatoes. Reduce the heat slightly and stir in the basil, salt, and pepper. 3. Cook, stirring occasionally, for about 20 minutes, or until the tomatoes are softened and the sauce has thickened slightly. 4. Stir in the red pepper flakes (if using). Remove from the heat. Let cool, then portion into 4 small storage containers. 5. Give your sauce a little room to breathe by selecting a container that will hold 6 ounces or more.

Calories: 153, Total Fat: 14g, Carbs: 15g, Fiber: 2g, Protein: 2g, Sodium: 176mg

Garlic Dipping Sauce

Prep Time: 5 minutes, Cook Time: 0 minutes, Serves: 4

1 cup nonfat Greek yogurt
1 tbsp. fresh dill, diced fine
2 cloves garlic, diced fine

1. In a small bowl, whisk all ingredients together. 2. Serve warm or cover and chill until ready to use.

Calories: 40, Total Carbs: 2g, Protein: 5g, Fat: 1g, Sugar: 2g, Fiber: 0g

Cinnamon-Vanilla Applesauce

Prep Time: 10 minutes, Cook Time: 5 minutes, Serves: 6 to 8

3 pounds (1.4 kg) apples, cored and quartered
⅓ cup water
1 tsp. ground cinnamon
1 tsp. freshly squeezed lemon juice
1 tsp. vanilla extract
½ tsp. salt

1. Add all the ingredients to the Instant Pot and stir to combine. 2. Lock the lid. Select the Manual mode and set the cooking time for 5 minutes on High Pressure. Once the timer goes off, perform a natural pressure release for 10 minutes, then release any remaining pressure. Carefully open the lid. 3. Using an immersion blender, blend the applesauce until smooth. 4. Serve immediately or refrigerate until ready to use.

Calories: 89, Fat: 0.3g, Protein: 0.5g, Carbs: 24g, Fiber: 4g, Sugar: 18g, Sodium: 98mg

Spicy Red Mexican Salsa

Prep Time: 15 minutes, Cook Time: 20 minutes, Serves: 12 (2-tablespoon) servings

2 large Roma tomatoes, cut into large pieces
½ cup water
½ white onion, cut into large pieces
¾ cup fresh cilantro
20 dried red chiles/chiles de arbol
1 large clove garlic
¼ tsp. sea salt

1. Prepare a large frying pan and heat it on high heat. Without oil, put peppers, garlic, onions and tomatoes in the pan. When the tomato skin and chili start to turn black, immediately remove the chili from the frying pan and put it in a small pot with water. 2. Cover the lid and simmer for 8 to 10 minutes to soften the peppers. When the peppers are soft, put the cooked ingredients and coriander in a blender. 3. Stir on low speed and cover the top with a kitchen towel so that the steam can escape, but the salsa will not explode from the top of the blender. Season with salt at the end and enjoy.

Calories: 10, Fat: 0.1g, Protein: 0.2g, Carbs: 2g, Fiber: 0.3g, Sugar: 0g, Sodium: 132mg

APPENDIX 1: BASIC KITCHEN CONVERSIONS & EQUIVALENTS

DRY MEASUREMENTS CONVERSION CHART

3 teaspoons = 1 tablespoon = 1/16 cup
6 teaspoons = 2 tablespoons = 1/8 cup
12 teaspoons = 4 tablespoons = ¼ cup
24 teaspoons = 8 tablespoons = ½ cup
36 teaspoons = 12 tablespoons = ¾ cup
48 teaspoons = 16 tablespoons = 1 cup

METRIC TO US COOKING CONVERSIONS

OVEN TEMPERATURES

120 °C = 250 °F
160 °C = 320 °F
180 °C = 350 °F
205 °C = 400 °F
220 °C = 425 °F

LIQUID MEASUREMENTS CONVERSION CHART

8 fluid ounces = 1 cup = ½ pint = ¼ quart
16 fluid ounces = 2 cups = 1 pint = ½ quart
32 fluid ounces = 4 cups = 2 pints = 1 quart = ¼ gallon
128 fluid ounces = 16 cups = 8 pints = 4 quarts = 1 gallon

BAKING IN GRAMS

1 cup flour = 140 grams
1 cup sugar = 150 grams
1 cup powdered sugar = 160 grams
1 cup heavy cream = 235 grams

VOLUME

1 milliliter = 1/5 teaspoon
5 ml = 1 teaspoon
15 ml = 1 tablespoon
240 ml = 1 cup or 8 fluid ounces
1 liter = 34 fluid ounces

WEIGHT

1 gram = .035 ounces
100 grams = 3.5 ounces
500 grams = 1.1 pounds
1 kilogram = 35 ounces

US TO METRIC COOKING CONVERSIONS

1/5 tsp = 1 ml
1 tsp = 5 ml
1 tbsp = 15 ml
1 fluid ounces = 30 ml
1 cup = 237 ml
1 pint (2 cups) = 473 ml
1 quart (4 cups) = .95 liter
1 gallon (16 cups) = 3.8 liters
1 oz = 28 grams
1 pound = 454 grams

BUTTER

1 cup butter = 2 sticks = 8 ounces = 230 grams = 16 tablespoons

WHAT DOES 1 CUP EQUAL

1 cup = 8 fluid ounces
1 cup = 16 tablespoons
1 cup = 48 teaspoons
1 cup = ½ pint
1 cup = ¼ quart
1 cup = 1/16 gallon
1 cup = 240 ml

BAKING PAN CONVERSIONS

9-inch round cake pan = 12 cups
10-inch tube pan = 16 cups
10-inch bundt pan = 12 cups
9-inch springform pan = 10 cups
9 x 5 inch loaf pan = 8 cups
9-inch square pan = 8 cups

BAKING PAN CONVERSIONS

1 cup all-purpose flour = 4.5 oz
1 cup rolled oats = 3 oz
1 large egg = 1.7 oz
1 cup butter = 8 oz
1 cup milk = 8 oz
1 cup heavy cream = 8.4 oz
1 cup granulated sugar = 7.1 oz
1 cup packed brown sugar = 7.75 oz
1 cup vegetable oil = 7.7 oz
1 cup unsifted powdered sugar = 4.4 oz

APPENDIX 2: THE DIRTY DOZEN AND CLEAN FIFTEEN

The Environmental Working Group (EWG) is a widely known organization that has an eminent guide to pesticides and produce. More specifically, the group takes in data from tests conducted by the US Department of Agriculture (USDA) and then categorizes produce into a list titled "Dirty Dozen," which ranks the twelve top produce items that contain the most pesticide residues, or alternatively the "Clean Fifteen," which ranks fifteen produce items that are contaminated with the least amount of pesticide residues.

The EWG has recently released their 2021 Dirty Dozen list, and this year strawberries, spinach and kale – with a few other produces which will be revealed shortly – are listed at the top of the list. This year's ranking is similar to the 2020 Dirty Dozen list, with the few differences being that collards and mustard greens have joined kale at number three on the list. Other changes include peaches and cherries, which having been listed subsequently as seventh and eighth on the 2020 list, have now been flipped; the introduction – which the EWG has said is the first time ever – of bell and hot peppers into the 2021 list; and the departure of potatoes from the twelfth spot.

DIRTY DOZEN LIST

Strawberries	Apples	Pears
Spinach	Grapes	Bell and hot peppers
Kale, collards and mustard greens	Cherries	Celery
Nectarines	Peaches	Tomatoes

CLEAN FIFTEEN LIST

Avocados	Sweet peas (frozen)	Kiwi
Sweet corn	Eggplant	Cauliflower
Pineapple	Asparagus	Mushrooms
Onions	Broccoli	Honeydew melon
Papaya	Cabbage	Cantaloupe

These lists are created to help keep the public informed on their potential exposures to pesticides, which then allows for better and healthier food choices to be made.

This is the advice that ASEQ-EHAQ also recommends. Stay clear of the dirty dozen by opting for their organic versions, and always be mindful of what you are eating and how it was grown. Try to eat organic as much as possible – whether it is on the list, or not.

APPENDIX 3: RECIPES INDEX

A

ACORN SQUASH
Simple Curried Squash	56

ADZUKI BEAN
Adzuki Bean and Celery Soup	69

ALMOND
Almond Cheesecake Bites	89

APPLE
Delicious Apple Pancakes	14
Healthy Apple Cinnamon Overnight Oats	16
Apple and Pecan Quinoa Salad	20
Toffee Apple Mini Pies	90
Crispy Apple and Pecan Bake	92
Crispy Apple Chips	91
Apple Cinnamon Chimichanga	92
Cinnamon-Vanilla Applesauce	97

ARTICHOKE
Artichokes with Mayonnaise Dip	78

ARUGULA
Pomegranate Salad with Avocado	39

ASPARAGUS
Spring Asparagus and Radicchio Brunch Plate	17
Vinegar Asparagus Salad	36
Roasted Asparagus with Apple Cider	91

AVOCADO
Quick Avocado Egg Sandwiches	17
Quinoa Bowls with Avocado and Egg	18
Farro and Avocado Bowl	23
Avocado Smoothie	83
Kale and Avocado Smoothie Bowl	84
Creamy Avocado Alfredo Sauce	94

B

BABY BACK PORK RIB
Maple-Glazed Spareribs	65

BANANA
Quick Protein Bowl	14
Healthy Whole Grain Pancakes	15
Fried Almond Butter with Banana	17
Apple and Banana Smoothie	82
Carrot and Banana Smoothie Bowl	84
Savory Banana Almond Smoothie	85
Easy Banana Mug Cake	89
Peach, Banana and Almond Pancakes	91

BEEF
Spicy Beef with Worcestershire Sauce	62
Beef & Veggie Quesadillas	62
Beef Picadillo	63
Parmesan Beef Burger with Carrot	63
Sloppy Joes in Lettuce	64
Cauliflower and Beef Soup	70
Beef and Eggplant Tagine	73
Meaty Spagetti Sauce	95

BEEF BRISKET
Beer Braised Brisket	63

BEEF SIRLOIN STEAK
Sichuan Beef with Vegetable and Almond Butter	62

BEEF TENDERLOIN STEAK
Beef Tenderloin Steaks with Brandied Mushrooms	62
Blue Cheese Crusted Beef Tenderloin	62

BEET
Chermoula Beet Roast	57
Italian Beets and Tomato	58
Delicious Roasted Beet Soup	70
Sumptuous Beet Salad with Vinaigrette	76
Beet and Grapefruit Salad	77
Fruit and Beet Smoothie	84

BELL PEPPER

Pearl Barley with Peppers	22
Pepper and Egg Oatmeal Bowl	22
Vegetarian Kidney Bean Étouffée	32
Roasted Colorful Bell Peppers	59

BLACK BEAN

Herbed Black Beans	28
Crispy Cowboy Black Bean Fritters	29
Super Bean and Grain Burgers	29
Easy Three-Bean Medley	29
Dandelion and Beet Greens with Black Beans	30
Enchilada Black Bean Casserole	30
Pepper and Black Bean Tacos	32
Triple Bean Chili	32
Vegetable Chili	56
Bean Tostadas	56
Black Bean and Tomato Chili	57
Black Bean Wild Rice Chili	70
Black Bean and Tomato Soup with Lime Yogurt	70
Healthy Black Bean Hummus	96

BLACKBERRY

Quinoa Bowl with Blackberry	18

BLACK-EYED PEA

Black-Eyed Peas Curry	30
Black-Eyed Peas with Collard	31
Black-Eyed Peas with Greens	77

BLUEBERRY

Healthy English Muffin with Berries	17
Spinach and Berries Smoothie	82
Quick Berry Banana Smoothie	82
Banana Blueberry Smoothie	84

BROCCOLI

Healthy Veggie Egg Scramble	14
Mini Basil Broccoli Frittatas	15
Delicious Baked Broccoli Rice Cakes	56
Creamy Broccoli and Cauliflower Soup	71
Baked Parmesan Broccoli Fritters	79
Garlicky Broccoli	79

BROCCOLINI

Green Broccolini Sauté	78

BRUSSELS SPROUTS

Garlicky Tofu and Brussels Sprouts	28
Balsamic Brussels Sprouts	58
Italian Roasted Vegetables	76
Roasted Coconut Brussels Sprouts	78
Brussels Sprouts with Sesame Seeds	79
Quinoa with Brussels Sprouts and Avocado	79

BUTTERNUT SQUASH

Barley Kale and Squash Risotto	24

BUTTON MUSHROOM

Mushroom Rice with Hazelnut	24

C

CABBAGE

Classic Coleslaw	37
Braised Cabbage	78

CANNELLINI BEAN

Tomato and Beans with Baby Spinach	28
Greens and Beans Stuffed Mushrooms	31
Spicy Cannellini Bean Ratatouille	56
Carrot and Bean Chili	69
Cannellini Mandarin Salsa	80
Cannellini Bean Dip	96

CARROT

Brown Rice with Collard and Scrambled Egg	20
Couscous with Veggies	23
Carrot Salad with Nuts and Coconut Flakes	39
Honey Roasted Carrots and Parsnips	59
Carrot, Celery and Barley Soup	69
Nourishing Vegetable Stew	70
Lentil and Tomato Barley Soup	71
Grilled Carrots with Dill	75
Thai Curry Roasted Veggies	77
Smoky Carrots and Collard Greens	78
Carrot and Banana Smoothie	84

CAULIFLOWER

Cauliflower Hash Brown	13

Roasted Cauliflower with Pomegranate and Pine Nuts	35
Rice Cauliflower Tabbouleh Salad	37
Cauliflower and Cashew Gratin	55
Cauliflower Tater Tots	55
Tandoori Zucchini Cauliflower Curry	57
Turmeric Cauliflower and Chickpea Stew	59
Spicy Cauliflower Roast	59
Cauliflower, Chickpea, and Avocado Mash	60
Creamy Vegetable Soup	72
Herbed Cauliflower with Orange Juice	76
Curried Cauliflower	76
Buffalo Bites	88

CELERY ROOT

Celery Root and Pear Soup	71

CELERY STALK

Healthy French Lentil Salad	35
Healthy Mushroom Cashew Rice	57

CHERRY

Farro and Cherry Salad	24
Old-Fashioned Cherry French Toast	89

CHERRY TOMATO

Za'atar-Spiced Bulgur Wheat Salad	25
Healthy Italian Pasta Salad with Pine Nuts	35
Roasted Cherry Tomato with Parmesan	88

CHICKEN

Chicken Breakfast Burritos	13
Homemade Breakfast Chicken Sausage	17
Fabulous Chicken Salad with Dried Apricots and Almonds	35
Chicken with Peanut Sauce	49
Lemon Chicken and Zucchini Soup	73

CHICKEN BREAST

Spicy Chicken Bulgur	23
Quick Summer Chicken Salad	35
Broiled Curried Chicken Tenders	47
Healthy Grilled Chicken and Black Bean Salsa	48
Chicken Cacciatore	48
White Beans Chicken Chili	49
Tasty Pita Sandwich with Curried Chicken Salad	48
Spinach and Mushroom Stuffed Chicken	49
Chicken and Apple Sandwich	49
Crispy Apricot Chicken with Steamed Baby Greens	50
Savory Orange Chicken with Brown Rice	52
Curry Chicken with Lemongrass and Coconut	52
One-Pot Creamy Tuscan Chicken	52
Slaw and Chicken Stir-Fry	53
Chicken with Crispy Kale and Artichokes	53

CHICKEN TENDER

Simple Oatmeal Chicken Tenders	47
Crispy Za'atar Chicken Tenders	52

CHICKEN THIGH

Easy Sumac Chicken with Cauliflower and Carrots	47
Harissa Chicken Thighs with Yogurt	50
Chicken Stew with Olives and Lemon	51
Italian Chicken Cacciatore	51
Stir-Fried Chicken and Broccoli	51
French Chicken, Mushroom and Wild Rice Stew	71

CHICKPEA

Chickpeas Curry	32
Italian Chickpea and Carrot Soup	69
Healthy Veggie Minestrone Soup	69
Roasted Chickpeas with Herbs	88

CHUCK STEAK

Beef Goulash	64

COD

Herbed Cod Steaks	41
Spicy Cod	41
Cod Cakes	41
Cod with Asparagus	45

CRAB

Easy Crab Salad with Endive	37

CRANBERRY

Cranberry and Almond Quinoa Pilaf	20

Wild Rice, Almonds, and Cranberries Salad — 24

CUCUMBER

Quick Quinoa Tabbouleh — 59
Gazpacho with Avocado — 72
Strawberry Cucumber Delight Smoothie — 83
Summer Cucumber Ginger Smoothie — 85
Roasted Harissa Cucumber — 88
Pita Pizza with Feta and Cucumber — 91
Authentic Greek Tzatziki Sauce — 94

D

DATE

Almond Butter and Dates Power Bars — 13
Date and Almond Balls with Seeds — 90

E

EDAMAME

Healthy Asian Quinoa Salad — 36
Roasted Za'atar Edamame — 88

EGGPLANT

Eggplant and Bulgur Pilaf — 22
Roasted Eggplant and White Bean — 30
Italian Eggplant Parmesan — 58
Roasted Eggplant Slices — 60

F

FIG

Nut Buckwheat Pilaf — 21

FLANK STEAK

Peppered Shredded Beef Salad — 39
Steak with Green Beans — 63

FLOUNDER

Crispy Baked Flounder with Green Beans — 45

G

GRAPE TOMATO

Healthy Mediterranean Pasta Salad — 38
Super Simple Tomato Sauce — 97

GREAT NORTHERN BEAN

Rosemary White Beans with Onion — 28

GREEN APPLE

Green Smoothie with Pear — 82

GREEN BEAN

Thai Green Bean and Soybean — 30
Green Beans with Shallot — 58
Tomato and Bean Stew — 69
Cranberry Green Beans with Walnut — 77
Green Beans with Shallots — 77
Spicy Green Beans — 79

GREEN CABBAGE

Braised Green Cabbage and Onion — 58

GREEN LENTIL

Green Lentils with Summer Vegetables — 29
Green Lentil and Carrot Stew — 70

GREEN ONION

Millet Pilaf with Lime — 22

H

HADDOCK

Veggie and Haddock Foil Packets — 41
Herbed Haddock — 45

HALIBUT

Halibut En Papillote — 42
Thyme-Sesame Crusted Halibut — 42
Curry Halibut — 45

J

JICAMA

Crispy Jicama Fries — 55

K

KALE

Kale and Black-Eyed Pea Curry	33
Lemony Kale Salad	39
Shakshuka with Red Peppers	57
Ginger-Garlic Spicy Kale	75
Classic Tex-Mex Kale	76
Braised Kale	77
Fruit Smoothie with Yogurt	82

KIWIFRUIT

Kiwifruit, Peach and Yogurt Bowl	14
Healthy Green Avocado Smoothie	83
Easy Strawberry Kiwi Smoothie	85

L

LACINATO KALE

Beluga Lentils with Lacinato Kale	31

LAMB

Black Bean Minced Lamb	64
Greek Lamb Loaf	64
Feta Lamb Burgers	64
Classic Lamb and Eggplant Tikka Masala	64
Braised Lamb Ragout	65
Icelandic Lamb with Turnip	65
Indian Lamb Curry	65

LAMB CHOP

Lollipop Lamb Chops	63

LAMB RIB

Air Fried Lamb Ribs	65

LAMB STEAK

Fast Lamb Satay	65

LEEK

Vegetable Fried Millet	23

LETTUCE

Egg Salad Lettuce Wraps	36

M

MAHI-MAHI

Mahi Mahi with Green Beans	44
Mahi-Mahi Fillets with Peppers	44

MINI PEPPER

Mini Peppers Stuffed with Black Bean	91

MUSHROOM

Farro Risotto with Mushroom	22
Wild Rice and Basmati Pilaf	24
Mushroom Farro Bowl	25
Asparagus, Mushroom and Tomato Frittata	59

N

NAVY BEAN

Navy Bean Pico de Gallo	31

O

OLIVE

Olive & Mint Vinaigrette	94

ONION

Easy Coconut Quinoa	21
Mint and Pea Risotto	21
Lentil and Bulgur Pilaf	22
Mushroom Alfredo Rice	25
Greek Yogurt Dressing with Basil	97

ORANGE

Orange and Peach Ambrosia	90
Citrus Vinaigrette	95

P

PEA

Pea and Carrot Rice	24
Lemony Peas	78

PEACH
Tomato and Peach Salad	38
Healthy Peach Green Smoothie	84
Vanilla Avocado Peach Smoothie	82
Peach Bruschetta with Tarragon	89
Coconut Yogurt and Pistachio Stuffed Peaches	91

PEAR
Healthy Green Smoothie Bowl	83

PECAN
Couscous with Balsamic Dressing	21
Spicy Nuts	89

PINTO BEAN
Instant Pot Pinto Beans	75

PORK
Egg Meatloaf	67

PORK BUTT
Pork Butt with Pear	67

PORK CHOP
Pork with Bell Peppers	67
Pork Chops with Peas	66

PORK LOIN
Paprika Pork Loin Roast	66
Indian Roasted Pork	66

PORK SHOULDER
Paprika Pork with Brussels Sprouts	66
Jamaican Pork Roast	66
Pulled Pork	67
Hawaiian Pulled Pork Roast with Cabbage	67
Pozole	72

PORK SIRLOIN
Mexican Chili Pork	66

PORK TENDERLOIN
Pine Nut Pork	67

PORTABELLA MUSHROOM
Creamy Spinach with Mushrooms	75

PUMPKIN
Pumpkin and Yogurt Bread	16
Lemony Spicy Pumpkin Dip	95

R

RADISH
Quinoa Salad with Zucchini, Mint, and Pistachios	35

RASPBERRY
Chia and Raspberry Pudding	90

RED BELL PEPPER
Mediterranean Scramble with Feta Cheese	15
Roasted Red Pepper and Dry Sherry	80
Red Bean with Pine Nuts	89

RED CUCUMBER
Cucumber and Roasted Pine Nut Spread	95

RED KIDNEY BEAN
Herbed Beans and Brown Rice Bowl	28
Red Kidney Beans with Green Beans	31

RED LENTIL
Quick Lentil Bisque	73

RED ONION
Feta and Red Onion Couscous Pilaf	20
Mediterranean Couscous Salad	26

RED SNAPPER
Herbed Red Snapper	44

ROMA TOMATO
Spicy Red Mexican Salsa	96

ROMAINE LETTUCE
Classic Blue Cheese Wedge Salad	37
Savory Mexican Summer Salad	36
Grilled Romaine Salad with Tomatoes and Walnuts	38
Savory Greek Salad with Lemon Vinaigrette	39

RUTABAGA
Rutabaga and Lentils Rice Bowl	32

S

SALMON
Dill-Lemon Salmon	41
Salmon with Lemon Mustard	42

Simple Salmon	42
Curried Salmon	42
Lemon Pepper Salmon	43
Lemony Salmon with Avocados	43
Salmon with Basil Pesto	43
Thai Fish Curry	43
Salmon Tandoori	43
Amazing Salmon Fillets	43
Salmon Cakes	44 |//
SHALLOT	
Herb Vinaigrette	94
SHRIMP	
Endive and Shrimp with Walnuts	38
Spicy Shrimps	42
Shrimp Magic	43
SIRLOIN TIP	
Beef Chili Bean	73
SNAPPER	
Snapper with Spicy Tomato Sauce	44
SPAGHETTI SQUASH	
Classic Spaghetti Squash	55
Tomato-Topped Spaghetti Squash	58
Pesto Spaghetti Squash	75
SPINACH	
Easy Breakfast Egg Burrito	13
Easy Breakfast Quesadillas with Egg	14
Air Fryer Breakfast Bake	15
Open-Faced Breakfast Egg Sandwich	15
Spinach and Tomato Baked Egg Cups	16
Spicy Egg Muffins	17
Quinoa with Spinach	21
Brown Rice Salad	36
Fresh Raspberry Spinach Salad	37
Apple Spinach Salad	39
Creamy Chocolate-Cherry Smoothie	83
Fresh Green Strawberry Smoothie	82
Quick Healthy Peaches and Greens Smoothie	83
Green Smoothie with Berry and Banana	85
Mint Chocolate Spinach Smoothie	84
Spinach and Banana Smoothie	84
Savory Melon Mélange Smoothie	83
Healthy Green Smoothie for Diabetics	86
Healthy Green Smoothie	83
Green Apple and Oat Bran Smoothie	86
STRAWBERRY	
Healthy Strawberry Parfait Oatmeal	13
Quick Healthy Strawberry Yogurt Smoothie	82
Strawberry and Banana Bowl	85
Strawberry and Peach Smoothie	85
Strawberry Sorbet	91
SWISS CHARD	
Swiss Chard with Black-Eyed Peas	33

T

TIGER SHRIMP	
Paprika Shrimp	42
Quick and Easy Shrimp	42
TILAPIA	
Chili-Rubbed Tilapia	45
TOFU	
Tofu and Mushroom Omelet	18
Sesame Taj Tofu	59
Kale and White Bean Soup with Tofu	71
TOMATO	
Greek Quinoa Bowl	20
Lentils with Spinach	25
Black Chickpea Curry	33
Pepper and Tomato Salad	36
Healthy Southwestern Salad	37
Garden Salad with Sardine	38
Moroccan Roast Chili Salad	38
Authentic Ratatouille Soup	71
Rustic Tomato Soup	72
Pasta Vegetables Stew	73
Basic Salsa	94
Fresh Tomato Basil Sauce	96
TUNA	

Healthy Tuna Salad	36
Tuna Salad with Lettuce	41
Appetizing Tuna Patties	45

TURKEY

Healthy Turkey Chili	48
Easy Quick Greek Turkey Burger	49
Chili Turkey with Beans	50
Traditional Open Face Turkey Burger	50
Tender Turkey Meatballs with Marinara Sauce	51

TURKEY BREAST

Healthy Country Breakfast Sausage	15
Sunflower Seed Encrusted Turkey Cutlets	47
Herb Turkey Cutlets	47
Turkey Scallopini with Creamy Lemon Sauce	48
Sauté Turkey Cutlets	50
Ground Turkey Spinach Stir-Fry	52

ZUCCHINI

Breakfast Zucchini	16
Veggie Stuffed Omelet	16
Zucchini Fritters	18
Sautéed Beluga Lentil and Zucchinis	21
Zucchini and Cherry Tomato Salad	39
Zucchini Balls	55
Mediterranean Air Fried Veggies	58
Ratatouille	60
Zucchini Noodles with Lemon Artichoke Pesto	79

W

WALNUT

Spicy Roasted Maple Nuts	88

WAX BEAN

Lemon Wax Beans	28
Saltine Wax Beans	55

WHITE BEAN

Crispy Parmesan Bean and Veggie Cups	29

WHITE FISH

Fish Fillets with Asparagus	44

Y

YELLOW ONION

Caramelized Onions and Garlic	76

Z

Made in the USA
Columbia, SC
16 March 2025